A SEASON IN MECCA

A SEASON
IN MECCA

NARRATIVE OF A
PILGRIMAGE

ABDELLAH HAMMOUDI

TRANSLATED FROM THE FRENCH
BY PASCALE GHAZALEH

HILL AND WANG

A DIVISION OF FARRAR, STRAUS AND GIROUX

NEW YORK

Hill and Wang
A division of Farrar, Straus and Giroux
19 Union Square West, New York 10003

Library of Congress Cataloging-in-Publication Data
Hammoudi, Abdellah.
    [Saison à La Mecque, English]
    A season in Mecca: narrative of a pilgrimage / Abdellah Hammoudi ;
translated from the French by Pascale Ghazaleh.
        p. cm.
    ISBN-13: 978-0-8090-7609-3 (hardcover : alk. paper)
    ISBN-10: 0-8090-7609-8
    1. Muslim pilgrims and pilgrimages—Saudi Arabia—Mecca.
2. Muslim pilgrims and pilgrimages—Morocco. 3. Hammoudi,
Abdellah. I. Ghazalah, Pascale. II. Title.
BP187.3.H2713 2006
297.3'52—dc22

                                                            2005052507

Designed by Debbie Glasserman
Maps by Joe LeMonnier

www.fsgbooks.com

1   3   5   7   9   10   8   6   4   2

The publisher gratefully acknowledges the assistance of Amy Jacobs
in preparing the text of this English translation.

CONTENTS

1. DEPARTURES 3

2. GOVERNING RELIGION 19

3. IN TRAINING, AND GHOSTS OF THE SELF 39

4. PRAYING AND SHOPPING 67

5. DEAD ENDS 94

6. DENYING THE SELF TO THE SELF, OR
THE ROAD TO MECCA 119

7. UNTITLED 142

8. THE UNWELCOME ARCHIVE 167

9. RESURRECTION BEFORE DEATH 190

10. MEMORY OF FINITUDE 221

11. MEMORY OF VIOLENCE 240

12. EPILOGUES 263

ACKNOWLEDGMENTS 291

Maps appear on pages 68–69.

A SEASON IN MECCA

DEPARTURES

MY DEPARTURE FOR ISLAM'S HOLY SITES WAS NO EASY MATTER. There were the time-consuming travel preparations, and then long weeks spent going through the procedures required for the pilgrimage—complicated further by my being a resident of both the United States and Morocco.

But this was the common lot of every pilgrim who in the same circumstances chose to undertake the trip to Mecca that spring of the year 1419 of the Hegira—that is, 1999. What took me by surprise was that a malaise engulfed me, and I couldn't tell whether it would intensify or disappear. It turned out to be lasting, so coloring my life that it became my future.

As the date approached that the Muslim calendar fixed for the departure, I felt not that I was moving toward it but that it was advancing, coming to meet me, catching up with me. This surely was the cause of my malaise. I was floating, tossed and turned by contradictions. Who exactly was this man setting off like this, whose life and activities had for decades found their meaning elsewhere? For me, the hajj had long ceased to signal salvation or a successful life. It was of course one of the famous five pillars of Islam—along with the profession of faith, prayer, fasting, and charity—established after the initial revelation, when the Prophet called for the teachings of Ibrahim (Abraham) to be restored, when as Muslim tradition has it, eternal Islam was rediscovered after the long period of decadence of pre-Islamic times. I had professed my faith, prayed, and fasted. I regularly gave to charity, and now I was about to go on pilgrimage. But all this was going on in a time frame that was not exactly mine anymore; it belonged, rather, to my identifying traditions, "beliefs and practices" attributed to the society I came from, which were objects of anthropological discourse—mine and other people's.

It was in this mindset that I had begun to plan this project the year before. I had wanted to approach it as I had the subject of sacrifice in my earlier work—by reporting on every last detail of what was said and done. I hoped that in this first stage I would come to understand the meanings that pilgrims gave to their actions and to the sequence in which they would accomplish them. I wanted to understand the relation between each action and those preceding and following it. And I expected this first part of my work, yielding new theoretical perspectives illuminated by what pilgrims said about their experiences, to transcend mere description. I thought I could thereby understand religion through one of its concrete forms, and understand those who practice it today. From experience, I knew it would be with my difference that I would achieve this "first description." As in my previous work on sacrifice and on masquerade, on rites of power and ritual power, my task would be to imagine Muslim religious life in the future tense, a religion in process whose traces I would follow in the past and present. And once again I knew my research would be very different from that of anthropologists who come to the study of Muslim tradition by other paths.

Still, as I made these plans, I had not foreseen the feelings that now I could no longer elude, for the more imminent and real my departure became, the more it seemed to authorize, even free up, certain words; I began to express my unease and anxiety in inadequate formulas that left much unsaid; but despite my regularly reminding myself and those around me of my worries, the reason for my malaise and for its persistence remained hidden, unknown. My diary from 1999 echoes this:

All four of us came back [from Morocco] to Princeton: Miriam [my wife], Jazia [our daughter], Ismail [our son], and I, on 5 January. My plan was to spend a few weeks with the family, to reassure everyone before returning to Morocco. We talk and talk about my hajj with our friends. Many allusions to it, many jokes as well: "You'll be a grand haj," says Chahnaz, the Turkish Muslim wife of an American friend who is an eminent specialist in international relations and an activist for Third World nations' political and cultural rights. The closer the departure, the more specific the questions.

Am I being completely straightforward with my friends [in Morocco] Lahcen and Fadma? They know I write books about my experiences and in fact don't ask questions. They surely understand that I have no intention of subverting the hajj or lying about what I'm doing. But I am not a believer like the others. I am approaching the hajj as I would a ritual from another religion. I am not contemptuous of religions; I believe that under certain conditions they allow for the expression of major existential dilemmas and encourage reconciliation on a grand scale. As with art, it's not so much about belief as about creating a palpable form (visual, audible, tangible) that reveals the future, creating by repetition (prayer, invocation, ritual) an image of self: first in outline, then more precisely, then coming into full bloom, as in a painting, an icon that exists only to fade away when another, more fully realized one takes its place.

I don't know if this way of seeing things will allow me to be in communion with the masses of pilgrims, or with Lahcen and Fadma, although it surely connects me with the forms of absorption in piety that one can see on faces and bodies, hear in words . . . Anyway, what does communion with the faithful mean? Is there any proof that communion implies identical experiences and expectations?

I have to acknowledge that the motive for my venture isn't salvation, and perhaps this puts me out of line with most of the pilgrims. On the other hand, my project is indeed one of initiation. I've taken risks to become who I am today, and this trip could change me, introduce me to an even harder life, a more difficult drama. So the malaise I feel as the hajj approaches, my own hajj, is not going to dissipate. Maybe that's the main topic of this journey to the end of the night.

It was in any case a journey to an ultimate destination—which the word "hajj" itself indicates, beyond its usual translation as "pilgrimage." It was to move along the traces left by the founding heroes—Ibrahim, Hajar (Hagar), Ismail (Ishmael), Muhammad. It doesn't matter to the existential quest of the men and women preparing for this journey that three of these four were or weren't known to Arabs before Muhammad's prophecy, or that Muslim tradition kept Hajar obscure for so long. These are the names spoken today, recited and sung, which have such great resonance. I decided for this reason to write them in ordinary transcriptions, though of course I mostly heard them in colloquial Moroccan Arabic. I preferred the conversational "distortions," shifts, and translations. Names migrate, too, as do the meanings of "migration," nor is this foreign to the very foundation of Islam or to the name "Hajar," which, along with "Ibrahim" and "Ismail," precedes and links up with the word "hajj" in the ultimate journey that should crown every Muslim life.

Our peregrination—this much is clear to everyone—had to end with a return, for once one has bidden the Kaaba farewell, one must quickly leave Mecca and go home. This last leg of the trip is also a migration, to be added to the others. Taken together, these migrations proceed—with the oscillating tension of to-and-fro, going and coming—to a double destination, in a round-trip punctuated with pauses, going to the source and then proving it by coming home. As if the later stages ought to anticipate the preceding ones. A paradoxical space of transmission: of course Ismail's name follows that of Ibrahim, but does it not also anticipate it, being the name of the father of Islam? Isn't "father," for that matter, defined after the fact by "son"? Besides, according to the Bible and the Qur'an, there is that impossible link between Sarah and Hajar, Hajar being the first mother, the first to make Ibrahim a father, whatever else her status may have been. This matrix, producing both father and son, links Muslims to Jews, and to Copts via an Egyptian parentage, through them to Sarah and Ishaq (Isaac); it links and harmonizes rich, comprehensive groupings. As the Arabic word for it, "*rahm*," indicates, this matrix gives us the word for mercy (*rahma*), it branches out via the different paternities in multiple directions, different yet all-embracing in mercy: the most frequently invoked attribute of Allah. It gives birth to possibilities and reversals—in short, to the characteristic paths of time and of narration.

On the eve of this departure, in any case, anxieties contended with introspection:

*The closer the due date, the more tangible become the physical
dangers I shall face on the hajj. The cold, the heat . . . the risk of
sunstroke especially. I tend to get heatstrokes, and being bald
doesn't help. The pictures of pilgrims being trampled to death
frighten me, too . . . Here, though, I navigate between anxiety
and fatalism. I've traveled quite a lot: in Europe, Mexico, the
United States, Canada, Tunisia, Libya, Saudi Arabia, Lebanon,
Egypt, Singapore, Papua New Guinea, Japan, not to mention my
constant trips to and from Morocco since 1960. Each time, of
course, I've felt apprehensive but always very excited about
what I was doing. I went to Yugoslavia to find out about its ex-
periments in self-management carried out against Stalinism
and to garner its "heritage" of unconventional Marxists—
Lukács, Axelos, and the people at Praxis (published multilin-
gually in Belgrade then). In Papua, I had my first contact with
people famously described in the old ethnographic literature as
primitives. In Saudi Arabia, I was thrilled and very curious to see
a country that is the virtual backdrop for Islam. And going to
Egypt was like going home and rediscovering bits of my own culture there, the songs I had loved as a child and the "classical"
art of Egypt's musicians and singers, which I had absorbed so
passionately when I was a student at the lycée in Marrakech.*

*The trip to Mecca isn't a trip like these others. It's the per-
formance of a ritual. It begins, as all travel does, when before
you leave apprehension wins out over exhilaration. Still, I know
that carrying out this rite of pilgrimage when I am so detached
from its eschatological meaning is going to force me out of the
self I have been constructing, with such great difficulty, over
the years—a self that will not accept blind submission, perse-
cution, ostracism, and that will therefore be able to gain access to certain types of knowledge.*

Knowing how truly *dangerous* language can be, I already
understood—I'd understood for some time—that I had to be

especially cautious in my research. I had to stand outside myself, retrieve my implicit concepts, the trace of my own footsteps mapping the world, before deciding to follow them
back to where they came from. This introspection, this turning back to symbolic forms, would make me address questions that the Islamic tradition posed for me in the present
about what kind of human community we anticipate or
dream of for the future.

To trace one's footsteps like this is to find oneself face-
to-face with one's own doubts. One of them was that my departure would seem more and more like a return, but by
another route on which my footsteps had left enigmatic
traces. Each step was taking me back, but by returning,
where was I going? What was making me do this? As I faced
toward Mecca, I did not know what the outcome of my trip
would be. Still, I quickly realized I was traveling to places I
had come from—which made for curiosity, confidence, and
anxiety all at once. I was going to walk in the footsteps of Islam's prophet and, before him, of Ibrahim, wasn't I? Put another way: I would be following the track of my tradition, a
tradition that knew where it was going, had given itself a beginning and an end, and had already thus defined my life—a
story within history, giving me a future that had already
taken place, brilliantly illustrated by the prophets' example.
This tradition constructed its past in the future tense or, put
differently, built its knowledge on the norm. Tradition was
offering me its moment of truth, which was also the moment
when it passed beyond truth. Like all foundational languages, it laid bare the lives of people, including me, feeling
their way toward the future, often blindly; it was a memory
in process, a record of all possible questions. Was I, without
really wanting to know it, on the verge of a decisive farewell?
Even the meaning of the question escaped me.

In the meantime, a title—*haj*—was going to be added to

my name. Would I know how to bear it? Who was this person whom I was about to dress in white and thereby place in
a state of ritual purity? Was such a move simply a way of
pledging allegiance? In the diary I decided to keep at the beginning of this experience, I expressed my preoccupations
thus:

> *In Morocco, this allegiance will translate into a "relearning" of
> the Qur'an, the prayer, the invocation . . . and will last
> throughout the pilgrimage and maybe even beyond. How should
> I confront the ambiguity? I'm going to have to carry the title
> Haj Abdellah! Yet haven't I been dissembling for years? People
> in my circle know perfectly well I'm not a practicing Muslim, do
> not observe the rites and do not obey the injunctions about
> food and drink. Something in this way of life is hiding in plain
> sight. I'm worried because basically this open secret is so
> volatile: What if a nation, a police force, or a group of zealots
> decided to tear asunder the magic curtain guarding it? I'm wor-
> ried because I have not yet decided what I would do in such a
> situation.*

I was perhaps even more worried about all the alleged transgressions I might commit. Was I going to bid "ambiguity"
farewell, confront it to leave it behind? A question haunted
me which a man had asked me fifteen years before in Imi
n'Tassaft, a village in the western High Atlas where I was
doing fieldwork: "What are you doing here? Why aren't
you with your people on this day of sacrifice?" At the time, I
answered that I simply wanted to see how the feast was
being celebrated in different regions. The man accepted my
answer in good faith, and I saw in his willingness to accept
my distance from religious practice a form of tolerance.
But I could not mistake the meaning of his remark: it was a

query about my religious identity and a plea for me to join him.

The man's words came to occupy the space that since adolescence had separated me from religion. For a long time revolution and demystification had been my chosen alternatives. But the dilemma between the freedom I sought and had been denied on the one hand and my attachment to Muslim men and women and their civilization, including their religion, on the other, became quickly apparent. It was tantamount to squaring the circle: Could one hope to separate these forms of life from their oppressive power over one? If one suspected a secret link between them and the absence of freedom, how could one continue to love them? There lay the paradox: Islamic forms were the only ones that I was intimately close to and claimed as mine, that were my true home, and yet, as the years went by, I felt more and more confined in them.

This departure for Mecca was not a departure from a certain belief system: I had done that long before, as everyone had seen. This new departure was turning out to be more painful: Would I remain hiding in plain sight? If I did, my "I" would have to continue to endure an inner exile, and the illusion this required would become more obvious every day. Exile of this sort devalued me in my own eyes. To live exiled within myself amounted to "pledging allegiance." In the end, it would impose on me a life incapable of generating its own representations. It would condemn me to living my own tradition as if it were "other," experiencing it as something that was not a projection of my own free will. I would be making a fatal choice, kept from mourning the past and from loving it as something lost. In turning my back both on time past and on new beginnings, I would satisfy myself with an illusion of totality, consent to live the story of the pilgrimage intensely while representing it to myself as only a story about simple survival. That would mean losing the way to truth, the way toward a truth of the self.

I had to go. As it turned out, I was taken aback by how easily my bewilderment about the departure relegated the anthropological truth about the pilgrimage to the background. All the theories I had spent years learning did not disappear, of course, and they still had worth in the effort to gain a certain knowledge. But this knowledge became of secondary importance. I no longer had the strength to make it my only goal. What I now wanted passionately to know, and what kept eluding me, was the truth about the anxiety of this departure. There were so many unanswered questions. Still, I could not claim to be participating in the project in an ordinary way, so I had to add simulation to my open secret. My only redeeming claim—a poor one at that— was that I was indeed attached to Muslim forms of life *as forms*. So I would be simulating something I had never ceased wanting to make my own. I knew I was seeking a truth of a different order from the one that interpretations of religion usually ascribe to it, which anyway end up sounding very much like the basic "truths" of existence as religion itself supplies them.

I was indeed in search of a truth of religion that could carry my life. In preparing for my pilgrimage to Mecca, I tried to imagine something that Islam might have evoked or reminded me of, something that might have been fading away, something even the very act of forgetting would have preserved as a memory. A sunlit desert stretched around me, giving the traveler no other signpost but his own shadow. I kept moving toward the horizon as it appeared and then was lost from view—from Princeton to Morocco or in my Holy Places, so long anticipated.

Princeton, 2 February 1999. The date of my return to Temara [Morocco] is approaching. Relief: to be leaving Princeton. Suffering: to be leaving my wife and children. Since I'm going to try to spend more time in Morocco, this dual sentiment will torment me for a good part of my life. Here I feel I'm walled in. I understand everything, but nothing speaks to me: not this magnificent, chilly campus, not my colleagues, not the trees everywhere, not this society, so often given to competition and violence. And on top of all this—contempt for Arabs. Alienation: I feel I am living more in the image of something than in the original. So, like a sleepwalker, I live between two images: that of Morocco and that of America, where I landed by chance and by necessity . . .

The relief is mitigated this time, though. I have to prepare for the hajj. This morning I was telling Miriam, "I don't know how to behave in this piece of white cloth" (the ihram,* and when I say the word, I think "shroud").

What does it mean to live "in the original"? What meaning should or could be attributed to the word "original"? People's occasional retreat into noncommunication is certainly real, too. I knew I did that myself, when something in me no longer wanted to talk. Was it that I lost the power or will to name things? The original is indeed the origin, the source, when it becomes communicable, opening onto experience that is hard to express or has perhaps withdrawn from language. No doubt knowledge and learning atrophy life, atrophy the will to live by simple attachment and filiation. They

---

*Ihram: the state of purity into which one enters by ritual ablutions; also the two pieces of seamless white cloth worn by men in *ihram*, one on the torso, one around the legs, with a belt tying them together. The footwear is sandals without buckles. The state of *ihram* includes, among other things, prohibitions concerning bodily functions, perfumes, sexual relations, and hunting.

create a "false address" but leave intact all the "addresses" of tradition—heedless of itself, inattentive to its own creations, preserving the momentum of compassion even as it denies it. To leave the "false address," then, was to agree to be homeless, to prepare to accept a new paternity, a kind of genealogy that moves perpetually toward its origin, both a question and a lack, both creator and fatal desecrator of norms and constitutions. It was to recapture the historicity of existence so as to highlight it according to the main marks of language. To agree to move toward this fracture line was not to imply—as people often do—that institutions are arbitrary or artificial but to feel in them the tremors of blocked creation. Was this what should guide my fumbling efforts to reflect on "my religion"? Perhaps, and that meant I had to move away from my predecessors, which complicated things, as I realized clearly the night before I left, when I reread a passage by a founder—a *re*founder—of anthropology about his relation to Buddhism. My diary reports:

> *Sunday, 14 February 1999. The passage in question is the one in* Tristes Tropiques *where Lévi-Strauss climbs a muddy hill in Burma to visit a Buddhist temple. This takes place in September 1950 near Chittagong. He has stayed in a village for a few days, marked by the rhythm of the temple gong. Inside the temple, everything feels "natural" to him—the customary ablutions at the entrance (he has walked barefoot in the mud and welcomes them), the simplicity of the place, the "barnlike" atmosphere, the priests' courtesy, the care with which they gather up the ceremonial instruments . . .*
>
> *Without hesitation he quickly declares his affinity for the place; this is a temple as he likes to imagine temples should be. In the name of his own civilization, he pays homage to Buddhism. At this point, though, the dividing line appears. He is in sympathy with Buddhism, but he is not a Buddhist; he hasn't*

been brought up in that civilization. It's a double line: one drawn by civilization, the other by the anthropologist's professionalism. The two dividing lines lead him to take a stand on what he should do in the temple. His companion makes matters easier. "You don't need to do what I do," he says, prostrating himself four times before the altar. The visitor tactfully follows the advice. Not sharing his companion's beliefs, he might have devalued the ritual had he prostrated himself simply to observe the conventions.

Reading this passage, I thought a lot about my own predicament. I am a Muslim, one who continually questions the religion's fundaments but fiercely maintains its ethos—which I want to sum up as solidarity and sharing, as the measured acceptance of worldly pleasures and the effort to free oneself from them. I don't know, though, whether this corresponds to the position taken by most pilgrims to Mecca. I share with them a love for the great achievements of Muslim civilization and culture, but I can only perform the rites knowing that I act simply for pure pleasure and the desire to understand—with respect, of course, for the pilgrims and for their beliefs, but unable to adopt the truths of absolute knowledge they profess.

The difference between the anthropologist I was reading and me is that his companion knew they did not share in the affirmation of a single truth. And the anthropologist wrote that he wouldn't have been embarrassed to bow down before the wisdom of the Buddha, wisdom that, according to him, his own culture could only confirm. But there's the rub: in my case, when I perform the ritual acts, I cannot affirm certain aspects of Islamic wisdom my coreligionists confirm every day, so there is a sort of falsehood in my situation: I will be making "as if"— and no one will ask me anything, and I won't have to explain myself. My confusion really stems from this: faithful Muslims will, in the name of Islamic truth, be offering me a bond of sol-

idarity and shared love; I will be receiving something precious I would have no way of reciprocating. Face-to-face with them, I will be no more than a fake . . .

No doubt I could partially remedy the situation by giving them something of real value to both them and myself: a kind of love going beyond a shared faith and an omnipotent God, a love of the sort that many cherish, especially in situations of distress, a love that overflows the religious framework. I could also claim that after all I both respect the hajj and am entitled to see what happens during it; I can say, if anyone asks, that I hope to follow the rites and write a book. I've taken other risks in my life, and I know that this time, too, I won't hesitate to abandon my position if a new experience leads me to do so. My trip is a quest in two senses: for salvation, and for truth. My work always has the mark of an existential quest. In consolation, I can tell myself that I shall not be observing the pilgrims and pilgrimage from an easy vantage point. Risk forbids this sort of comfort.

I realized that the humor and jokes, the hesitations and the shilly-shallying, as well as the writing, were efforts to deal with an insoluble problem. Since I could find no rational solution for it, I would at least change some of its terms, displace it, throw it off center.

It was not that I might threaten to devalue the pilgrimage rite—an issue that always came up whenever I performed a ritual solely to understand it or even just to participate in a life-form from which I certainly did not want to cut myself off. Rather, it was that the rite posed questions for me that I couldn't always answer. When because of social or political fear I couldn't give a public answer about what I was doing, it was my self-esteem that I felt had been devalued, the more so since the balance of power was unfair. As an anthropologist studying my own culture and religion, I had always been protected by the postcolonial system prevailing in Muslim countries, since my academic specialty was left largely free of religious regulations and the conventions by which they were implemented. To the degree that the state operated along several different lines of logic, and inasmuch as its systems postulated several coexisting worlds—among them the world of scientific research—I as a researcher was always privileged in comparison to practicing believers. My activities were accepted, albeit with varying degrees of enthusiasm or resignation. But I knew that traditionalists despised me or, at best, placed me low in their hierarchy of human paradigms. Thankfully, my value varied from one world to the next, and thus I benefited from a kind of compensation in other spheres of my life.

Nothing could turn me into an anthropologist from Europe or America taking this trip so as to be initiated into Islam or edified by it. Since my coreligionists did not ask me for mere respect, I could not adopt a researcher's posture toward them without transgressing their norm. I couldn't possibly be an observer plain and simple, whether hostile and distant or friendly and admiring of Islam. And there was another divide, which my Muslim colleagues in anthropology and I never mentioned: the suffering caused by the distance we had to put between us and the communities we decided to study. Distance, translation, treason?

This reflexive return to religion and identity, with the suspicions and contradictions surrounding them, was subverting the participant observation I had planned on. The risk-taking, the possibility of returning to Islam or being further distanced from it, was acceptable only to men and women who put themselves in positions like or near mine. I knew there were more of them every day, not to mention those who transgressed Islamic rules even though they could not imagine life without them, and, of course, all the skeptics. So the odds were that only a minority of men and women might feel authorized to call me to account—active and resolute, but still a minority. It was also clear that religious policies and the structures for managing religion developed by Muslim states forbade free individual initiative. Yet I no longer thought, as I once had, that only fear was holding me back or deterring those who, like me, felt their will to live in a different atrophying. To think differently from other Muslims, deep within oneself, for oneself, whether alone or with others—this was common enough. In private, one simply denied tradition; but denial left it intact, living on in its burdensome, oppressive way. Could it be that my anguish stemmed from the confused feeling that somehow I could no longer avoid this issue?

GOVERNING RELIGION

THE PILGRIMAGE WAS, UNCERTAINLY AND PAINFULLY, BECOMING my own. And yet which was taking possession of which? The research plan I had thought appropriate for mastering the pilgrimage was being thrown into increasing disarray by its unsuspected powers. The hajj was unmanageable and becoming more so by the day. But had it ever been governed by individuals or states? It is well known that from early in the history of Islam, pilgrims dealt with multiple power centers. Nothing in the chronicles or travel literature suggests that people had emotional qualms or crises of conscience because of this division of the *umma*, the community of the Muslim faithful. Difficulties in traveling, concerns about security or supplies, problems to settle with the agencies in charge: these were what pilgrims most often experienced—as if, then and now, intention and ritual escaped the structures of power.

Still, as administration of the pilgrimage has developed steadily since the nineteenth century, the pilgrims' autonomy and room for maneuver have shrunk. At the very end of the twentieth century, I found I had to adjust myself to the ever more finely meshed grid on which our national governments, fitting heirs of colonial rationalism, force our lives and map our biographies in advance. A new reality became clearer by the day: I was becoming the unwitting subject of a hajj government. Unlike other governments, this one was present at every border, mobilizing the machinery of many nation-states to define a religious identity that nonetheless none of them could control—an identity situated not on a territory but in a *holy land*. And, as if a powerful, invisible hand had wanted to ensure the most extreme degree of complexity, that *holy land* and the gates to it belonged to Saudi Arabia, a particular nation-state: theocratic in appearance, totalitarian in actual fact.

To obtain a place in the Moroccan contingent of the hajj, participating in the ritual cycle of the year A.H. 1419 (March–April 1999), I had to start procedures in the summer of 1998. My situation was a special one: I lived and worked in the United States, and I wanted to go to Mecca with my friends Lahcen and Fadma. Lahcen had helped me years before with my research among the Berbers of the Ait Mizane, a tribal group living in the western High Atlas, when I was studying ritual sacrifices and masquerades there. I had proposed this plan to them, and they had accepted enthusiastically. I had told them of my project to write a book about my experience; they had simply replied, "You must do as you like—intention is what counts."

So I went to visit Lahcen and his family, planning to make a few treks in the high mountains and find out how to register on his region's lists for the pilgrimage. Since the 1970s, the "guardians of the Holy Places"—in the present circumstances, the Saudi government—have imposed a quota for every country from which pilgrims might come to Mecca or

Medina. In Morocco, this quota is shared out among the provinces, then divided all the way down to the smallest territorial units, which are managed by state administrators and comprise several subdivisions, each under the authority of a *shaykh*, one of the local notables of a village, tribe, or city neighborhood. Each *shaykh*, in turn, is responsible for several sections, run by the sheikhs' deputies, *muqaddims*. It was to one of the administrators—educated in the modern school system (quite alien to the local populations and their native leaders)—that I had to address my request to register on the lists of Haouz province, a dependency of Marrakech. His office was in the mountains, in a town where a market drew crowds every week.

We went there on market day. At nine in the morning we were at the door of this administrator, who bore, like his counterparts everywhere in Morocco, the ancient title of *caïd*. I hoped to benefit from Lahcen's influence. In a few short years, he had done very well in the local tourism business; along with a European partner, he had turned the remnants of an old manor house into a "Field Study Center and Auberge," which attracted many young tourists. Lahcen had also become a real trekking entrepreneur, with a flotilla of vehicles, a permanent group of guides, and a small stable of mules; he had opened an office in Marrakech with a telephone, fax machine, e-mail, and an agent responsible for liaising with travel agencies and airports.

Despite the aces I thought I held—Lahcen's growing influence, my personal reputation, and my identity card that showed I was a professor at Princeton—I couldn't quite rid myself of the inevitable feeling of helplessness that overwhelms me at the door of any government department, especially those of the Ministry of the Interior. That morning, on 9 July 1998, the feeling jolted me back to reality, with disturbing effects on my behavior. For a long time, I'd suffered from what seemed to me a powerful bureaucratic neurosis.

"The *caïd* is a nice young man from Casablanca," Lahcen told me. Trained at the national civil service school, wearing a suit of vivid blue and a red tie, he not only ran his district but also adjudicated its civil cases in the presence of local leaders: he sat at his desk, and they sat in two rows in front of him, facing each other on either side of a low table. People were brought in by a guard under the gaze of this group and, standing, pleaded their cases. When they could not speak Arabic—Berber being the region's language—the local leaders translated for them, and often intervened to ask questions, corroborate testimony, or challenge the plaintiffs' claims.

We waited for a long time before being shown in, like the peasants around us. This was government by waiting, or waiting as a means of administration. Waiting meant, first, being made aware of difference: I was waiting because I had to understand, in case I hadn't yet grasped it, that the person I was waiting for held the power, that he was everything and I nothing. The peasants seemed to have been waiting outside that office since the beginning of time, especially the poorest ones and the women. Many people waited in vain and went away without having had their business attended to, without even having seen the *caïd*. And then there was the guard, the *shaoush*, who that day, strangely, was accompanied by a young man in civilian clothes. The two of them officiated at the door; they performed triage, listened, asked questions, and ushered in whom they pleased: first important and powerful men, then those who paid up, and, at the end, the others if there was time. Lahcen was an important notable. As for me, wasn't I one, too? As soon as the court left the *caïd*, we were shown in. His welcome was friendly and sympathetic.

"Lahcen is a friend," he said to me. "We know each other well. But registering you poses a legal problem. As you know, there are provincial quotas, and often we can't satisfy local demand. So to register someone who is not from the region poses a problem."

To myself, I readily admitted that I was hoping for a sort of unfair privilege. Still, the discussion continued courteously enough: "What address do you have on your ID?"

I showed it to him.

"Ah! You're a professor? You live in America?"

"Yes," I replied. "And Lahcen is like a brother to me. And I have no relatives with whom I could go on this pilgrimage."

"All right, we'll see. Maybe the best thing would be for you to get a certificate of residency in the district. I'll take care of it. Lahcen should come and see me two months before the date of the pilgrimage."

I took leave of the *caïd* and went out. Lahcen stayed with him for a while, then joined me, having done "what I do every time I go to a government department," as he explained. "The 'fastener' is indispensable." In this way, he said, he did business peaceably, and whenever he needed something, like a passport for his son, he got it immediately.

So now Lahcen and I were future *haj* (pilgrims), an ancient category. It instills respect and gives status and a role to those who occupy it. Still, I was not a little surprised to discover that it was far from incompatible with a certain form of corruption. True, it was not I but my companion who had offered the gift to smooth our departure. When I asked about this, Lahcen at first seemed not to understand. Later, when I told him I feared such an action might stain the rituals of devotion, he said he couldn't do anything about it, this was "the way of the *makhzan*,"* and it was for God to judge

---

Makhzan: from "magazine" in the sense of "warehouse" or "treasury," as in "state treasury," a term that many Moroccans use to designate the central government.

these "cursed customs." "Religion is clear and obvious for whoever wants to follow its path," he concluded forcefully. Thus I caught my first glimpse of a tension line that I was to see often again.

The category of *haj* developed over centuries. Throughout the history of the Arab world, from North Africa to the Fertile Crescent, it was always part of the vocabulary of Islamic order and ordering, used by the forces who occupied the power centers. Rulers had the duty, among others, to protect religion and preserve the forms of worship—hence their attention to the roads and caravans used by the pilgrims, to relations with the territories across which the caravans passed, to supplying and managing the pilgrimage. Today, central authorities still control the hajj, but with vigorously renewed means. I realized when I became a "pilgrim" that this particular category of Muslim has been profoundly reshaped by the modern nation-state.

To get into this category, I had to have my name on the list drawn up by the local and regional offices of Morocco's Interior Ministry. Once registered, I had to fill out *the file*. I therefore left my friend Lahcen with the promise that I would obtain a *file* in his district and province. In Princeton, where I started teaching again after the summer, I received an urgent demand for twenty-four photographs and official copies of my birth certificate. The administration needed these documents in order, I was told, to put *the file* together. Along with these documents, I had to send photocopies of my ID. In Morocco, we all have a national ID card, and it, too, is made up on the basis of another *file*, which is kept at the central archives of the national security services. Yet one must prove one's identity over and over again, handing over more and more copies of everything as one grows older and when one needs to renew important *documents*.

In order to be registered as a *haj*, one has to be located

on a census map, within a duly counted and identified pop-
ulation, and with an address guaranteed by a certificate of
residency. Pilgrims are divided into distinct groups for all
matters of transportation, lodgings, and organization for the
rites, groups that must reflect Morocco's administrative map,
with its rural and urban territorial units and subdivisions, especially those regarding sanitation and religion. But my ID,
issued in New York, bore my Princeton address. After all the
efforts I made to go on the pilgrimage with my friends from
Haouz, I learned in early November from Lahcen that the
subdivision chief could not register me on the Haouz list
with my U.S. address. "We would have to make you an ID
card in . . . It's difficult. No one dares to, especially since
you're a professor." I had to resign myself to registering on
the list for another province, the one where I owned a house.

Now I had to get back to Morocco in a hurry, giving myself a four- to five-month head start to prepare. This much
was clear: I absolutely had to be on the scene when the registration lists opened. I finally understood the situation: demand was always greater than the number of places available,
and I might miss my chance if I didn't fight to get listed.

My first attempt, around 15 November, failed. The secretary responsible for my subdivision said the registration
wasn't open yet, and in any case I had to renew my ID. I did
so in a few days—with the help of a low-ranking government
employee who agreed to work for me in return for a certain
sum, which we decided to call "alms." He was already addressing me by the prestigious title of *haj* and referred to
every payment I made as *baraka* (a blessing).

When I returned to the same secretary on 30 November
to resume my efforts, I was surprised to receive the same
reply: "Registration isn't open yet." Yet an announcement
I was carrying with me said registration opened on the
twenty-fourth of the month (a date corresponding to

1 Sha'ban A.H. 1419). *Al-Ittihad al-Ishtiraki*, a well-known daily paper, had published it in its 21 November issue:

THIS CONCERNS MOROCCAN PILGRIMS. REGISTRATION BEGINS NEXT TUESDAY.

The Royal Commission on Pilgrimage and Umra Affairs met the day before yesterday, Thursday, in Rabat. At its meeting, it decided that registration for the next hajj "season" [*mawsim*] would be open from 24 November to 15 December.

The number of Moroccan pilgrims authorized to carry out their pilgrimage duty has been set definitively at 24,000, and the number reserved for travel agencies at 5,000. The price of a round-trip plane ticket has been set at 7,650 dirhams and [baggage] weight at 40 kilograms per pilgrim. Excess luggage must be paid at a rate of 10 Saudi riyals per kilogram.

During this meeting, the Ministry of Waqf [pious foundations] and Islamic Affairs . . . called once again upon those who are in charge of these operations to prevent the registration of anyone suffering from a contagious disease and anyone who last went on the hajj less than five years ago. Furthermore, it is forbidden to organize trips by land to the Holy Places.

"Yes, the announcement did come out in the papers, but we haven't yet received instructions from the governor." Rumor had it that the Saudis had set the number of Moroccan pilgrims at twenty-seven thousand for the current year, but the royal commission had given a lower number. I was determined to be one of the nineteen thousand who relied on the services provided by the Ministry of the Interior.

At an impasse, I resorted to my middleman, the government agent. When guards tried to stop us from seeing the administrator, he took me by the hand, opened the door, and showed me in. The order was given to register me immediately. Then we went back to the secretary, and miracle of miracles: there indeed was the list, and names on it already! The man's calm demeanor impressed me: he saw nothing amiss with having this list, which had not existed moments before, suddenly materialize before our eyes.

The registration had been open for quite a while, in fact, for men and women who were willing to pay. The quota system was a gold mine for a whole host of bureaucrats, I realized, and for these specialists in "mining," every citizen, including me, was a rich vein of ore, the value depending on circumstance and services rendered, in my case registration for the pilgrimage. My name was therefore now "provisionally" on the list "until the other papers are provided."

Once I had negotiated this first hurdle, I told the middleman how discouraged I felt. "I'd like to keep some time to work and write," I was surprised to hear myself say. He answered: "Go study. I'll come and get you at four o'clock for your [final] registration . . . You'll go to Lalla Makka [Holy Mecca], and I'll do everything needed to sign you up." After all, I was—was I not?—the person he had been talking about when he told the administrator, "This is Professor Hammoudi, our professor. He lives here. I have very few people and he must register." My locally prestigious summer address at Temara was working to my advantage.

Thirty photographs, six copies of my birth certificate, a certificate of residency, a "duly completed" form for the spe-

cial hajj passport: Some of the copies and photos went to renew my national ID card, without which nothing could be
confirmed. The rest was for *the file*, kept by the provincial
department in charge of organizing the trip and "taking care
of everything." In the meantime, I had to visit the "community sanitation headquarters."

"Be there at ten in the morning with a photo and your national ID. The others are for *the file*." This new obligatory
photo would stay in my "medical file."

A nurse wearing a djellaba and an "Islamic" headscarf
stuck the photo on a form she filled out in front of me.

"Why do you need a picture when I've already given the
provincial headquarters thirty others?" I asked.

"To identify you . . ."

"But I am identified on lots of documents! There's a
photo on my national ID and a photo on my passport!"

"I don't know. They want a photo. [Silence] All right,
there, now wait for the doctor."

"Oh, he's not here?"

"Hold on! There are people ahead of you! He'll be here
around eleven o'clock."

"Are you sure, at eleven?"

"Well, I'm sure I can't say! Usually he comes in at eleven.
There's no staff doctor here. After he's seen his own patients,
he comes here."

I went walking around town to kill time. When I returned, and after a long wait, I was examined by a young volunteer doctor, along with one of his colleagues. Both did
their work scrupulously. Unfortunately, the third doctor
wasn't there.

"The certificate is ready. But we need a third signature to
validate it. The third doctor isn't here. Come back tomorrow!"

On 4 December, having finally received the medical certificate, I went to find my middleman ("the facilitator," as some say) to give it to him.

"Finally, *the file*'s ready!" I told him in relief. I asked him to hand it in and bring me the receipt.

"What receipt?" he asked, astonished. "You're registered; you're one of the six people I'm allowed to register from your neighborhood."

Before leaving, I repeated my request for a receipt, but not before having paid him another "alms" installment. It was getting hard to predict how much I'd have to pay *in toto*.

Many people were turned away. "No room left" was the most frequently cited explanation. Registration closed on 15 December, and I couldn't return to Princeton to be with my family as long as I didn't have the document: I was afraid my *file* might be "forgotten" or "misplaced."

The middleman disagreed: "What receipt? Consider yourself there, in Lalla Makka. You're already there. Why do you need a receipt?"

"I'd like to have some peace of mind when I go back to America," I snapped.

"Yes, but you have to return for the vaccinations anyway. No date has been set yet. And also for the hajj classes at the Ministry of Islamic Affairs. You'll have to be there when they call you . . . maybe in the middle of Ramadan, or at the end . . ."

No matter how I tried to imagine it, I couldn't really see myself in Lalla Makka without proof that *the file* with my name on it existed somewhere. When I handed in the thirty photographs, to my surprise I had found myself thinking about the many pairs of eyes that would scrutinize my face to verify its features: the Moroccan police, the Interior services, the sanitation department, the royal commission, the Ministry of Islamic Affairs, border control, customs, smuggling and drug control officials, the Saudi embassy, the Saudi Min-

istry of the Hajj—no doubt I was leaving some out. I was
agreeing to let my picture pass before the gaze of countless
examiners bent over piles of documents, who would stare at
it as long and hard as they chose, in real places that were,
nonetheless, like dream space, inaccessible.

"I trust you completely," I told the middleman. "But you
know, there are the others. Papers go from one office to another . . . you never know. I have to have that receipt before
I go."

He replied, "Listen, I'll get it. He has to sign it! You'll
have it by Friday, for sure. Do you have a hundred dirhams?
I haven't got any money on me."

I resigned myself to making this small gift, an installment
of the "alms." *Baraka* seemed to be inflating the middleman's
aspirations and, to my surprise, deepening my pockets. But
these miracles did nothing to reassure me about the pilgrimage trip, slipping from my grasp just as I drew close to it.
What could I do? Should I have gone to see some high-
ranking provincial official or a "national figure"? I hated that
sort of thing.

I decided to tell the grocer my troubles, and it turned out
to be a good idea. Many officials did their shopping at his
store. He promised to help me, encouraged me to persevere,
and told me to put pressure on my middleman.

"I know him. There's no problem," he said, "but we're all
'children of the *makhzan*.' He's got to give you a receipt. You
can never be too sure."

On the eve of my return to Princeton, I finally got a certificate confirming I had handed in my *file*. To reach this
point, I had invested more than forty days in my efforts, in
the time spent outside offices, shilly-shallying, asking for information, procrastinating, and bargaining. The middleman
reminded me I wouldn't be in Morocco for Ramadan. I
replied that I wasn't afraid of Ramadan, or of Islam for that

matter, and asked him if he fasted during Ramadan. He stammered something and changed the subject.

Back in Morocco in early February 1999, I had to return to this business immediately. At provincial headquarters, the passport department was dealing with hajj matters. "You're late, professor!" shot a mustachioed civil servant in dark suit and red tie. He was seated, I was standing.

Nonplussed, I didn't know how to reply. Yet my memory told me I had some capacity to endure this—not enough, though, since memories of past facts are not the facts themselves. When the facts return, we are no longer in them; we've already been through them, and their unfolding and consequences are no longer unpredictable. Of course, they haunt us nonetheless, but at that point they are part of what we're living through in the present. So my previous dealings with bureaucrats did little to protect me, especially since I had tried to ensure I never habituated myself to them.

I took refuge in a sort of painful, worried patience. Because I felt fragile, my manners became clumsy and my speech hesitant. Without warning, my energy abandoned me; I had only enough to hold myself together, to hold up my body, to keep me at least presentable. So I could not hide my worries with my questions about the departure date, the tickets, the airline company, the lodgings, and probably (someone might add "in all objectivity") I deserved the answer I got: "You're late, professor. I sent your special hajj passport to the exchange bureau to get currency. It will be here on Friday. You'll come and get it, and then you'll go get your shots at the old pound in Rabat. Do you know where the old pound is?"

"No," I replied.

I don't know if my words were heard. Were they even audible? Ending the conversation without further ado, the civil servant told me I had to bring him a stamp, to come back four days later to get my passport, then to get the vaccination certificate inserted on one of its pages. The precious document, along with the money, would then be transferred to the Saudi embassy, because pilgrims in my category—that is, the vast majority—paid a fixed sum to the Interior Ministry for a package deal on the hajj (including the trip, the stay in Saudi Arabia, and the rituals) arranged by specialized Saudi companies.

On the afternoon of 15 February, I waited outside an office at the old pound (as this free clinic was called) with a green passport titled "Document of Passage for the Hajj of the Year A.H. 1419—1999 After the Birth [of Jesus]."

The nurse who came out was surprised to find me there: "Let's see now, what can I do for you? . . . Ah, the vaccination!"

She took the passport, which reassured me. She would certainly help me, I thought to myself. She took a stamp from her drawer and stuck it on a blank sheet of paper. I was finally going to get my shots!

"There are no pilgrims here today," she said. "There have to be ten pilgrims," she added. When she saw that I didn't move, she repeated loudly, "Come back next Monday, and if there are ten pilgrims, we'll give you your shots!"

"Ten pilgrims? Why?"

"Because the vaccines only come in packages of ten. We get them like that from the Pasteur Institute in Casablanca. If we open a package for one vaccine, the others are lost. A package of ten costs 850 dirhams . . . you understand . . ."

"Can I buy one at a pharmacy?"

"I don't know. You can always try . . ."

It was pointless to insist. I ran from one pharmacy to the next. Each time I heard the same negative reply and hurried off again, until one pharmacist, perhaps a slightly more charitable one, took a good look at me and announced, "There's

no use rushing around. You won't find any in the pharma-
cies. They're only available in the clinic at the old pound."

On 22 February, dejected and acquiescent, I was back in
the clinic waiting room at the old pound. A man was there
whom I had met frequently in the past. He was from Rabat
and had an Andalusian name such as one finds here and elsewhere in Morocco, especially in the coastal towns (Piro, Mu-
lato, Sanchez, Bargash, Fanjiro . . . the list goes on). A real
city dweller, he was married to a woman who worked in
town. Now I no longer knew how to classify him. Which
was he? A Rbati, or Andalusian Rbati, or maybe Rbati-
Andalusian, Moroccan Rbati-Andalusian, Muslim Andalusian Rbati Moroccan? Things assembled and reassembled in
my mind and perturbed my spirit. I started thinking of special Andalusian cakes made for Ramadan, of Andalusian Arabic accents, of a certain type of Andalusian endogamy. Was
this an urban tribe? Other men from Rabat were there, too,
in very well tailored European suits, and women with "city"
hairstyles and close-fitting djellabas of a "modern cut." And
then there were those who, like me, came from elsewhere,
like a man from Zaer, a tribe settled near Rabat, who sat next
to me. He was a "countryman," as they say here.

"I hope this will go well!" he said, addressing us all.

He got no response and looked at me. I answered distractedly that there was nothing to worry about. Another man,
quite young, spoke up, telling him it was best he carry out
the rites properly. "Otherwise," he said pointedly in a strong
Tétouan accent, "the hajj is invalid." He advised the fellow
to take part in the "exercises" organized by the regional Islamic Affairs administration.

The "countryman" continued to talk to the room. "You all
know how to read, we don't. Let's hope someone explains!"

We were shown, two by two, into another room, where
the meningitis vaccinations took a few minutes. I struck up a

conversation with a man who gave the impression that he knew all there was to know about the pilgrimage and its regulations.

"It lasts for a whole month," he confirmed. "And what's your intention?"

Taken aback, I was slow to retrieve an answer from my theological-legal readings. It is imperative to establish one's "intention," or *niyya*, to make clear what kind of a pilgrimage one "intends," and it is essential to affirm it to oneself in order to validate going on the pilgrimage. When I replied that I intended (God willing) a *qiran*, he immediately undertook to enlighten me.

"What do you want with *qiran*? That's for people in a hurry. Maybe Saudis." With that type of pilgrimage, he told me, "you have to stay in *ihram*. You can't wash or walk around properly. You should do *tamattu'*. If you can, make a sacrifice. Of course, if you don't have any money, then *qiran* is all right."

The root of *"qiran,"* *q-r-n*, means to bring together, to do two things at once, and in this context to do the rites of *umra* and hajj together.* But how can one translate *tamattu'*? Literally—if one can believe in words having a literal meaning—it signifies "enjoyment." The man I was talking to, who said he worked at the Ministry of Islamic Affairs, was advising me that in the *tamattu'* type of pilgrimage one is allowed to leave *ihram* after completing the *umra* rites, so that one can enjoy the benefits of living in a regular way for an interval, unconstrained by prohibitions, especially those concern-

---

Umra consists essentially of the circumambulations of the Kaaba and the *sa'y*, running between Safa and Marwa, together with the prayers and invocations appropriate to them. The circumambulation includes the salutation at the Black Stone and the invocations at the place called Hijr, where, according to tradition, the baby Ismail was left while his mother, Hajar, ran between Safa and Marwa searching for water to save him from dying of thirst. To these the faithful add the drinking of the waters of Zamzam and the prayer at the station of Ibrahim.

ing personal hygiene and sexuality. Then one enters *ihram* again for the pilgrimage proper.

In such ways, then, the hajj is indeed governed. To accomplish the pilgrimage is a religious duty, but, more than a duty, it is also a desire, a deep aspiration, which for some Muslims becomes an irresistible resolve and total self-sacrifice, a will that ends by merging with the very will to live. Some people, like me, also seek knowledge, while others want wealth and prestige. And these desires are what nation-states work on in order to turn each of us into a controllable subject. First by means of long procedures requiring waiting and pure expenditure of time. For weeks and months, life is shaped around these administrative procedures and learning how to deal with them—which involves becoming intimately familiar with government departments, clerks' counters, and waiting lines. Being ruled means being prepared to wait, knowing how to wait, agreeing to wait, right there, without moving, or to wait between coming and going. The coming and going were also part of the waiting, going around in circles like a mule at an oil press. For those who did not show enough submissiveness, the common rebuke was: "Let him wait, and he'll see." One waited for everything, all the time: for the administrator, the doctor, the nurse, the clerk, the department head, the announcements, the decisions, the end of the month, Ramadan, the Feast of the Sacrifice, rain, the harvest season, the Feast of the Throne, Youth Day—the list was endless. The point was to await the awaiting: I finally began to understand this.

To govern, in this concrete sense, did not mean to give orders and be obeyed, or to seize and preserve "a monopoly on the legitimate use of violence." To govern was, first and foremost, to set oneself up as the guardian of the passageways leading from people's desires to the satisfaction of them. This guard had its spaces and positions: corridors, waiting rooms, antechambers. And the people waited, standing or seated, alone or in a group, in a cluster or a line, with or without "agents," "cadres," or "high-ranking officials." This made the discrepancy between the protagonists' formal prerogatives and their sense of self brutally clear, stripping them of their humanity and put face-to-face as powers.

Governing by manipulation of information was the other aspect of government by making people wait. Giving me instructions drop by drop, in dribs and drabs, or according to carefully calculated coincidences, the authorities made me come and go as they pleased—"as many times as necessary," they liked to repeat complacently. I had to come back to wait for "the masters of time," as the old expression has it. Every procedure required that I find a trustworthy source, get to know people and have a relationship, some interpersonal connection that would guarantee success in the transaction. There was a monopoly and also a radical imbalance in what I was experiencing, both being of the essence of the modern authoritarian state in a society like Morocco's that had been powerfully transformed by European colonialism. Through both its actions and its silences, the Moroccan state, working to produce a quantity of information unprecedented in its precolonial history, busied itself making that information scarce. By restricting it to certain bureaucratic and political circles, channeling it toward certain groups and depriving others of it, the state distorted the information circuit and repeatedly created spaces from which information was absent.

A venerable technique, known throughout human history, was thus used to capture information and money—rare and eminently desirable goods. A hunter-gatherer society once again showed its efficiency: one had to cull the prey, clear it from elsewhere, and concentrate it in a propitious part of the forest. Such was the case with the registrations for the hajj;

such was the case with having the most banal form be "made available to the public" the better to disappear. Once scarcity had been created, every copy of such a form went into a kind of open black market. This could indeed be called government by corruption. "People eat, and they feed others," I had often heard said in exoneration. Thus was corruption associated with generosity, and it wasn't only that the psychology of gift-giving was linked to guilt about "winning." Beyond this, the "cycle" of material operated according to a slogan suggesting the cyclical order, *al-tadwira* (from a root that is like a plant whose seeds spread in all directions): *dar* means to turn; *dawar* is to spin, to encircle, to draw a circle around; *dawara*, the viscera that cyclically process food (a turn, or cycle); *dar*, a house: *dawaar*, an encampment (once a circle or semicircle of tents) or, simply, a human settlement. Doesn't the cycle of receiving and giving open up to all the cycles of the universe? Does it not open a window onto the order of things, onto what can be lived, uttered, and seen in the world?

At any rate, the hajj was forcing me to deal with what is usually called corruption. The middleman and I had called it "alms," or "grace." The ease of this shift from one register to another was somewhat surprising. The point, yes, was to obtain a service by means that might be unjust: exposing myself to the risk, if not the reality, of taking someone else's place, I was violating the principle of justice. True, all Muslims who prepared for the pilgrimage had similar, if not identical, means, and therefore any of them could buy "easy terms." In a way, everyone was treated according to the same criteria, so there was a sort of equity in generalized corruption, a game that everyone played and lost in turn (*dawr*). Besides, the roulette game was acceptable in God's name. Here corruption and sacrifice met: what we handed over, "like any loss, was for God." Pilgrims were only striving "along God's path." Corruption was therefore no crime, inasmuch as the sin could not affect the person who gained the venial advantage, and the sacrifice itself erased it! Here was the cyclical logic: of all the rites of the faith, the hajj was the one created to "wash away one's sins" and to return one to the state of "a newborn."

Generalized corruption simply didn't much stain one's "religious intention," then. As a technique for governance, it took over the hajj by making it yet another activity inescapably caught in the grip of the nation-state. If one wanted to look for the ideology with the most adherents in my country, one would not be surprised to find it to be something very like corruption. It's a secret, but a public secret that everyone is in on. And, like any recipe for political conduct, its secrecy derives from the consensus supporting it. In this it resembles the supernatural, and, as in the case of worship devoted to the latter, its very denunciation is a matter of ritual.

3

IN TRAINING, AND GHOSTS
OF THE SELF

I OFTEN FEEL LIKE THE GHOST OF MYSELF. WAS THIS WHY I insisted on seeing multiplicity when others saw unity, and why I skipped from difference to difference when I should have wanted identity? At any rate, here I was, on 17 February 1999, becoming a new kind of apprentice. I had spent a good part of my fifty years taking classes or giving them; now I was a student once again, and under circumstances I could never have imagined a few years previously. How had I gotten here? What invisible hand was guiding me? Once I started to search for a way to build my identity freely, ending a religious practice that had been inspired by fear, my interest in religion had seemed to disappear, but now I was quickly discovering that it had only been dormant.

It had reawakened imperceptibly and indirectly, disguised as science, in the 1970s, and now I could no longer dodge the inescapable questions—how? why? When I submitted to such questions religion suddenly took on a disconcerting mien; its practices and commandments became objects.

When I started studying the rites instead of performing them, I kept my familiarity with them, but it was a familiarity colored by distance, suffering, and sadness. I envied those who practiced their faith in more or less the same way as they got up in the morning, put on their clothes, ate breakfast, and went to work—as part of the order of things and therefore in the order of their being, so to speak. I didn't rule out the possibility (how on earth could I?) that others, too, might be skeptical or uncertain, might feel detached, or, conversely, feel a burning sense of quest. But I envied the coal man's faith as much as I did Pascalian practices.

I was on the wrong foot, as so often, and this disturbed my serenity. I had taken the faith in which I was raised and turned it into an object to be reflected on, which, in turn, became a means of intellectual and moral deepening. The practitioner of old gave way to an anthropologist who wanted to understand but was divided within himself. I wanted to know what religion meant for others, but I realized I could not stop there and had to question myself on the meaning of my own views on it. Besides, the researcher's self—simultaneously obscured and exposed by all the many postures of the participant—was not my most daunting ghost. So as not to lose heart, I told myself over and over that nothing kept a pilgrim from having other objectives, beyond religious obligation, and that nobody was interested in my efforts to explain my projects anyway. I was sent back repeatedly to my "intention" and to my relation to God, the ultimate standard by which actions were measured. And in the end, Islam was my home. No one and nothing could forbid me from inhabiting and visiting it as I saw fit.

The difficulty, then, lay not so much in the integrity of my project (although I frequently worried about this) as in my having to move around among all these ghosts. Such was the frame of mind in which I attended what the Ministry of Islamic Affairs called the "training program for pilgrims of the year A.H. 1419/1999." (All the dates on the program, apart from this first one, followed the Gregorian calendar, I noticed, not the Muslim one. So I wasn't the only one dragging ghosts about.)

In Rabat, just beyond the Gate of Chellah (Bab Shellah), I reached the neo-Moorish building in the medina, next to the city walls and not far from the old Jewish quarter. I crossed a large courtyard under an enormous *darbuz* whose windows gave light to the space below, and reached the conference hall. In the vast octagonal room, a big audience had already gathered, facing a stage where three scholars of Shari'a law sat. In the hallways and courtyard and auditorium, the din of people milling about was incessant. We were about five hundred persons of middling or modest means, a good third of us women. Few were younger than thirty, and most were probably older than fifty. Many were from the country. Upper-class pilgrims did not need these classes. They could learn what they needed on television, without help from official guides and travel agencies, and could read the many manuals available to them on their own. Their situation was very different from that of the people here, who had come to learn the rituals from state-trained instructors.

The chief scholar, or *'alem*, was a member of the Rabat Ulema Council, a man from a powerful family, and of a venerable age, but alert and well turned out in a djellaba and immaculate white burnoose. He was sitting between two other well-known scholars dressed in traditional garb, one whose clothes were marked with small urban details, the other with rural ones. The one on the right made a rather garbled presentation in a mixture of classical Arabic and Moroccan colloquial dialect. His Andalusian accent didn't make things easy for the people in the audience, most of whom came from outlying working-class districts and the countryside.

I thought I understood him to be emphasizing the difference between the "pillars" and the "obligations" of the pilgrimage, to be telling us there were four of the first: *ihram*; the circumambulation of the Kaaba (seven times); the *sa'y*, running seven times between the two hills of Safa and Marwa; and, most important, the station at Arafat. He kept repeating that any mistake made in carrying out these four pillars, or a failure to perform them, invalidated one's hajj. A defect in performing the obligations, however, could be compensated for by paying alms or sacrificing an animal. Having summed up the rites, the expert went into detail about the conditions under which pilgrims should perform them: purifying the body through ablutions and purifying the spirit through an exclusive concentration on the worship of God; consecration of the whole person by entering into *ihram*. Last, he called attention to the differences between men and women: men must exchange their normal clothes, sewn with thread, for the two pieces of seamless white cloth, but women did not have to follow this rule, and wore ordinary clothes, which did not have to be white, their only obligation being to cover their entire body except their face and hands; women can simply walk between Safa and Marwa, while men must run between the two points; and at all times, women must avoid "ostentation"—the word I use to translate *tabarruj*, the invariable term for a bearing that is deemed immodest or conspicuous, a hieratic stance. The speech, which had thus far been quite routine, suddenly turned into a homily, then a threatening sermon:

No ostentation, and may God keep you in his mercy! No commerce between women and men, no courting, no flirtation; abstinence is absolute during *ihram* and the rites. Guard your mouths and eyes with vigilance. God asks us to be serious, to show brotherly feelings, to help each other, and to avoid aggressiveness and quarrels. Don't forget: in the Holy Places you will be guests of the Merciful!

The silence grew heavier.

"At Arafat you are before God, and *ihram* is your shroud. Between the hands of the All-Powerful, the Eternal, nothing can help you, not riches, not prestige!" Voices rose, chanting, "Allah! Allah! Allah!" and drowning out the preacher. Then the voices faded into silence and the crowd's murmurs ceased as he concluded:

There, there are no classes, no distinctions, the world of vanity fades away in the presence of God. Therefore worship him, fear him, and call upon him for your salvation, for the salvation of those who are dear to you, of the community . . . And don't forget to pray for His Majesty the King; pray for His Majesty! Peace be with you!

After a brief moment of silence and reflection, we heard a second lecture. When the chief *'alem* said he would give it in colloquial Arabic, he was roundly applauded. "People must be able to understand," he said, overriding his colleagues' reservations. "Those who have not had the benefit of an education, those who never went to school, must understand. We must speak to them in the language they understand; we must teach even in the language of the streets!"

He went over the practices of the pilgrimage, detailing each with great precision:

The white cloth is not for women. *Ihram* means to cover oneself in the white cloth and the *futa*. These go around the hips, covering the knees, and around the torso, with the right shoulder bared. A white belt around the hips holds the *ihram* together. There are pockets for money, because you need money, and in *ihram* underwear is forbidden. You have to clip your nails and clean your hair with the ritual ablutions that prepare you for the state of *ihram*. After that you say: "To thee, my God, to thee, hajj or *umra*, according to what is chosen." Men say it out loud, and women say the same thing but under their breath. Circumambulation seven times, and then running seven times between the two hills. Failing to perform this pillar while reciting the well-known verse invalidates the ritual. It's the same for the other pillars. The third is Arafat. "Hajj is Arafat," says the hadith [saying or tradition attributed to the Prophet]. Still in *ihram*: that's imperative. It's a very, very big place, a place chosen by God, with the Mount of Mercy right there. People push and shove to reach this blessed mountain. But all of Arafat is a station, and in *ihram* the prince and the pauper are one and the same. If you have millions, you will leave them here. Arafat is the day of gathering before God, the great gathering before God, and it is a great day . . . Arafat is for oration and prayer; God sees his angels and the prayer is accepted. Afterward, you go back to Mina by way of Muzdalifah.* You collect pebbles for the stoning [marking the places where Satan intervened] and the sacrifice [in emulation of Ibrahim] if you are in "enjoyment," because you start with *umra*, and after that the pilgrimage proper. You don't need to make the sacrifice yourselves. You can give money to people who will do it for you, and it will be noted [on your account]. Direct sacrifice doesn't add anything. The reward is the same.

---

*Mina: a valley a few miles from Mecca, with a small urban center in the middle of it, turned into a vast camp during the hajj. Muzdalifah: a site between Mount Arafat and Mina.

Like the first lecture, this one ended with a sermon:

> Each pilgrim must help his fellow pilgrim. No arguing and
> no quarreling during hajj. You must not leave enmity or bad
> blood behind you at home when you go on hajj, and honor
> the rights that people have over you before you go. No
> turpitude and no sinning during the hajj. The hajj comes af-
> ter Ramadan. During Ramadan we learn patience and en-
> durance. Let us use that patience during the hajj to practice
> piety, brotherhood, and courtesy! That is the law of God.
> Avoid this especially: there are those who leave as friends
> and return as enemies . . . Forgive him who steps on your
> feet! And pray without shouting . . . Prayers are for you,
> your family, the community, and His Majesty King Has-
> san II, may God grant him victory. During the prayers, lis-
> ten to the scholars; also listen to your guides! If someone
> changes his behavior, "may God assist him," but don't let
> him influence you. We are on a jihad. We are with God's
> Messenger, and may God's blessings and salvation be upon
> him. We are sitting with the Prophet now, so let us behave
> morally. Among our brethren we can see those who are lax
> in this regard and those who are forceful and arrogant . . .
>
> We must enter [the mosque] through Bab al-Salaam, the
> Gate of Peace, and stop in front of the Kaaba . . . Don't
> press against the Kaaba or cling to it. Don't shout, O my
> brothers, these things must not occur . . . Women must not
> uncover their hair; angels do not approach women whose
> hair is uncovered. Each effort deserves reward; God for-
> gives all; pilgrims must be pure and free from sin in word
> and deed. May God help you, and peace be upon you!

After the lectures on theory came "practical applications."
We were asked to move into the covered courtyard. There
we stood in a circle around a miniature Kaaba set up in

the middle. Five volunteers—three men and two women—
"rehearsed" the ritual under the supervision of a "guide,"
who led the small procession in replicating the different
stages of the circumambulation; we heard him recite the prescribed verses and invocations through a loudspeaker. He
also acted out "the run" several times, inviting us to imitate
him, which we did as many times as he asked.

I left after these exercises, quite tired out. Everything I
had seen and heard was familiar. I had taken no satisfaction
in this apprenticeship and had no sense I was truly com-
muning with the others. These sessions, indeed the whole
experience, far from giving me the happy sense of confirmed
faith or deeper intelligibility, were forcing me to turn back to
the past. I was rediscovering, with the reassurance and pleasure of familiarity, an old self—in actions, words, metaphors,
accents, gestures, costumes, spaces—rediscovering disgusts
and hardships, rediscovering goodwill, confidence, trust, acceptance, and the tranquillity of belonging. Nothing—not
critical analysis, not philosophical reconsideration, not even
my doubts about the lexicon of separation that a certain
pharisaism constantly underlined (women-men, believers-
infidels, pure-impure)—had succeeded in eliminating this
former self. The mixed but very real pleasure I took in our
reunion was the best proof: this being from the distant past
was indeed active in the present. I thought he was behind
me, where I had sent him, but no, he was right there on the
horizon. Which of us, then, was the other's ghost?

There were undoubtedly more than two ghosts. They
met often, shifting the signposts, which then had to be re-
positioned again, lest I fall out of time into a sort of torpid,
dulled present with no future. How to stay on course? My
steps kept taking me back to my country, to its languages, to
its various types of worship, to its women and men in their
daily lives, especially in their religious practice. Each time I

felt brought back to the center after having veered away. Here something was manifesting itself that could not be resolved by understanding. The effort at intellection itself seemed to be loosening the vise that had gripped my life, a life now seizing the rare opportunity to breathe in open clearings that had been there long before. But perhaps this life had only been deflected? Where had its inexorable forward movement and its many forms gained their capacity for expressing former lives? Was the pilgrimage—was religion— a window open on the future perfects of the past? I felt sure that my own will came from it, giving life to one ghost after another.

How could one think that this will of mine was part of the crowd practicing the pilgrimage? Nothing in the session could have genuinely fused individuals together, except perhaps the brief moments when the preacher evoked Arafat, the presence of God, and the Last Judgment. The others kept to themselves, as I did. Many of them were illiterate and concerned mainly with memorizing what the preachers taught. They were understandably anxious, since they ran the risk of violating "God's law" as inscribed in "the Book," which only scholars could read and understand. We knew perfectly well that some of the details in what was said changed depending on the commentators' relative competence. But if "ignorant people" left out part of the ritual, they would have to do the pilgrimage again or, if they could not afford it, live with this "failure" and cross into the otherworld without having accomplished the fifth pillar of Islam. Their concerns were echoed in the professional attitude of the trainers who presided over the hajj preparations. All in all, there was not much fervor, let alone a fusion of collective consciousness in this run-through of the rite.

People's fears fed a general desire for knowledge just as great as mine. On a Friday in February there were perhaps even more of us for the second afternoon of preparation. This session was devoted to practical points and "legal statutes." The coordinator was a young official from the Ministry of the Interior. He warned us that the hajj wasn't "tourism," and that when we traveled to Saudi Arabia, there would be six or seven of us per room, with men separated from women; the Saudi Ministry of the Hajj would be especially vigilant about this, since Morocco had been criticized for allowing mixed groups. He emphasized that religious counselors, assisted by security agents, would travel with us to maintain order. He reminded us not to forget "to pray for His Majesty." Then there was advice regarding hygiene and health. A physician told us to wash fruit and vegetables, to drink a lot of mineral water, to avoid staying in the sun and getting sunstroke, and finally to get enough sleep: "The prayers and rituals take place during the day and early evening. So rest at night. Hajj isn't about worshipping during the day and shopping at night!"

People started chattering again, timidly at first and then so loudly they drowned out the doctor. I couldn't hear what he was saying, and his gestures gave no clues. Soon he fell silent, and the entire hall did the same when the microphone was turned over to the representative from the Ulema Council, who was going to give us a summary of the pilgrimage and its "legal stipulations." Between Wednesday and Friday, as the timetable showed, people who had questions about the ritual had had to submit them in writing (those who could not read and write had the services of a scribe). After pronouncing "the name of God," the 'alem flipped through the questions as through a catalog:

Will and testament: obligatory before departure. Pay your debts and make a record of what you are owed.
Rid yourself of financial obligations and debt . . .

Prayer: he who does not pray does not go on pilgrimage. Order your family and your children to pray.

Repentance: you must repent sincerely.

You must stay together for prayer, meals, and company. And morality: our crisis is a moral crisis. You must reconcile with your parents. There is no grace for men and women who are not on good terms with their fathers and mothers.

Hajj: three types—*tamattu'*, *ifrad*,* and *qiran*.

For the first, one enters *ihram* before entering Mecca. One states one's intention: I answer thy call, O God, *umra*! In this type of hajj, circumambulation comes first, then one drinks from the spring of Zamzam, one prays at the station of Ibrahim, and finally there is the run between Safa and Marwa. Only the first and last of these are indispensable. *Umra* is like a pilgrimage, but it does not replace the hajj, for it washes away only those sins committed during the year.

After the running, there is *taqsir*: cutting the hair short.

One leaves *ihram*. *Ihram* clothing for men only. Women: ordinary clothes. Anyway, at this point everything is allowed again. You may "go to" your women lawfully. But fear God: no dancing, no turpitude, no fighting.

Talbiya: this consists in repeating aloud, "I answer thy call, O my God, I answer! I answer thy call, O my God! I answer thy call, there is no God but you, praise and thanks to you, there is no God but you!" As soon as one sees the Kaaba, the *talbiya* stops.

On the eighth day of Dhu'l-Hijja,† one enters *ihram* again, repeating the *talbiya* without stopping. One goes to Mina and spends the night there.

On the ninth, Arafat until sunset, then return to Muzda-

---

*The type of pilgrimage in which the faithful does only the hajj (i.e., without *umra*).

†Dhu'l-Hijja: the sacred, twelfth month in the Muslim lunar calendar.

lifah. There, perform the evening and night prayers together, [each] with only two prostrations. Then gather
seven stones at Muzdalifah and three times seven stones,
twice, anywhere. They have to be the size of a bean!

On the morning of the tenth, you will stone the third
pillar, and then return to the tents to wash and shave: this is
the lesser permission.* But careful: don't touch a woman,
don't hunt, and don't use perfume.

Second day of the Feast [of the Sacrifice]: stoning again,
each of the three pillars with seven stones.

Third day of the feast: stoning. Then the second running between Safa and Marwa, and the greater permission:
everything God allows is permitted then.

Second type of hajj: *qiran*: same thing, except that one
leaves *ihram* only at the end.

Third type, *ifrad*: hajj without *umra*.

With the "enjoyment pilgrimage" a sacrifice is necessary.
During menstruation no circumambulation.

Earache: stop it up with cotton [before performing the
ablutions]. Outer ear? Then *tayammum* [dry ablutions, performed with sand or a stone].

Breaking wind during circumambulation? Do the ablutions [and circumambulation] again. If the person is sick,
then *tayammum*.

In the "enjoyment pilgrimage," does a sacrifice make up
for all the things done incorrectly? No, each rite is counted
independently.

Circumambulation is obligatory both in the "enjoyment
pilgrimage" and in the *qiran* type.

The pilgrim is not obliged to carry out an Ibrahimic sacrifice. The immolation [that he must do] is called an "offering," not *udhiya* [victim substituted for Ismael].

---

*To do what is prohibited in the state of *ihram*.

Hajj on behalf of someone else is not valid, even if one gives one's own father money to do it for him.

Pills to avoid menstruating during pilgrimage? Yes, they are permissible.

A break in the state of purity due to breaking wind or otherwise during the run between Safa and Marwa? This is not a problem. Ablutions are not obligatory for the "running." But if there is a break in the state of purity during circumambulation, one must repeat the ablutions.

Invocation before the journey: God is great! God is great! God is great! Praise to him who made this possible!

Can the invocations be translated into colloquial Arabic? Yes, that is permitted.

Reading the invocations and the suras from a book during circumambulation and while "running"? Yes, that is allowed.

Ihram? No penetrating perfume [*tib*]. Before *ihram*, yes, but during *ihram*, no. Rose water? Opinions differ on that subject. Any women's perfume is forbidden because it lingers on the body.

Umra for a deceased father? Yes, that is allowed.

A barren woman asks another woman to go on pilgrimage wearing her belt for *baraka*. That is not forbidden. Abu Zayd al-Qayrawani performed the circumambulation with his famous *Epistle* to pray for those who had helped him learn science and acquire prosperity. Therefore, it is allowed to go around the Kaaba wearing a friend's belt to obtain *baraka*. People used to wear the Prophet's clothing so as to gain *baraka* and, if they were ill, to get well.

Expiation (compensation) only in Mecca? It is preferable in Mecca, because death might intervene. That is, if possible. Otherwise, one can do it at home after returning.

Changing one's ihram clothes during the "enjoyment pilgrimage"? Allowed.

Buttons? Yes for women. No for men.

A belt? Allowed.

A partnership for the sacrifice? No, according to Malikite doctrine [followed in Morocco], one lamb for each man; one lamb for each woman, in case of pilgrimage with one's wife. According to other doctrines, a partnership for the slaughter of sheep and camels is permitted. Sheep must be (at least) a year old, cattle three, and camels five. For cattle and camels, seven pilgrims must form a partnership.

Lotion? Forbidden, whether perfumed or not.

Everything in the hajj may be carried out while menstruating except entry into the Holy Mosque. The circumambulation takes place after menstruation and ablutions.

Humans are full of sin. We live in sin, always. Even joking is a sin. So repentance is necessary, and remorse for the past.

Avoid disobeying [God] and repair the wrongs [you have committed].

Kissing the Black Stone is recommended. But you must avoid pushing and shoving. If you cannot draw near to the Black Stone, you must be content with saluting it from afar. As for seeking grace by touching and clinging to it, that is not a duty, not even a sound tradition. Avoid it.

Running between Safa and Marwa? Only between the two "posts."

When the session ended a little before sunset, men and women rushed to the stage to ask the experts further questions. Despite the presentations, it was hard to remember the precise details of the different rites, their order, and the correct observance in all circumstances. Some among the engineers, civil servants, and teachers I encountered were familiar with the rituals; others had gotten information in the

countless guides available, and a good many of them had listened to the radio or watched television to learn more. But
very few had the skill necessary to study the rituals' many
aspects, and the question-and-answer session had only
scratched the surface. I exchanged a few words with one of
my former students, whom I ran into with his mother. We
were both having difficulties, though we were well versed in
matters of religion.

For a great many pilgrims, illiteracy posed a serious ob-
stacle. Men and women repeated the same questions over
and over. "Did you understand everything? Do you know
what we have to do?" a man asked me. "No, not everything,"
I said, "but I'm going to read a book. They said a guide
would be with us to advise and orient us." The man (he
turned out to be a horse dealer who wanted to go to Mecca
with his wife) retorted, "That's what they say. But . . . well,
you know how to read. We don't. My wife will do as I do.
We want to do everything according to what the 'Book of
God' says, but how? And everyone is like us, we can only
learn by listening, and we need a *faqih* [religious scholar] . . ."
All I could do was advise him to seek out the company of an
educated pilgrim. We said goodbye, exchanging invitations
to meet again in Medina or Mecca, *insha' Allah!* He headed
toward the stage to ask his questions.

I was struck by the technical nature of the presentations
and questions. Apart from a few rare moments of fervor,
everyone focused entirely on learning the acts and words
they would have to reproduce at the prescribed times and
places during the pilgrimage. This was no time for contemplation, justification, or enthusiasm. First and foremost, one
had to have a precise idea of the strict observance of the ritual. Apart from a few general remarks regarding good and
evil—"Our crisis is a moral crisis," or "We live in sin"—the
speakers, like the audience, were concerned mainly with ac-

tions and words as God had ordained them in "the Book." Obviously my preoccupations, once again, were not those of the others, given my contemplative and analytical stance. My intellectual interest had led me to think of religion as a field of knowledge, but I realized that in reality I was basically dealing with commands and acts.

There was no way of knowing if I was the only one going on pilgrimage with a desire for knowledge so clearly different from that which I detected among my interlocutors. Of course I didn't presume they weren't trying to think and analyze, too. But their way of going about things apparently proceeded from a certainty that action both demonstrated and created, whereas mine, hesitant and very unsure, evolved within the "beliefs and practices" of my profession as an anthropologist. Where would I locate the will from which to draw energy to go on? I was beginning a new apprenticeship, learning about a part of being that subordinates knowledge to will.

Another pilgrim hailed me who, like so many others I was meeting, wanted details about the rules the better to follow them. I knew those rules more or less, but I was interested more in what they meant. For him, their meaning lay in submitting to God's orders as the experts had explained them; as for any hidden meaning, only God knew it, but following the commandments at least reassured him that he was on the correct path. Tradition, in relating an act to a result—rather than relating an act, word, or symbol to a meaning—linked everything to a source of life. This sort of "maneuver" was not a down payment on reason's total (and future) credit. The designs of Providence remained mysterious. Rational meaning—even that which had resulted from the human difficulty in thinking holistically about one's worldview, in contemplating paradoxical ultimate goals—could not help me here. What my companions desired was self-fulfillment, the crowning achievement of long practice and a lifetime of learning. The diligence with which they applied themselves came less from an archaeological formation of their identity than from an effort to open it up to what it was not. Everyone, including me, was on a quest for traces. The rituals laid out paths whose many directions were readily recognized. We each were going to create a sacred body of our own.

The men and women I met were here to learn how to "give themselves to God." The rules they were trying to learn by heart were actually meant to exclude ordinary life from the experience of the pilgrimage. But wasn't ordinary life already given order by the fundamental commandments of religion? Yes, certainly; however, something in it could occur only in the framework of rules, intervals, and limits. Ritual was the source of theoretically infinite regulations that, by touching on every detail of life, also gave anxiety its due. Beyond anthropological beliefs and practices, I was rediscovering the inspiration of the Muslim mystics I had read: Jalal al-Din al-Rumi, Ibn al-Farid, and Ibn al-'Arabi. The first of them taught that religion is a cord which requires us to draw close to one another but which on its own has no direction; in other words, everything depends on lived experience and on an ethical will above and beyond the ordinary practice of religion. Anxiety, as well as the meticulous preoccupation with ritual that unintentionally reveals it, forced me to go back to the "lived experiences" of Muslim mysticism, those whose paths William James and Henri Bergson had in their own ways rediscovered.

"What does the Book say?" Both apprehension and taking care of detail came through this question, repeated constantly during our days of apprenticeship. We were all together in this: working-class people, people from the countryside and the city, teachers, government employees, engineers, artisans, shopkeepers. The ceaseless back-and-forth between "Scripture" and the spoken word was the main thing, far more important than the limited amount of secondary written material. Everyone knew how to make the profession of faith, how to pray, fast, and so on. But "legal alms" posed a "technical" problem which sent us back to the "experts." The hajj has its distinctive singularity: it was incumbent upon the faithful only once in a lifetime, and then only if it was within one's means.

The crowds at these training sessions wanted something specific: to register God's orders. How did one do this? The orders were "written," "inscribed," "prescribed" in "Scripture." So, very specifically, one had to "listen," "hear" an authoritative word about these commandments spoken by an authority, Authority itself, a powerful orthodoxy with a monopoly on the knowledge of origins. The spoken word, far from being in opposition to the written one, added to its aura, generalized it, the more so since this was after all a society founded on "Scripture." We were a writing society, ordered by and according to the written word; that is how our society was and is defined. In these apprenticeship sessions, one could be an engineer or a civil servant literate in Arabic, French, or English, but one still had to come and *hear* what the *Word*, graphically inscribed, allowed. The situation is comparable to that found elsewhere with the Church and its exegetes. The need is the same, and only those who can claim "scriptural" authority are in a position to fill it. In this sense, there were no authors, and the scholars' legitimacy came from their professional, practical familiarity with the founding text and its interpretations. Scriptural authority has long endured in an unstable but well-marked relationship with power (one that in retrospect seems to have been fairly effective) and with power's means of dominating, defending, and representing the community. Today, authoritarian states extend their governmental sway over the very management of orthodoxy.

Preparation for the pilgrimage was intended for a public shaped by the laws drawn from these writings—laws long obeyed and assimilated into a tradition. On the one hand, one could see that the assimilation had not been the same for everyone. On the other, there was evidence that people had also well incorporated different texts, and that this perturbed the textual authorities. For instance, one could both respect the knowledgeable theologians and challenge them by attending the training sessions in garments that showed off one's curves, the beauty of one's neck, face, or hair. What was decisive was not the authority of Scripture or its assimilation over a lifetime—a process both incontestable and full of gaps, differences, and incoherencies—but the fact that all these fully realized Muslims bore expectations with regard to it.

The farewell ceremony preceding the departure, another phase in the pilgrimage preparation, made this obvious. I had the opportunity to participate in one in a community in the High Atlas, far from Rabat, as a guest of my old friends Lahcen and Fadma. Lahcen, who can read and write, is a pious, open man who does his work scrupulously. He had taken me into his family when I worked with him in the mountains in the 1970s, and Fadma, his wife, cared for me as a sister for her brother. When I decided to undertake the pilgrimage experience and suggested they go with me, they had accepted, saying, "We would be happy to go together and to talk about it with you, as usual. You are free to do as you like—intention is what counts. And our intention is to do our duty toward God."

On Wednesday, 24 February 1999, I arrived at their house. I gazed around at the peaks turning pink in the late-

afternoon light. Once again, this mountain had the power to
calm me. My friends welcomed me so warmly that I came
alive again after a long day of travel and introspection. After
we had tea, they gave me a present: a complete *ihram* outfit, with a white belt, a white djellaba, and yellow slippers.
"Here, we did this to save you the trouble of going to buy
these things yourself." I hugged them, gladly recognizing
their gift of friendship. Thanking them, I told them I had
been intending to acquire my outfit in Arabia, when we arrived. "Oh, it's so expensive there!" Fadma replied. "Everything is very expensive in Mecca." They told me they had
gotten this outfit in Marrakech, in the well-known market of
Mouassine; they had bought it from a merchant of *ihram*
cloth who was himself a *haj*. Then Fadma told me how to
put the things on, and Lahcen cheered me, smiling.

Lahcen and Fadma settled me in a room so that I could
rest before the farewell ceremony. I closed my eyes, thinking
of the *ihram*. It seemed sinister; thankfully, I didn't have to
wrap my body in it right away. I couldn't get used to the idea.
The more I read about the pilgrimage, the more I became
obsessed—and ever more specifically—with the outfit's mor-
bid associations. *Ihram*: "shroud." No doubt about the equa-
tion. When I wrote these words in my diary, I also thought,
naturally enough, of "ghost." Then I understood: besides the
misery of abandoning hope in eternal life, in the here and
now I also had to renounce a life in one piece. Had I
changed so much that I was my own ghost? Sometimes my
entire life unfolded before my eyes like a voyage through
foreign worlds. Tribes, cities, countries. Dearth, plenty, ignorance, knowledge, language, marriage. Bourgeoisie, peasants, downtrodden urban masses. And what of the different
forms of thought and feeling, of doubts, and, first and foremost, of learned religion? It was such a fragile edifice: an
identity constructed at great pains, always fractured. One

had to gather strength and initiative to grasp life as it flowed through one's hands—grasp it first, and make something of it later.

At around seven in the evening, Lahcen came to get me for the ceremony, the *sadaqa*. It was cold and dark around the big inn that my friends ran. We reached the large rectangular room directly to the right of the front door, furnished in the Moroccan style, with cushions on low wooden benches along the walls. Hung on the wall were watercolors, a gift from an English tourist and a rarity here. Men were sitting on the benches, among them six Qur'an teachers, *tolbas*,* at the back of the room. One of them, still in training, was not a day over fifteen. Si Mhand (as people called him, using "Si," a mark of respect), a *taleb* from Targa, didn't recognize me straightaway. Lahcen reminded him of the discussions we had had more than ten years earlier. He embraced me. I was tense, and the general mood was reserved and stilted. The elderly men were all wrapped in gray djellabas, their heads covered by skullcaps or turbans and drawn into their hoods. It was winter, and chilly. It came to me slowly that in contrast I was bareheaded, dressed in American pants and a jacket. Somewhat reluctantly, I accepted the image I projected. I had to resign myself: these men had an image of me I could not control.

Si Mhand mentioned our old theological conversations on the subject of sacrifice and the character of Ibrahim, "the father we share with the Jews, the first to benefit from the revelation that brings us together . . . that primacy is theirs . . . [as is] even revelation, [the Bible], the closure of which is ours." Then Si Mhand added, "But how close are we today? Look at the injustice, the way the Palestinians are humili-

---

Tolbas, from *taleb*, a person who learns the Qur'an by heart and is versed in some Islamic learning. *Taleb/tolba* is how the words are pronounced in Moroccan Arabic.

ated, the way their rights are violated." The conversation
gradually spread to the rest of the room. Each person spoke,
in his own way, of the wars in the Middle East. Si Mhand
and I chatted about our mutual acquaintances, particularly
the Qur'an teachers: Si Abd al-Karim, from the "upper" village, who had died a few years before; Si Sa'id and Si Umar,
of the Sufi brotherhood in Sidi Fares, on the northwestern
slopes of the Oukaimeden plateau, a once active center that
was now deserted. "Everyone's gone to Marrakech or Dar-
al-Baida [Casablanca]," he said.

Soon the *shaykh* arrived, with the school principal and
other men. A group of women gathered with Fadma in the
next room. A conversation began with the principal, whom I
was meeting for the first time. "My wife lives in Casa with
the children . . . I'm on the road, have been for years . . . Do
you speak Berber?" "A little," I replied. He was speaking
Arabic with the guests, who out of courtesy responded in
that language. The usual language exchange was being set
up: the people here spoke Berber among themselves and addressed the principal and me in Arabic. Other men arrived,
wearing the same gray wool djellabas, all of them middle-
aged except for two young men with well-clipped beards like
those of the new radical reformers (usually, and incorrectly,
called Islamists or fundamentalists).

Lahcen later confirmed that the two belonged to underground groups, of which I did not learn the names. "Yes,
they're in the Muslim Brotherhood: they went to the Marrakech lycée. They're often in town. They try to talk to people here, but no one listens. One of them is my maternal
cousin. When he approaches, I leave immediately. My religion is a matter between God and me. Here on this mountain, people don't want those sorts." The two young men sat
near the doorway and avoided greeting me.

The atmosphere warmed up, and we even exchanged a

few jokes. Around half past eight, there was silence. A vigorous young Qur'an teacher struck up the recitation of holy verses, and we all promptly joined in. We recited a quarter of one chapter of the Qur'an three times. This lasted half an hour, and when it ended, the conversation began again.

A man from Taourirt n'Ufella, a neighboring village, teased the principal with his expectations of Casablanca-style hospitality. "Come stay at my house for forty days!" the principal replied. "Yes," someone else said to the man from Taourirt, "you can go to all the cafés, hotels, and restaurants you like!" People laughed. The principal went on: "It's on me for three days, and then I'll give you a separate kitchen!" More laughter. "Three days, the Prophet's hospitality!" concluded the *shaykh*. We carried on drinking tea and nibbling cookies from Marrakech.

Then the recitation resumed, followed by another pause, followed by another recitation: this time of well-known verses about the hajj, about the end of the world, the Last Judgment, and the horrors of hellfire. We also recited the verses about the "proofs": the orderly succession of day and night, God's knowledge of "what is in the womb," the matrices, proofs that confounded unbelievers and polytheists, affirming that God had no associates, is everywhere, sees everything, knows everything. That "verily," He knows the Hour [of the apocalypse].

A certain sadness drifted across the faces of the men gathered for these recitations. We went on to the evening prayer, after some uncertainty regarding the exact direction of Mecca. My body resisted the prostrations, but I managed to make it do them as best I could. Si Mhand immediately began a sermon in which he discussed the hajj as well as other holy places to visit: Medina, Jerusalem. Then he spoke about the four other pillars and, regarding the pilgrimage, the essential "purity of intention." He reminded us that "there we stand before God. There is no intercessor, no power, no money . . . Nothing protects you . . . You possess nothing." Si Mhand spoke in a loud voice so the women in the other room could hear him. He spoke to us in Berber, switching to Arabic for the verses and hadiths he had chosen. The hajj "is an essential pillar for those who have the means." He urged us to profess our faith, pray, fast, and give alms. Alms are "the right of the poor." Si Mhand distinguished between two categories of sin: sins toward the creatures of God, and sins toward God. "God forgives the first kind only if the creatures forgive them. As for the second kind, God forgives them because they concern him and mankind." It was imperative, therefore, to repair wrongs and ask members of the community for forgiveness before leaving.

Si Mhand then elaborated on the three foundations of religion: Islam, faith, and good conduct. "Islam: that means to profess there is no god but God, and Muhammad is his messenger, to profess faith that the Almighty has no associate. Faith: that is faith in God, his prophets, his books, his angels, and Judgment Day. Good conduct: that means practicing the four pillars and acting for the good. This is more general than faith. As for the Last Judgment, it is a certainty, but God alone knows its time." His tone changed when he spoke of the harbingers of "the coming of the Hour." Taking us as witnesses, he cited "the confusion which makes it hard to know who is a man and who is a woman. The incessant building, which covers the earth, the excess of building—that, too, is a sign." Then he suddenly stopped and turned his joined hands, palms up, toward the sky, a gesture we all imitated. He prayed to God at length for forgiveness.

Profound silence followed this sermon. Thanatos reigned: the faces were somber and grave. But when the couscous was served, some life and animation returned to our group. "Only couscous suits *sadaqa*," Lahcen remarked, as if addressing me. Many dug in with spoons, but the Qur'an teachers didn't use them, and with a plain, unassuming gesture Si Mhand refused one. We ate, discreetly, parsimoniously. After the meal, Si Mhand carefully gathered the grains of couscous that had fallen on the tables and swallowed them humbly, looking straight ahead.

The plates were cleared and the accoutrements for tea laid out again. Si Mhand started the session of invocations. First, for Lahcen: for his religion, health, family, belongings, and successful pilgrimage, which he begged God to accept. He asked the Almighty to reward him for the *sadaqa* and implored God to grant him a safe return, as well as the patience and endurance he would need. Meanwhile, Lahcen discreetly placed a sum of money in the hands of the officiant, who continued with invocations for Fadma, for the prosperity of the household, and for the children's happiness. Prayers were also said for me, but the inventory was much shorter, which made me quite uncomfortable. Then a friend of Fadma's came in to give alms, and further prayers were recited for her, her daughter, and her son-in-law, who had earlier sent a gift to the Qur'an teachers.

In the midst of these invocations, Lahcen signaled to me to follow him. "Come see the others in the courtyard," he said. The "youngsters" had, as usual, gotten together outside. The group within was made up of "household heads" (and the two "reformers," who, their youth notwithstanding, did not wish to mingle with this "lesser assembly," as it was habitually called). Here there were jokes and cigarettes aplenty. A few of the Qur'an teachers joined us, and the whole gathering said a long prayer for Lahcen, after which we went back inside and rejoined the principal group. We recited the opening verses of the Qur'an, and then people left, kissing Lahcen. A few, Si Mhand among them, did the same with me. We said our goodbyes, and we forgave each other. Lahcen and I had coffee with a small group of men who lingered for a while, along with Fadma and a few other women, all of us standing in the outer courtyard.

I stayed with Lahcen and Fadma, having answered a few questions from a young peasant, the head of a nongovernmental group dealing with rural development. And I looked at the books and brochures left behind by European visitors who came to this high valley, not far from Mount Toubkal. A photo album contained pictures of villages turned into a Tibetan backdrop for Martin Scorsese's film *Kundun*. (Lahcen and Fadma, who knew the local logistics well, had been active participants in the film's production in 1997, and they had kept photographs, mementos, and memories of that experience.) "Those people in the movie are like us: mountain people, with a religious leader they venerate . . . Movie people are so powerful! They set everything up here: you should have seen the cars and the helicopters . . . Billions!" Fadma said. The shoot had briefly and spectacularly transformed Berber peasants into Tibetans gathered around a Dalai Lama. Changing the subject, I congratulated her on a very successful party.

"*Sadaqa*," Lahcen answered. "It was good. Without *sadaqa*, there's no hajj . . . You invite people. Tonight there were ninety people, all told, from our villages, but also from the tribe's other villages. When you come back, they're with you . . . If they don't come, if you don't do this, you don't have a hajj . . . You'll see, for days and days they'll come here, dancing, and they'll leave in the same way. That's the custom; and besides, each of us does what he has to. The *tolbas*, those who come to recite the Qur'an, what do you think? They also come because they make money." Smiling: "I'm happy to be going on this hajj. May God accept it!"

I left Lahcen and Fadma the next day, soothed by the friendship they had shown me and the ties that still bound me to them and to others, like Si Mhand, with his hair going gray like mine.

While writing these lines, I reread a passage from my diary about leaving Rabat for the mountains. Heading south on the highway to Casablanca, I had realized that my reflexes were slow, that my hands and feet were lagging in their transmittal of commands to the machine. I was aware of the danger. And although I knew for sure that the ocean was to my right as usual, I was moving along without signposts. The world was somehow receding. My reasoning faculties were engaged, but I wasn't. Things seemed to be receding, but in fact I was. This kind of exile into the void lasted at least an hour. When it finally released me, I inhaled with the joy of a renewed presence to the world.

For many long years, I had worked to keep a distance from my Moroccan forms of life while preserving an existential link to them. But now, having spent no doubt too much time exploring their contours, I was getting lost in them and often lost even a sense of exteriority. My identity then seemed about to coincide with a "return" of things in their indecipherable naturalness, indifferent to the call of death. But at this point, as after the apprenticeship sessions in Rabat, something saved me—or so I felt. Beyond the questions and the postponed choices of theological reason, I was sharing with my fellow pilgrims a particular form of humanity, a humanity prior to humanism, a sort of pre-acquaintance with it, which had made me the gift of life and of the will to live borne within and ahead.

Worship sent the vibrations of this human prerequisite coursing through me. It had no pretension to universality, but kept the memory of a gestation and a deployment without memory. In short, it linked me to a filiation that one could call symbolic if one cared to look for it in a regained exteriority, in the contemporaneity which is always already

there, before we realize it, of our being together. Tradition
looks like a text and a body of texts, with their institutions of
authority, transmission, practice, and discipline sustaining in
constant apprenticeship the evidence of life-forms. And
whatever else may be said of them, these inscriptions, in and
through their bodily imprints, have never achieved the uniformity ascribed to them. The men and women with whom I
had the chance to share these matters did not experience
Muslim virtues uniformly. Tradition and its texts continu-
ously metamorphosed in the flux of the word-of-mouth
communication that was the stuff of worship. The spoken
word implied not simply the origins, the source, of all things;
indeed, in its manifold dispersals, it took us back to the shifting temporalities of our own existence.

4

PRAYING AND SHOPPING

AL-MADINA! AL-MADINA AL-MUNAWWARA! . . . THE CITY! THE City of Light! At sunset, the bus decked with the Moroccan flag set off for Medina—peerless Medina with all its enchantments, city of the Prophet, his home, locus of his triumphant life and accomplishment. I always imagined it nestled in a green oasis, with an infinite multitude of minarets projecting their lights into the distance—the only lights that would sustain across space the power of their source.

Our vehicle, chartered by a pilgrimage company, was full. We had been promised an air-conditioned bus, and ours had fans, but with its narrow seats and so many passengers it quickly became uncomfortable. When we left the Jeddah airport, light from the setting sun was still flooding the vast gray desert plain beneath a clear sky, but night fell quickly and soon everything disappeared into shadows. We navigated slowly along the invisible highway, as though on a vessel plunging along in darkness. From time to time, I could guess at the skeletal outline of a tree or other dark form. The

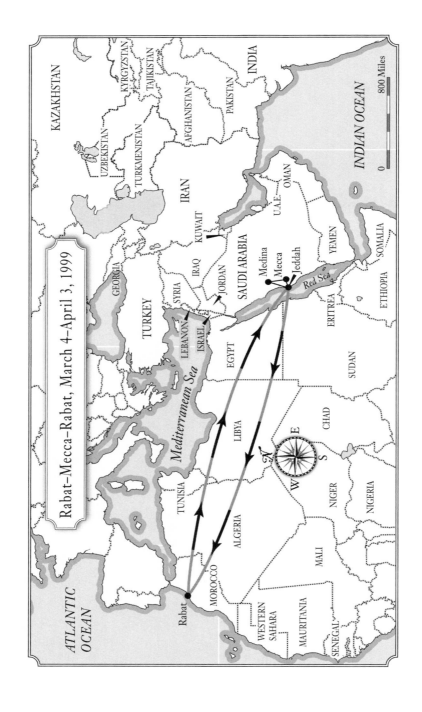

Rabat–Mecca–Rabat, March 4–April 3, 1999

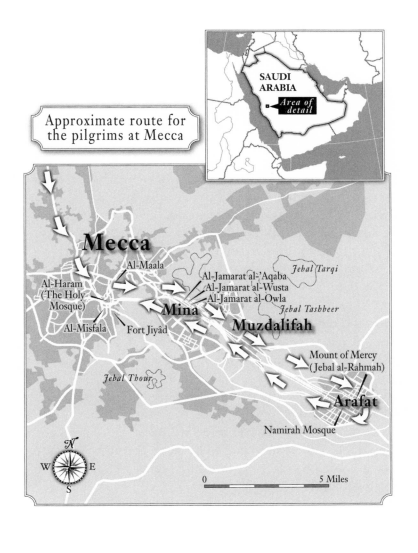

Approximate route for
the pilgrims at Mecca

SAUDI
ARABIA
Area of
detail

Mecca

Al-Maala

Al-Haram
(The Holy
Mosque)

Al-Jamarat al-'Aqaba
Al-Jamarat al-Wusta
Al-Jamarat al-Owla

Jebal Tarqi

Al-Misfala   Fort Jiyâd   Mina

Jebal Tashbeer

Muzdalifah

Jebal Thour

Mount of Mercy
(Jebal al-Rahmah)

Arafat

Namirah Mosque

N
W   E
S

0   5 Miles

rigors of the flight from Rabat to Jeddah, the humid heat, smells of sweat, the slowness of the vehicle, and monotony all exhausted the pilgrims, and they soon succumbed to torpor and sleep.

Where exactly were we going? The slow progress of the bus, rumble of the engine, unending taped Qur'an recitations on the PA system . . . I knew we were heading north—but toward what? To the Radiant City! Was it the city I thought I knew so well, whose valley and mountains I could describe, whose green dome I could already see, framed by its Ottoman-style minarets, whose tomb I had always imagined, beneath its rich catafalque? I knew that city well: the one that gave the Prophet asylum, the one of his biographies, of his battles and his victories, the one where a multiconfessional constitution was invented—I had always lived in it; or perhaps it lived in me.

Along the way, another Medina was taking me by surprise. Was there any way I could imagine the city I was about to see? I realized quickly there was not. What kept coming back was the radiant vision from travelers' stories I had read or heard. Here I was, then, sailing toward an unknown place, drenched in sweat, my ears buzzing with the mixed sound of the engine rumbling and Qur'an chanting. I felt doubly alone when I told the man next to me how I was feeling. He made no effort to hide his surprise, and let me know brusquely that our conversation was at an end. Know nothing about Medina? What could such a confession mean? Didn't I know—as every Muslim knew—what Medina the Radiant was?

I was sent back to myself and refrained from further attempts to communicate. The bus rolled on. After the Qur'an recitation came sermons. At the end of each one, the driver or a passenger would pass a new tape to the travelers. Because of the noise, it was impossible to follow these lessons and sermons, though now and again I managed to catch a phrase or sentence or paragraph. They pertained to the hajj rituals. It would be an exaggeration to say that I listened to them; they reached me intermittently as I hovered between sleep and waking. A voice was saying: "Men do not pray behind women; it is the women who pray behind the men. As for *ihram*, it is for men only, while women wear ordinary clothes, their hands and faces uncovered without ostentation . . . The *talbiya*, recited aloud, for men only; running, for men only . . . "

We had been on the road for two hours, and I was gradually becoming accustomed to this new situation. I was a pilgrim traveling with other pilgrims toward the City of Light, Medina the Radiant. I had to be satisfied with that. I could see nothing from the window but a few neon-lit buildings here and there, not far from the road. They seemed like pieces of scenery hanging above an invisible ground. At times I imagined I was the one suspended—in a vessel floating toward a city with unknown coordinates, a city hidden within a different, familiar one. During my childhood and early youth, I had learned to assess the world in light of its own light. I called its heroes by their first names and, with assiduous attendance upon them, came to know the inhabitants' individual personalities, their families, clans, alliances, parties, intrigues. I knew if they were loyalists or traitors, believers or "hypocrites," "émigrés" or "partisans."

Thus was I transported—crammed in with the others like a package—to an unknown place concealed, as if backlit, by Medina's intense brilliance. I was a piece of merchandise, a mere pilgrim and nothing else, denuded of any other identity—my cards, passport, and plane ticket had all been taken by the company that took charge of us for the whole trip—a pilgrim, identified by name, nationality, and address in Medina, information duly recorded by the many overlapping

Saudi authorities. I had been delivered to the pilgrimage market, thrown on the road to save the expense of a night in Jeddah, following a capitalist law bridled only by the limits set in "God's Book" as the Wahhabis interpret it. We had left Morocco on Thursday morning. After a flight of about five hours, we had spent the rest of the day praying and waiting in the area at the airport reserved for Moroccans. Like the other nationalities, we were set apart by our flag and guarded by a national task force and local bureaucrats.

It was late at night when our bus left the road and stopped in front of a few neon-lit buildings—three or four coffee shops in "modern" concrete shacks such as one can see in every Arab city today: rectangles with walls painted white, makeshift bars at the back of big rooms crowded with wooden, iron, and Formica tables and chairs. I crossed one of these rooms to reach the toilets at the far end, but I couldn't get through the crowd and went off in search of another restroom. Crossing a vacant lot, I had to pass between tiny enclosures protected by meter-high walls, so white they stood out sharply in the lucid darkness of the night. I found out these constructions were made for women to pray in, and this greatly surprised me—and not because of the segregation of the sexes, which is widespread in Morocco and which in my own way of life had only lately been abandoned. I was used to it, everywhere and always, in ordinary places as well as in places of worship. I was surprised, rather, because here the segregation of women was made manifest in a sort of strange creation resembling nothing I had ever seen before. It was, as a matter of fact, an original creation, from which the white cubes drew singular power—a hitherto unknown form coming into the usual field of vision, among the familiar ways of praying. So women addressed God like this, each one all alone, in a space that could in no way be compared with any space used by men. In a mosque, an ultimate presence is invoked in a shared ground, and even when it is divided, it remains a commons nonetheless. Here it was fragmented. What order were these divided little lots supposed to signify? Had it been decided that God would receive women separately?

After a long wait, I finally managed to get to the toilets. The smell was unbearable and the filth intolerable, at least for me. I made rudimentary ablutions and, along with a few other men, went to pray in a dusty mosque. Dinner was some fruit and, to drink, a choice of Fanta, Pepsi, and other North American soft drinks.

We were back on the road late in the night, which seemed endless to me. My awareness of time was wavering. Silence overtook us as the pilgrims fell asleep. I no longer knew if it was Thursday, 4 March, or already early Friday, 5 March. The two days were melding into a sort of magma in which memory was caught. Existence itself, my existence, was seizing me from the outside: Qur'an recitations in burning Saudi accents, strident Egyptian ones, pensive Moroccan ones, sermons and lessons on the hajj given by agents of the new Saudi ministry created by King Fahd, "custodian of the two Holy Mosques, to supervise worship and worldly transactions, to enjoin Good and forbid Evil, and to suppress corrupting games in religious affairs." Voices of the speakers, reciters, and preachers blended with the engine's hum, forming webs of sound that spread as far as the eye could see, as far as the ear could hear. I was woken twice from my half sleep by the bus stopping for "routine checks": someone from the Saudi company and a policeman would count us, check our first and last names, and then let us go on to Medina.

We were woken up at a checkpoint at the entrance to the holy city. After the usual verification, we went along a new road for a while, then stopped in front of an administration building. No one asked us to disembark. Through the window, I had my first glimpse of Medina—buses parked in rows and rows as far as the horizon. We were given badges with our passport numbers and addresses. With these formalities over and with no further explanation we were driven—along wide streets lined with concrete structures—to the back of a large, high building. Other pilgrims there were disembarking from their hellish vehicles at the same time. It took a while to get organized: we had to form into groups of six, men carefully separated from the women. I had joined a group of two couples and a woman traveling alone. I knew both men, one a technician and the other an artisan with whom I had worked a decade or so earlier; sometime before our trip, they had suggested that I join them. My companions now had to go into a long negotiation to avoid being separated from their wives because of this "law." The crush of people in the halls, on the stairs, and in the elevators was beyond description. The body didn't give up its rights, not even a few dozen meters from the Prophet's tomb. Each time goods or services were distributed, each time a goal had to be reached, the religion of Me, Me first, Me before everyone else pushed Islam to the edge. This religion, too, had its rituals, incantations, and moments of rapture.

We six, like the other groups, were put in an apartment room. Each of us got a piece of foam rubber that was a meter and eighty centimeters long, sixty wide, four thick, with a pillow of the same stuff, and a sheet. A piece of cloth was strung up, to divide the room in two and to enforce separation while we slept and changed clothes.

Our first Friday in Medina! To enter the Prophet's city on a Friday—what a special occasion! After a brief rest and snack, we went to wait our turn outside the communal bathroom—a shower, a toilet, and two sinks—reserved for about thirty of us. Once we had performed our ablutions, we left the premises to attend the communal prayer. The building where we were staying looked onto the central avenue of Medina which leads to the Great Mosque, and we walked for a while toward this vision. And then, there it was, the mosque that had lived in my memory forever; for an instant, it showed us one of its many faces. As in a kaleidoscope, these changed, shifted, reassembled, and gave place to new epiphanies. There it was in its immensity, with its minarets like giant chandeliers charging the sky. It seemed for a moment to be floating in the firmament, suspended from it by the sanctuary's green dome. This was no doubt the kaleidoscopic memory of it, which in a sort of powerful ensemble movement gave it a strange mobility—the same mobility, perhaps, that carried it in words and images through the ages. Yet obviously I was seeing this mosque for the first time. I knew it was new, in its current dimensions, with the Moroccan Andalusian style of its doors, the Oriental curvature of its domes; and that it owed its new incarnation to spectacular renovations done by the Saud dynasty. But the certain knowledge that my steps were carrying me toward it for the first time did not keep me from feeling that this was the second time I'd seen it, that my "first" images of it would come to inhabit those which I saw as I walked toward it.

Moving in a white-clad throng, we men soon left the women, who entered the mosque by a side door on the south while we approached it, walking east, to enter through the main door. Soothing shade welcomed us within after the punishing sun and its light burning our eyes. We looked for a while for places among the faithful, who knelt in serried rows between the marble pillars topped with gold capitals, or beneath the vast wrought domes, where Byzantine windows filtered the light and gave it its celebrated serenity. We moved forward to get as close as we could to the Prophet's tomb in the middle of the southeastern section of the mosque. Finding places beneath a dome, we sat down and spent a long time reading the Qur'an in the Wahhabi kingdom's official edition.* Then there was the call to prayer and sermons before the two required prostrations.

The preacher's loud voice rang out vehemently in the silence. "Islam means to give oneself to God and to testify to him by being pious and repressing the demons of the pre-Islamic era, an age of ignorance and associationism. Among its acts of worship, the hajj crowns the effort to repent and return to God. It must be done with lawful money, for divine punishment is at hand." This peroration introduced the theme of the second sermon: "The Muslim community has remained attached to its religion and its noble ambitions despite conspiracies, despite what is being hatched, against it. The gathering [of the hajj] brings together the glorious past with the present, the painful present, when the *umma* is threatened, divided, and challenged by its enemies." The voice rose higher, shrill and injured, finding proof of Islam's eternal mission in this gathering of all peoples, in all their diversity of race, color, and language, around the superior principles of this religion of "justice and equality." No difference among nations or between rich and poor—all are equal before God and his law. The crowd gathered here has come to link the glorious past to the present, to express the permanence of Islam's mission and community, to pronounce the *talbiya* "in plain Arabic."

In the holiness of this day, it was a propitious time to visit the Prophet's tomb. We approached it from the Bab al-Salaam, the Gate of Peace, on the southeast side, squeezing

---

*The Wahhabi interpretation of Islam (named after the founder, Muhammad Ibn Abd Alwahhab) is a literalist school. It carries literalism to an extreme, rejecting other interpretations outright. Indeed Wahhabi doctrine almost systematically condemns change as impious innovation.

into a human column that narrowed as it approached the threshold. My feet barely touched the ground. The column moved slowly, watched by vigilant guards in military uniform. Inside, we were jammed together, each of us waiting for a space to be freed up to begin praying. Near the place where the Prophet prayed, marked by a baldachin on four marble columns, facing the *minbar*, the pulpit marking where the Prophet had preached, the faithful were massed so closely as to be virtually piled on top of each other. Yet despite the pervasive danger, prayers took place in absolute calm. Plunged in meditation and seized by fierce questions, I could hear my neighbors imploring and weeping, felt their chests swollen by emotion. Everyone wanted above all to prostrate himself where the Prophet had done so, to put his forehead on the spot where his had touched the ground in a sign of utter submission to the Eternal. The souls who opened their hearts here were in search not of the deepening of their ideas or theories about divine or human nature, about revelation or the afterlife, a sum of beliefs or evidence, but, rather, of the deepening (if one has to use the term) of their faith, the confirmation that through mutual testimony each individual had made the same choice, proof that the chosen path led to salvation after all.

After prayers, I walked along the grille separating the mausoleum proper from the mosque, and tried to see through the holes pierced for that purpose. I thought I saw something like a large catafalque and next to it two smaller ones, which sheltered the Prophet's remains and those of his companions Abu Bakr and Omar. But I couldn't be sure whether I really saw this or whether it was purely a product of an imagination nourished by years of learning.

I recognized the emotions shared by the faithful around me. Those of my companion Abbas touched me, especially

as I was feeling more and more fragile myself. Leaving the
sanctuary, Abbas, alone with me, said nothing. Mutual
recognition flowed through us. "You wept a lot," I said.

"I asked for intercession from our Lord Muhammad. Men
in their youth don't understand anything . . . They do things
. . . like drinking wine, seducing boys, bearing false witness
. . . May God have mercy upon us!" I could see Abbas as a
young man from a small town in northern Morocco, appren-
ticed to a carpenter according to the law of his generation,
moving early on to a big city on the coast and fighting to
make space for himself in Morocco's new society; then finding modest but unhoped-for success—a job as an artisan
working for the government—and the rest following naturally: marriage, getting a home and education for the children, some of them undertaking long and promising courses
of study. With his life coming to its fulfillment, he gave the
impression of self-acceptance.

I couldn't say the same of myself. Yet the tumult carrying
me forward seemed to be coming to a head, and that was a
source of relative tranquillity. I realized suddenly the inanity
of my efforts to get away from it. Surely I had to regulate it
as I went along so I could continue to live in it. That was all
I could do if I was to preserve the illusion of permanence on
the way to the unknown, to that which remained secret even
as it was revealed. It meant gambling on the places that our
languages attributed to God, on the satisfactions gained
from an earthly stroll at their verge, on the negatives of their
images. The terms of this wager were now becoming unexpectedly, vividly clear. As I moved in immediate proximity to
the tomb of the Prophet, walking in some way in his footsteps, as close as possible to his resolve, where it had melded
with that of his creator, my own resolve transcended the reasons I had given myself over the years.

This flash of intuition projected all around me the light

and contrasts of an open clearing. I felt a joy like no joy I had felt before. I had rediscovered a specific humanity at last, and was now experiencing what spoke to me in all the names that say the universe: heaven and earth, plants and animals, distant and imaginary lives, objects and machines, here or yet to come.

Alas! Exaltation and compassion gave way to unease when the fresh memory of the Friday sermons returned. Was I really in Medina? Certainly. Among these crowds at prayer, in the sanctuary and all around it. But what of these modern avenues and what of the sermons? This wasn't exactly a discovery. A strange sense of familiarity at a slight remove colored everything. I was hearing language that had saturated our lives for decades, about justice and equality before God and before the law, yet differentiations as to status, race, and gender were blindingly evident everywhere. What of justice? What of implementation of the law, as codified by the Shari'a? How could one rely solely on the piety of a *qadi* or notary? What became of equality among peoples, races, and languages if it was necessary to answer God's call "in plain Arabic"? What about Persian, Turkish, Farsi, Parsi, Urdu, Kurdish, Tamazight, Swahili, Wolof, Malay, Indonesian, Chinese, Russian, French, English, German, Spanish? What about the other languages spoken on the planet, almost all of them now languages spoken by Muslims? What, then, of Aramaic, Latin, Hebrew, Navajo, Quechua? No need to continue. Was I in Medina or somewhere else? In a mosque in Casablanca, Algiers, Cairo, Khartoum, Kano, Hamburg, or Lyon, where Muslims are taught about the "glorious past" and "painful present" of our "divided community," about "conspiracies," "external and internal enemies," where "the might of Islam" is measured by the density of the crowd?

Mutual recognition encounters here the damage that institutions wreak. Instead of putting ideas into practice, we come to prefer radicalizing them as ideals. In the absence of unity, the hajj is offered as unity itself; its incantations about union or preparation for it blot out the individual voices of leaders, of pupils and college students, of workers, merchants, of Islam's multitudes of men and women. Suddenly I felt there was no place distant or deserted enough for me to flee from these imprecations. This sovereign discourse, detached from all humanity, from everyone, invaded everybody here and poured out over everyone according to its own rhythms and logic; it became the very ground I trod in the day and at night gave me such restless sleep.

Near the Prophet's tomb, it hit me full force with all its Wahhabi virulence, this denial to Muslims of any right to live their faith differently. I was willing to acknowledge that in the presence of so many dangers, Islam had to return to the past and to its sources. Muslims must find the necessary energy to survive and renew ourselves if we are to offer anything to the world and our contemporaries. This unique gathering was proof of Islam's incredible vitality. But all the signs suggested that this mutually communicated power, as currently presented, bred impotence everywhere. Thankfully, questions and answers diverge; here as elsewhere, even in the Arabian Peninsula, many men and women suffer in silence under the yoke of this totalitarianism, which, I reassured myself, would surely fall one day. Its cynicism and its hypocrisies were guarantees of an inevitable collapse. In the meantime, one had to bear the brunt of these voices of preachers, veiled in their keffiyehs, long-bearded or goateed depending on policy. This state of religion, or religion of the state, devoid of compassion and merciless to God's creatures, besieged us on all sides. Every time I tried to imagine the Wahhabi *umma* as it is incarnated in the Saudi system being expanded across the entire globe, I succumbed to panic. Thankfully, anger would ensue.

The muezzins' call to prayer interrupted my thoughts. I met up with my companions Abbas and Salah for the mid-afternoon prayers. After the four requisite prostrations, we were asked to pray for those who had died in Medina during that day. This time it was a child. Then, in Indian file, we left the mosque. The wave of humans trickled slowly through its doors, smoothly and silently.

We walked past the shops on the northern and southern sides of the square in front of the "House of God" but did not stop at them. Their windows were bursting with gold, diamonds, precious stones, all sorts of jewelry, and brand-name watches. Men and women were rushing into the stores and pouring out into the nearby streets. I was surprised at the size of the markets: much larger than I had imagined. Going past these endless piles of merchandise, I wanted to see if the business section actually had a limit and one could eventually get to the "old town." I hoped to see a place that would link me to "Medina the Radiant" in my imagination and to the ancient city of Yathrib beyond it: the city before time was invented. But markets followed more markets, so I stopped a taxi driver to ask where the old town was. "You mean the regular town?" he replied. Repeating the same words two or three times, he showed me ordinary residential quarters across a highway. It was a familiar urban landscape: concrete cubes punctured with windows and empty balconies decked out with countless satellite dishes. "No," I said, "the old town! . . . old buildings, old mosques; traces, monuments left by the ancients . . . Such as we have in Fez." I added this detail because I felt the man understood my words without knowing what I was referring to. But the word "Fez" meant nothing to him, either. "This is the city! This is Medina!" he told me, driving off.

We went deeper into the markets. My companions examined the goods in detail, discussing their quality, price, and origins. Saudi and Pakistani vendors did not willingly accept this game; Moroccan-style bargaining was not to their taste, and my two friends saw this reluctance as ungracious and arrogant. To them, our Moroccan bargaining was surely universal. Abbas threw himself into an intense discussion about an *ihram* outfit. The salesman turned away to attend to other customers. Abbas pulled us into another shop and started again. The Pakistani salesman didn't budge. We went on like this, looking at shopwindows and displays: carpets, caps, sheets, turbans, sandals, belts, watches, compasses, radios, tea sets, coffee sets, shirts, dresses, blankets, shoes, televisions, VCRs, computers, calculators, perfumes, incense, aromatic plants, framed calligraphy, fans, parasols. Abbas and Salah overcame my weariness by the sheer force of their encouragement and friendly gestures. Then we reached the luggage market, where they hurried in, looking for suitcases in which to carry home their purchases. We spent a while examining handbags, trunks, and briefcases, assessing the leather, canvas, and metal, trying the locks. Abbas and Salah had to consult with their wives about the amount they could spend, so they were checking things out first and would come back later to buy. Then sunset prayers brought an end to our leisurely walk.

We went back to our lodgings to drop off our packages and wash for prayers. But as soon as the sunset prayers and prayers for the dead were done, we left the mosque and like thousands of other pilgrims returned to the markets. This time the women accompanied us: Abbas's wife, who ran a hair salon; Salah's wife, a lab technician; and Farida, a physician from a family of urban notables who was on the pilgrimage under the supervision of Salah, a friend of her husband's. Farida soon left us for the elegant jewelers' boutiques under arcades; they reminded me of the great department stores in Paris and of specialized jewelry bazaars. Our group headed for the fabric shops, which took up an entire neighborhood not far from the mosque. The foursome looked at cottons, wools, and silks, compared textures, colors, the size of swatches. They went over their lists of recipients: relatives, friends, neighbors, colleagues. The value of the gift had to be commensurate with the relationship. They talked of living rooms and bedrooms, of curtains and bedspreads. They considered what their children needed. Vendors assailed us constantly, shouting: "Worm! Worm! Worm silk!" I understood they were talking about raw silk, which, one vendor explained to me, Moroccans always wanted. "Do you know Moroccan Arabic?" I asked him. He said yes, and I heard his colleagues speaking it with my companions as other salesmen, too, attracted the attention of onlookers by mentioning *"douda,"* "worm," the word that had drawn my compatriots. I soon discovered that Medina's shopkeepers speak all the world's languages—Moroccan, Egyptian, Persian, Farsi, Urdu, Turkish, Indonesian, English—but when I tried to continue any conversation, I was given a clarification I was to hear again and again: "My knowledge [of languages] is limited to business terms."

After the initial surprise, it was clear that for centuries pilgrims had divided their time between mosque and commerce, that long practice had forged these techniques and rituals of contact, almost as formalized as those of "visiting the sanctuary." I realized what kind of rapport I had to establish with people here during my stay: short, pragmatic, limited to questions of transport, lodging, security, and purchases. Medina was not Babel. There was no clamor of tongues. Everything had a price. Each transaction, it appeared, was clearly conceived and easy to express. We were at the height of the pilgrimage season, and the enormous number of pilgrims led to a spectacular increase in business. For that matter, weren't we ourselves commodities in the hands of Saudi Arabia's agencies? From now on, I could be only a worshipper or a customer.

Our steps led us back to the mosque for the last evening prayer, followed as usual by prayers for those who had died. Afterward, we walked along the city's central avenue, looking for a place to have dinner. We decided on meat roasted in the Syrian-Lebanese style; after the meal, we went for an evening walk in the markets, men alone this time. We reached neighborhoods in the northwest part of the city, far from where we were staying. There, too, even at this late hour, an infinite number of shops were open, selling all sorts of accessories and instruments. There were also ready-to-wear clothes shops, bookstores, and people selling posters— of Mecca and Medina, always the same ones: of crowds praying or walking around the Kaaba in its covering of black cloth embellished with gold. And in these shops, as elsewhere, prayer rugs were king. Medina's markets never slept.

Day after day, our life followed an immutable rhythm: awake at dawn, before five o'clock; a long wait in front of the perpetually crowded bathroom; morning prayers at the mosque, entirely lit up at this early hour; back to our lodgings for a Moroccan breakfast of green tea with mint, biscuits with oil, butter, and honey; then sleep and rest before the noon prayers and lunch. As our sojourn continued, the countless comings and goings between our living quarters and the markets tended to take place in the afternoon and the evening. Prayers marked out the passage of time; with each one, we recited a further section of the Qur'an.

I gradually discovered other shopping malls in luxury buildings along the main avenue, with elevators, air-conditioning, restaurants, cafeterias, ice-cream vendors, all American-style: self-service, cardboard plates and cups, plastic forks and knives, menus and prices displayed on neon-lit boards. One day I had lunch in one of these establishments, where I was made to sit in the men's section. When my eyes grew accustomed to the dim lighting, I noticed tables tucked away behind curtains. A man was eating at one of them with his wife. There were several couples, too, with and without children, eating in this reserved section, separated from each other and from the single men. Pervasive Americanism was thus accommodating men from the Gulf states and their wives. Other American habits were transposed to Medina, too, like the cigars a few husbands were quietly savoring.

After the long siesta time, which I devoted to writing, my companions asked me to go pray with them. We first endured the usual long wait for the toilet and showers, where the smells were growing stronger every day. Constant use of the sanitary facilities had damaged them, and we never saw the slightest effort at repair. When we finished our ablutions, Abbas, Salah, and I walked toward the mosque, Salah leading the way. As we moved through the crowd under a leaden sun, Abbas asked me if I prayed in everyday life. I told him I had ceased doing so when I was fifteen or sixteen, except for a few occasions like religious holidays or burials. "God forgive you" was all he said.

We managed—this was now our habit—to arrive early at the mosque, and chose a corner after taking a Qur'an from the shelves of them available for that purpose. I was rereading a few passages I had selected and, occasionally, entire chapters, rediscovering the beauty of the text, its haunting images and sophisticated, supremely asymmetrical rhythms. I began to leave this world, walking into these stories toward horizons which pleased me with the intact freshness of all beginnings. We recited the canonical morning prayers, followed by prayers for the dead, by now a regular feature. After each service, two, three, or more deaths were announced—men, women, children. The ranks thinned slightly, and we performed the two customary prostrations.

Prayer and the presence of death did not, however, lessen anyone's ardor for commercial transactions, which we plunged into as soon as we left the mosque. I was looking for a watch to give my wife. We went from one display to another around the mosque, through arcades where women were busy shopping. I noticed the Indonesian women especially, all in white but with their faces made up and their lips painted red, many of them wearing espadrilles or fashionable (Western) shoes. There were also many Moroccans, men and women easily recognizable from their clothes and the women's predilection for the "gold shops," as we call them. On the other hand, I rarely saw Turkish women and no Iranian ones at all: I glimpsed them only from afar, near the mosque, always entirely covered in black and surrounded by their menfolk.

In one very active street, we met a crowd of Moroccans busy choosing silks and upholstery material—clearly for resale, not as gifts to offer visitors when the pilgrims went home. Among these merchant pilgrims, some obviously had special relations with Medina shopkeepers. We often found them sitting together at the back of a store, talking with the owner while the apprentices attended to making up packages just as they would in Casablanca, Marrakech, or Fez. I introduced myself to one of them, an educated man in his well-groomed sixties. Without hesitation, he told me he was from the Sousse region, had come on pilgrimage several times, and this time with the same intention: to carry out his religious duty *and* to do business. He wasn't the only one, as he pointed out: "Everyone knows there's nothing wrong with combining trade and worship for *baraka*."

After sunset prayers, we went to the suitcase market; my companions bought many items, which we quickly dropped off in our rooms before running off to the evening service. Once prayers were finished, Abbas chose two roast chickens for us to have as dinner in our room, but it had been invaded with more and more luggage every day. I had bought nothing, but my companions' suitcases and bags were piling up everywhere, and available space for eating and sleeping was shrinking. And suitcases often marked the horizon of our conversation, as well: small, medium, big; hand luggage or checked in; leather, plastic, cardboard, canvas, metal; reinforced at the corners or not; with a padlock or a combination lock? Was it better to buy all the suitcases in Medina or wait to choose others in Mecca? Would there be enough room to go back to Morocco with all this? Those who had bought neither suitcases nor other goods had to help out the others by carrying stuff. Mutual love nourished by shared piety thus passed among us quite naturally via the suitcases.

With this as the normal rhythm of our stay, we once went to the bazaar late at night for a quick look around. I was lagging behind the others and soon, being tired and bored, lost my sense of space and time. What I had been experiencing came through in my memory like a slow-motion film: endless lines of shops, bits of sentences, words, voices commenting and bargaining, national costumes in mixed-up colors, faces passing by one after another, short beards, long beards, goatees, jawline beards, black, gray, white, and everything wrapped in recitations of the Qur'an, Egyptian inflections, sermons, chatter everywhere filling the ear. I felt I returned to myself only at around two o'clock in the morning, when I finally lay on my foam mat and sleep delivered me from the cult of shopping.

On the third day in Medina, my companions woke me at 3:30 in the morning. We wanted to offer some prayers early, before the canonical worship service. The mosque appeared to me the instant I stepped from the door of our building—bathed in light, floating on the surface of a human tide. When we got there, no sooner had I seated myself in the midst of the enormous crowd than I was seized by a feeling of religious fear. This state of mind had not visited me for three decades, if indeed I had experienced it before. I tried to reason with myself, but in vain. I had trained myself not to fear my desires or the emotions they could arouse, but this time the upsurge was too strong for me. Was my rationalist self succumbing to a spell? A fateful moment. Who was this person who'd been suddenly taken over and possessed? Was the face I believed was mine crumbling in contact with prayer, with the ground? The duel returned, with unprecedented sharpness. Was I just a name—and what name? Abdellah, "God's slave," he who worships God. The name burst into sharp, murderous fragments. But what were they lacerating? Did I still have a body? These turbulences, these ebbs and flows (which crashed together in the heart of the mosque, near the Messenger, Islam's living inspiration), were followed by a paralyzing fear: that the earth would explode beneath my feet at any moment and a hot, violent wind would blow, scattering the desiccated fibers of this body which no longer belonged to me. It is difficult to grasp the evidence of nothingness, because we imagine it all too often as a vacuum. Yet I felt I was drawing closer to it, in the tangible dust that the wind carried away. Each time the image gripped me, the body relinquished its desire for survival and refused to hear the heart beating. The body's ruins were collapsing in on its foundations, on the ground; it was nothing more than an incarnation among others, a self that walked, talked, prayed, ate, slept, and followed the others rushing to buy things.

We gulped down breakfast. Salah, Abbas, and I were going to spend the morning in the markets in search of more suitcases. Everyone had told us Medina was the best city for shopping, and said its people kinder and more polite than the people of Quraysh, the Prophet's tribe, the merchants of

Mecca. In the hallway, we were surprised to smell a *tajine* simmering in the next room. A group of men were staying there who had come on pilgrimage without their wives—a technician from the Ministry of Agriculture, a driver who worked for a hospital in Skhirat, and a cattle breeder-dealer from the Rabat region. They shopped and cooked in turn.

"Goodness, the women had better start cooking!" Abbas remarked to Salah. "We've got everything, for God's sake! Couscous, canned meat, oil, and all sorts of olives. Everything's from Ouezzane—the best!"

We had talked about cooking with the women. Farida, the physician, had argued that our time in Medina should be devoted to prayer, that piety demanded we satisfy ourselves with simple food from the cafeterias. Abbas had insisted that the women, "as in the other groups, could make an effort" to prepare meals. Some Moroccan women did wake up before their men, make breakfast, and tidy the rooms before going off to the mosque. When they had done their morning prayers, they came back and got lunch started before going to the shops.

Salah agreed with Abbas, but he wanted to avoid direct conflict with Farida, a bourgeois lady whose good opinion he sought. As for me, I said little, but every time someone asked, I supported the anti-cooking party. The issue was poisoning relations between women and men, though, and between Abbas and Salah. Because he was illiterate and from a modest background, Abbas felt dominated by Salah, a high-ranking engineer and the owner of a "splendid villa," as he described it.

"Ah! A little Moroccan food would be good," said Abbas, smiling, "a *tajine* or some calves' feet . . . oh, great couscous!"

The cattle breeder-dealer spoke up. "There are seven of us. We buy a rooster for twenty dirhams. They kill and pluck it for us . . . and we've brought everything with us: olive oil, even Lesieur oil, butter, spices, and onions. Everything. Moroccan cooking is absolutely necessary. Make sure you don't buy lamb here, though; it's too fatty. Chicken, or some beef for ground meat."

"Smells good! But let's go finish up our business at the souk. We have to get more suitcases," said Salah, heading for the door.

The other men insisted on serving us a quick cup of tea. While I was smoking a cigarette with the ambulance driver, the suitcase vision returned powerfully. Everyone knew a "reasonable" number of suitcases could make or break a successful return home. At the airport, these suitcases would be unloaded from the plane, and the crowd of people who came to meet the new *haj* would see them, as would everyone else when he went back to his village or neighborhood, of course.

When we returned, we found the women asleep in our room. They had been feeling sick from the pills they had taken to stop menstruation so as to be in "a state of purity" during the hajj. We woke them for a quick snack before the midday prayers. Then we pushed our way through the crowd as we always did, and in front of the mosque in the burning sun we heard the sermon booming from the loudspeakers. Guides stood at the doors of their mobile cabins, hammering away with their reprimands, answering questions put by the faithful, and selling books of "doctrine" regarding the hajj and diverse other subjects. Near the front the women left us to go to their side door. This time when I went in, I noticed the wooden divider separating us from them. It was impossible to see through or above it, and the doors leading to their enclosure were locked. They were opened only when the staff cleaned the whole mosque, I learned later.

Murmuring voices rose among the columns and filled the mosque's enormous galleries. They ascended, undulating beneath the ceilings and domes—recitations, invocations, prayers, supplications. For the first time, I noticed certain differences: there were those who said a *takbir** at each prostration, those who prayed with their hands alongside their bodies, those who crossed them over the belly, Malikites who uttered the final salutation with their index fingers raised, and yet others unacquainted with this practice.

The atmosphere of powerful, contained piety was disrupted from time to time by invocations and declarations of faith. My neighbor constantly repeated, "Yea, the Hour is come." Tears flowed everywhere, deep and calm. I could not know if they expressed remorse, honesty about the self, unlimited and unconstrained, or a judgment with no court, judge, or lawyer. There were also, as I was told several times, tears of *shawq*: of nostalgia and anticipated reunion, of longing for a paradoxical reunion, as when one cries before leaving for Mecca although one has never been there before. Tears for an age of innocence, or for the time of deliverance? In this vast, somewhat Hollywoodesque palace, the Muslim voices rising in the air saved the place from vanity and from imitation, wresting it away from the plans of the powers who built it. The voices rose, inhabiting the building and making it theirs, intertwining as they floated toward the heavens.

At the call to prayer, the serried ranks fell silent in communal submission. The imam's clear voice brought each of us to attention. Then came the tender, dreamy psalmody. I thought I saw my father's white cloak open and close around the child pressed against him. Time and space were for once defeated.

The announcement about prayers for the dead following the regular offices said this time that prayers were being said for "men, a child, and a woman." Later we learned that six

*The formula "God is great," "*Allah Akbar*," which initiates the call to prayer and the prayer itself. It is also said at the moment of cutting an animal's throat, for sacrifice or for consumption, and before battle.

Moroccans were among them, killed in an elevator accident. (According to the most widespread version, crowding and shoving, of which my compatriots are fond, had led to an overload; when the cable gave way on the fourth or fifth floor, the elevator had gone crashing to the ground.)

Lunch was once again grilled chicken. We had already tried most of the restaurants, and we were getting tired of their menus. Many of the places copied McDonald's or Burger King; others had nothing more than some *shawarma* at exorbitant prices; the most popular establishments resembled feeding troughs—long, narrow, and always crowded. One had to sit at a greasy table to eat the same old chicken, grilled on charcoal or on an electric range. For a change, we had rice with a Pakistani stew of vegetables floating in a thick red or yellow sauce which seared the palate. There was no way to have a conversation, especially with the women around. In any case, we were always in a rush to get away from the stifling heat of these places, where customers were squashed in between the grills at the front and the kitchens at the back. Increasingly, we preferred to take food to our lodgings after buying tea or a Pepsi at the corner grocer's. I was surprised to find myself thinking that these various restaurants fulfilled a worthy function: they edified the faithful by presenting them with an unadulterated version of hell.

After siesta, mid-afternoon prayers, and prayers for the dead, we went through the markets we had already explored, toward Sittin Boulevard, where I bought a coral red fan that opened to reveal the declaration of faith. I spent some time looking at toys, clocks, trays illustrated with the mosques of Mecca and Medina or with the Kaaba. There were also prayer beads in wood, imitation ivory, or phosphorescent stones; and, of course, the ubiquitous prayer mats, some of them equipped with compasses to show the exact direction of Mecca wherever one happened to be. Every time we left the covered galleries we found ourselves back in the stifling streets, light-headed from the sun, the crowds, the noise of cars and trucks, not to mention asphyxiated by the dust mingling in with petrol fumes, the Egyptian voices "chanting" the Qur'an, spewing some doctrinal truth about this world and the hereafter, emitting morals as empty as they were sonorous. These predatory voices, launched from some dusty Cairo studio, were assaulting the whole Muslim world. I knew that these voices reached every one of Islam's markets. Was anyone really listening? Certainly their lugubrious religiosity saturated the atmosphere.

5

DEAD ENDS

I DECIDED ONE DAY TO GO ALONE TO THE PROPHET'S SHRINE for another visit, once the mid-afternoon prayer was accomplished. After meditating there, I went to the big cemetery called al-Baqi'. I wanted to be sure not to leave Medina without stopping at the tombs of the Prophet's companions, hoping to create a link with them and, despite the time separating me from them, to draw moral benefits from their virtue and knowledge.

The famous cemetery was surrounded by a high semicircular wall, along which ran a wide promenade. Enormous screened openings with vaulted tops somewhat broke up the monotony of the wall and, through their reinforced-concrete latticework, afforded a view of the innumerable black stones marking the graves. Women hung on to these pierced dividers to contemplate the interior of the cemetery, which they were not allowed to enter.

I paused for a moment near what I had been told were the tombs of several important Shiite imams, among them the particularly revered Ja'far al-Sadiq. From this vantage point, one could see the whole vast place—circles, squares, or rectangles of large black stones in the foreground, beyond and below them, barely visible, other traces of tombs. I took a walk along the main path. An Indian pilgrim, who had a map with the key in English, showed me the grave of Ibrahim, the Prophet's only son, who died in infancy; then that of Uthman, the third caliph, who was assassinated and left behind him a reputation for piety (and nepotism). Farther on was the tomb of Zaynab, who breast-fed the child Muhammad ibn Abd Allah in the desert encampments. At the gate, on the left, was Aisha, beloved wife of "God's Messenger" and "mother of the faithful." While pigeons pecked about for the seeds visitors threw them among the gravestones, religious policemen in white robes waited to stamp out the least sign of "tomb worship," as Wahhabi idiom calls it.

I lingered near a group of Iranians with their mullahs. Gathered around graves of their imams, some seated, the others standing in a circle, they started to chant poems in Persian; then, imperceptibly, the declamations became songs of mourning and contrition, interspersed with tears and sobbing; the crowd attracted the religious police, who came over and abruptly dispersed them. A policeman ordered me to move along and to watch out for "these barbaric Shiite practices, this veneration of persons and all worship of tombs." I left the cemetery, ashamed that one sect of Islam could with impunity repress other Islamic practices, could show such contempt for the religious sensibilities of other Muslims, could call them *ajam*, the Arabic equivalent of "barbarian." I willingly agreed to discuss this with a mullah who came up to me in the shadow of the outer wall.

"You were there when they made us leave. Are you Shiite?"

"Yes, I saw. I disapprove. I'm not Shiite; I'm Moroccan."

"Ah! *Sunna*. Maybe you don't know. It's the same conspiracy as it always has been against us, partisans of Ali . . ."

"Conspiracy?"

"Yes, conspiracy, today just as before; you've seen for yourself. In the time of the Prophet, the plot was already being hatched. Abu Bakr and the others twisted everything, set everything in the direction they wanted so they could push aside the legitimate caliph, Ali."

Thus did I receive my first direct initiation into the history of "the dawn of Islam" from a Shiite perspective, and in classical Arabic. The mullah who delivered it invited me to visit him one day in Shiraz. I suggested that he might consider the caliphate and its quarrels as things of the past, that perhaps it might be better to evoke the caliphs as reference points for interpreting democratic institutions *today*.

"Do you really think so?" my interlocutor demanded, staring at me.

"Yes."

"Well, we are awaiting the return of the [Hidden] Imam. The Well-Guided One is in his mother's womb. As we wait for him, scholars must watch over religion. He will return with the mission of restoring justice. His return is certain. In Iran today, we have the *vilayet-i faqih*.* That's the most important institution; it protects Islam by its ordering of the Good."

Before going our separate ways, we repeated to each other that there was no difference among Muslims. I walked along the open-air market next to the cemetery, passing the inevitable scarves, bonnets, bracelets, pendants, prayer beads, candles, perfumes, incense, prayer mats, and such, and met

---

*Rule of the Supreme Jurist. The Iranian constitution of 1979, written after the revolution, gives supreme power to this religious authority, which supervises all aspects of the government to ensure its conformity with Shari'a law as interpreted by the party of Ayatollah Khomeini.

up with my compatriots. We turned to Sittin Boulevard, where another exploratory trip was needed to complete our purchases. I also hoped to find a bookstore where I could order a few important works on Wahhabi doctrine.

The very extensive market had several different groupings, some entirely Afghan. "I'm Afghan but not Taliban," a man said when I asked where he came from. I explained that we were Moroccan, which he didn't seem to understand very well. Nor did we know how to translate "Maghreb" or "Morocco" into Afghan. His neighbor was devouring a piece of bread, which made me very hungry. He quickly offered me a piece. "*Tannour* bread, Afghan bread, our bread," he said, showing me a nearby oven.

We waited by the oven for a long time while the man first served Afghans and took no notice of us. He was indifferent to our displeasure. When we protested more loudly about this "un-Islamic behavior," our Afghan brothers withdrew into their language and carried on; we were served only when their compatriots left, bread under their arms.

The incident underscored something I had already noticed: pilgrims rarely mingled, but kept to themselves and spoke their own languages. We were all grouped by nationality in any case. Naturally, each group also wore its national costume. Since the *ziyara*, or "visit"—a rite quite distinct from the *umra* or the hajj (and not an obligatory one, though most pilgrims try to do it), which entails praying at the Prophet's mosque and meditating near his sanctuary—does not require ritual garb, it was easy that day to distinguish among Indonesians (men in caps, women in immaculate white hooded dresses), Pakistanis (baggy pants and tunics), Turks (khaki uniforms with flags pinned to their lapels), Moroccans (djellabas and white caps), Iranians (men in capes, women draped in black), people from the Gulf states and Arabia (various styles of keffiyeh), and the gallabaya-clad

Egyptians. Language and national identity separated these crowds of Muslims, who rubbed shoulders without making much contact. With the bread vendor as with others, one had to remember the hadith "No quarreling during hajj!" Conflict was not unknown, but everyone made a steady effort to keep the peace. Worship and commerce, by mobilizing energy, also worked to this end. Contact or discussion with pilgrims from other nations was brief and sporadic. We spoke only of what brought us together, and parted ways after an embrace or a clasp of hands. At least, that was my experience as a man. The women in my group confirmed my impression that this held for them, too.

Nothing was missing in the ongoing, intense activity—not even begging. I was stopped by a young Pakistani who appealed to my faith in his request for assistance. If one was to believe him, he wanted to go home but was alone and penniless. Other people hoping for alms aimed for the fat envelopes offered by rich Saudi families. As the hajj drew close, these quests intensified and sometimes attracted beggars of an unexpected type. We learned that a former member of the Moroccan parliament had been arrested for flagrant begging.

The circulation of merchandise, like the circulation of pilgrims, animated a very active labor market. Hajj transportation and the shops in Medina functioned largely thanks to the non-Saudis hired to do the work: mostly Afghans, Pakistanis, and other Muslims from poor countries. Egyptians drove the buses packed with pilgrims during the hajj season, while Pakistanis ran the shops under contract with Saudis who put up the capital. I got to know one of them, who ran a shop selling watches and pictures: a young man from the Karachi region. He told me he worked at the store for 250 Saudi riyals a month as well as food and lodging. He added that several members of his family—himself, his brother, and

his father—worked in turn for two months each. Exploring
Medina's markets further, I met other Pakistanis, Afghans,
and Indians who were wage workers or had the same kind of
deal. The fact that Saudi proprietors gave them food and
lodging often meant these "wage workers" were also working as domestic servants.

Everything was on the move: masses of human beings,
currents of thought, merchandise, images, profound and su-
perficial wisdom, doctrine, discourse, prejudices, and stereotypes. The diversity of nations and languages was making
nation and language relative. Arabic, being the sacred language related to worship, was for non-Arabs identified with
that particular domain in their lives. With Indonesians, Pakistanis, and other pilgrims from Southeast Asia, I spoke
English. At the mosque, we chanted the official Saudi version of the Qur'an. We already knew what we had come to
tell each other in this holy place, and we communicated by
means other than ordinary voices. But what were we saying?
"God," "message," "unity," "faith," "Islam"—these words
were plucked from theological and philosophical exchanges
and commentaries on the life and histories of Muslims. But
ritual put an end to this gleaning, because in it we moved
without discussion toward certainty, toward God, faith, Islam. We could meet without mingling, concur without
agreeing. We did not pretend otherwise, and the career path
of the words followed.

So the words of a tradition converged in one place, a center of intensity, and the same went for the things that filled
the spaces around the mosque in their hypnotic—to me, unbearable—profusion. This was a debauchery of merchandise,
indicating desires that moved implacably from one object to
another. Among all creatures, only human beings consume
the world as an image and are consumed by it. This is not
the case with spirits and angels, who are shielded from it.

But, like us, Satan is not thus protected, and for this very reason we were going to stone him to death.

Medina's beating heart had two chambers: the mosque and the marketplace. Some of the merchandise spoke the language of the Qur'an—books, prayer rugs, verses printed in gold letters under glass—but the goods mostly proliferated in English, French, Japanese, Korean, Chinese. And if in this era of general circulation one thought about capital, about placements and displacements of production, one could sense an invisible chemistry melding the language of the Qur'an with those of the Torah, the Gospels, Confucianism, and a few others besides.

All these commodities, offered so abundantly to the eyes, nose, ears, finger, tongue, and even sixth sense, sloughed off their provenance here in Medina, as well as the identity of their makers. Even the scriptural words on them lost importance and were deciphered only with an eye to price and quality. Their future efficacy and their oracular air removed them from their producers, and they became a scriptural palimpsest thanks to the grace imparted by prayer and the call of memory. In transit, like the pilgrims, these goods took on the beneficial potency of fetishes. Yet here "commodity fetishism" did not mask labor (as Karl Marx said it did); on the contrary, it disavowed it in the name of prior gestures of gift giving and debt.

This was not immediately visible, and for a good reason: the act of giving came *at the end* of the commodity, at the end of its production as merchandise. First an object to dream on, an object to produce, then a produced object, an object for selling, an object for consumption. What took place before seemed to come into play afterward, and vice versa. As time machines that could represent the past in the future, these goods put parenthetical marks around the traces humans leave in matter. Gift and sacrifice did not mark the same boundaries here as elsewhere. Nor could one detect their efficacy—even supposing this term was ever a religious one. Nor could one find a boundary between the human and the divine, between work and leisure—as might have been the case in ancient Greece. In Medina's practical memory, what men and women had to do, beyond work, was to receive and to give so as to gain recognition for a third term: the gift without precedent. There, to be clear, was a difference which came (through intrigue and violence) in the form of transcendence and hierarchy.

Transcendence was achieved in the community. It was there every day, gathered in the mosque of the Prophet. It took the form of the milling crowd, the mosque, the sanctuary, the Qur'an. It kept itself in being as power, delegated and regulated by religious knowledge—hence a hierarchy dependent on genealogical accumulation and on effort. The scholars were at the apex; then came men assigned to bear arms; and last the people, organized hierarchically according to birth and occupation. Still, it was not a world defined by caste, and nothing in this world was immutable. On the contrary, every individual asserted his or her rights according to the rules of a justice that treated each person individually and also according to what his or her status contributed, in theory, to the whole. Debts and gifts transform goods, and thus they play their part in humanity's journey infinitely projected onward. We make our way together, accepting the loss of our shared time spans, thrown to a region beyond ourselves. An intuitive sense of order corresponds to something necessary, not to something arbitrary beyond our grasp.

Medina, I realized as the days went by, set a limit on the general circulation of goods as goods; instead, it produced a hierarchized circulation of meanings. When I realized this, I saw that many other words could translate *"ziyara"*—the visit to the sanctuary and to Medina the Radiant, and also the prayer "near the Messenger of God." In that place one came upon the whole world, all nations reunited in the name of a universal creed. In the past as now, the circulation of this creed encompassed the global movements of people, of meaning, and of merchandise.

With colonial and imperialist globalization, goods, languages, images, and imagination became inextricably intertwined, and they ramified in unexpected ways. Translations and writing made for transverse paths. *Ziyara*? Gathering, devotion, market, debates—a straining toward a meaning yet to come, yet to be summoned. By meditation, psalmody, shouts, tears, or all of these at once? Unstable forms followed other unstable forms, each profiting from a moment of forgetfulness, from the moment it takes for a new configuration to emerge. *"Ziyara"* in the sense of a very peculiar visit shifted and jostled other meanings: visit, visitation, journey, passage, tourism, meetings, business. It also brought them together. *Ziyara*—first step on the journey to an outer limit and toward a house of God, at the limit of the globe and globalization. At the limit of what it means to travel, to circulate, and to pass through, at the limit of "global time," which gets its bearings here before setting out again. The journey to the limit stretched out a pattern that opened onto loss—that is, a will to live, a universal will.

All but two of my companions in this cramped room had traveled in Europe and elsewhere. They had spent long periods of time away from Morocco—at university, on training courses, or on holiday—and this meant they spoke French or English. I wasn't very different from them in this respect, since I had lived and studied in France. Of course, I also knew a good number of Arab countries fairly well, and life had taken me to North America, where I lived and taught in a university. Working trips had familiarized me with other European countries: Germany especially, Spain, England,

Italy. Japan and New Guinea had allowed me briefly to experience non-monotheistic societies. In Mexico, I saw the interplay among Mayan and Aztec universes, Hispanic Christianity, and Arab-Berber features (evident yet suppressed); archaeology in Mexico aptly revealed, in a sort of involuntary irony, the Algerian blood injected there during the Second Empire; and there was also its Syrian-Lebanese diaspora. About a year before my trip to the Hijaz,* my family and I were in Puerto Rico, where we lunched in a Palestinian restaurant whose windows had been broken, we were told, by Haitians—"slaves," the owner called them. The place was next to an uninteresting small mosque, and both buildings nestled discreetly in the sordid chaos of the place—another repression—no doubt the better to be forgotten.

Raised in Islam, I had seen Muslims at times triumphant, at others diminished and cringing, sometimes tolerant and serene, sometimes vindictive and exultant, sometimes as persecutors, and sometimes persecuted and killed by the thousands. Modern war machines had been grinding them down, and for some time their lives had seemed to count for less than those of Jews and Christians. My companions shared this view, but they also espoused, besides beliefs that simple faith would have consigned to the scrap heap, political and social doctrines that I didn't accept. Every passing day revealed our differences more clearly. I ended up, my fears notwithstanding, accepting that illusion and dream were the surest means of delivering me from rational theologies and authoritarian right thinking. I had also known, for some time, that my life was changing in condensations whose

---

*The western region of Saudi Arabia, bordering the Red Sea, which includes both Medina and Mecca. Briefly an independent kingdom, it was conquered in 1926 by the neighboring kingdom of Najd (homeland of the Saud family) and in 1932 became part of Saudi Arabia.

meaning I could only grasp retrospectively, in the past tense. I now guessed that *ziyara* and hajj were projecting me into one such condensation, which, in a sort of photosynthesis, bore me toward images of life that I would frequent as others did. But once again what was going to happen seemed already to have occurred, and the brilliance of life appeared in the colors of the past. The strange familiarity I had felt while living through every past moment of my life story was there to remind me that these futures were not futures at all.

In Medina, then, I found much that was familiar yet that I had never known. It was not simply because I came to this city carrying with me imagined Medinas, superimposed one over the other, forming deposits and overlaps; I saw Medina in these ruins of cities. The familiar countenance became a strange one, and I would have to hold steady to survive in the Medina of my *ziyara*, to avoid making a fatal slip at the thresholds separating it from the other Medinas and uniting it with them.

This journey was throwing me into a transitory, precarious, itinerant mode. It was nothing like tourism, with its swapping of snapshots, its trading of youthful paradises, nothing like a far-flung trip that takes you out of yourself, dissolving your identity in the endless disparities of translation. I had left my home and was going to another home, built on a boundary. This journey differed from others not only in terms of its destination: its unprecedented, ineffable character lay in the fact that something sacred inhabited a certain space found elsewhere, at an outer limit; it came into being only through human movement, in the past on foot and today by means of mechanized transport and communications technologies which stopped, as if thunderstruck, at its gates. The human movement came to a halt at the boundary of ancient time and touched there something whose genesis it could not trace, but that it knew to have been the

origin, here. As a pilgrim, therefore, I was leaving my home
to go to my mythological home, the only one I could inhabit, the one that accepted me as a being adrift in the
world: a home of eternity where I have always been, there
with the ancient. The first home and the last—which was en-
folded by the other? We were far from the new Babel, with
its claim of keeping languages separate.

The people of Medina supplied both imams and shopkeepers. Lucre could rule freely, and its passions could sustain the Medina of trade and those who served at the shrine
of this divinity. The universality of such an operation made
for simultaneous gathering and isolation, fusion and separation. We could bargain in Moroccan Arabic with Saudi, Pakistani, or Afghan merchants, but beyond the marketplace
each individual fell back to his own territory. Everywhere,
our clothes set us apart from each other. The garb of the old
Muslim nations, reintroduced in honor of the religious life
of various modern nation-states, showed a tense accommodation to Western clothes—which, for example, the Indonesians and Turks wore with some modifications.

Occasions for mutual irritation, explicit or implicit, were
numerous. I found it very hard to sustain prolonged contact
with Saudis and pilgrims from other nations, apart from a
few Iranians and Indonesians with whom I could speak modern standard Arabic or English. In contrast, relations were
closer among Moroccan men, who became companions and
neighbors; contact with the women was very limited and
intermittent. In the market as at the mosque, we learned
to treat each other with restraint, not by denying otherness
but by adjusting to it. The ritual of communal prayer, while
it alternated with the other communion, that of merchandise, preserved its primacy, which authorized unity and
dispersal.

We fell into routines. For a change, we decided one day to

go to the date market. One of our neighbors had heard it mentioned back home in Morocco—pilgrims gathered as much information as they could before going to Arabia. After sunset prayers, we left the mosque by the Gate of Peace and headed for this market. Immediately on our left, between the great cemetery and the highway, was the imposing building of the Shari'a court, its flag fluttering in the wind. I shuddered as I usually did when I saw such institutions—not out of fear, but because of another sensation, which I had also experienced on the airplane from Rabat.

I had been handed over with my group to Saudi Airlines as a matter of course. Somewhere in the sky between the Nile valley and the landing in Jeddah, I opened the company's sleek in-flight magazine: beautiful pictures on glossy paper, boring articles, advertisements. I was dozing off when I noticed an item I had never seen in publications of this sort: a warning that whoever brought drugs onto "Saudi soil" would be subject to the death penalty. Reading it—and now seeing this court of "justice"—in my imagination I began to reel off scenes of Wahhabi-style executions, not a realistic film of things I might have seen but a surrealistic sequence that perhaps brought me close to a certain reality: a colossus with muscles of steel, sword drawn; the condemned man, bound and bent, unable to guess the position of the angel of death; then very quickly the tip of the sword stabs his back, the neck stretches out, meeting the blade that descends upon it in the blink of an eye. The literalism of official Saudi doctrine, purportedly reducing the use of metaphor, revealed its murderous transparency. For instance, it might readily argue that "sword"—in the literal sense!—meant merely the "cutting instrument" used to mete out justice. Outside these sinister buildings, I began to think that I had perhaps committed crimes and could at any moment be sent before

well-trained judges (in the literal sense) and executioners
with immaculately pure swords.

Walking to the date market, I was overcome by disgust.
Disgust at the thought that a human being could thus be led
before a *qadi* who would dictate life or death on the basis of
how he chose to understand the divine edicts set down in the
time of the Prophet. Disgust that some people gave themselves the right to make an absolute interpretation of
prophetic precedent and, in the name of that interpretation,
the power to deliver absolute judgments. And then, the
house of God and the house of the law were too close together. Was the mosque no longer the place and time of
peace, of protection, of a mercy greater than the law, no
longer that place and time when the faithful recognized all
their lapses, all their misdeeds, not as crimes but as sins before God and his mercy—in anticipation of forgiveness and
not of a sharp blade?

I crossed the highway quickly so as to leave the dreadful
vision behind me. Streets of the neighborhood we were
headed for came into view. Oh, the peace and comfort of
that date market! It was a vast space, a large courtyard with
modest walls and pillars, divided lengthwise by a permanent
row of stalls built on either side of an openwork fence. All
around were open shops sheltered by a roofed arcade. It was
both busy and peaceful. The dates, piled in generous heaps,
were resplendent in the light and in all the colors they offered up to us: gold, honey, velvet brown, rust turning to
aubergine, silky black, ivory turning to ocher. All their
forms: long and slender, short, thick and faintly ribbed, fat
and somewhat round, flat, wide at one end and pointed at
the other like little peppers. All their textures: hard, firm,
soft, sticky. What deliverance was in those dates, glowing
with a thousand gentle sparkles! What relief! After the gold,
the diamonds, the global electronic junk, the hamburgers,

the *shawarma*, the self-service joints and restaurants, and the Saudi city. Pilgrims, hosts of Pakistanis and Indians, were buying dates both to enjoy their blessing and as provisions. Seeing their faces, peaceful and appeased, I forgot for a while about those who rummaged night and day in the galaxy of merchandise.

I tasted a date, then another, and a third: the perfumed sweetness woke my palate to dormant flavors it had first known long ago. They radiated like colors, and as I strolled slowly along an arcade, my eyes stopped on a sign that hung above an office door: "*Shaykh* of the date sellers"! I gazed into this face, framed by a keffiyeh held in place around his head by a black cord: a sensitive face with noble lines. The benevolent smile accentuated the delicacy of the man's features. Like the market, this face exuded *baraka*.

Every thing and every being can possess *baraka*. Much has been written about the word. Perhaps it has not been said often enough that it refers to an active principle, which is dormant at times, alive and virulent at others, at times in decline or even failing in effectiveness. Nor has its ambiguity been emphasized enough: it is both noun and adjective, and has both transitive and intransitive verbal forms. Passive and active, then: through contact and friction, it can lodge itself in beings by sheer contiguity or just pass through. Beneficial, and dangerous as well. Such a principle moves about freely and is subject to no law. One can receive it only under certain conditions. Certain gestures and functions favor its transmission: touch, kiss, caress, ingest. Share and ingest.

Dates, barley, and milk—substances imbued with saintliness—are particularly recommended in these places. It was not this sort of contact I was seeking when I tasted the dates I admired in the Medina market, although this religiosity by exhalation, rooted in immemorial tradition, was more to my liking than the Wahhabi religion. Wahhabi zealots, pushing "God's oneness"—of which humans, after all, know nothing—to absurd extremes, have transformed being into a simple abstraction. They have brought the Qur'an and the Prophet's example down to the level of a recipe book and consigned its implementation to militias. Rather than God being a principle and a call, he becomes a general in white robes and keffiyeh, pitiless and solitary.

The Wahhabi reform, supposedly intended to restore vigor to Muslim creativity and rationality, has in fact expelled sacredness from the creatures on this earth. Nothing escaped its devastation: not the hills or the desert sands, not the palm trees of the oases, not the animals, not the sanctuaries, not even the cities of venerable antiquities. Not even Medina. The lands from which the fluids of life flowed were treated without compunction; sanctuaries were torn down, and old cities razed to the ground with their old mosques, their streets, their houses, all these creations that bore the trace of human gaze and feeling since Adam. Even the bones that prayed, in their silence, for resurrection by the Verb— even these were reduced to ashes. As if recognizing a God imprisoned in power alone required that beauty be banished from the cemeteries which returned by the slow work of decomposition to wilderness; as if one had to curb the energy of past generations that graves and cemeteries gave to us!

The dates and palm trees saved me; I took refuge with them. This was henceforth my place, the place where I could be, a place that totalitarian and policed urbanism could not disfigure. The palm trees and dates were a consolation for almost everything: for the mosque of Tuba, the oldest of those the Messenger himself had built; for the mosque called "one of the two-*qibla*," where he pronounced that prayers should be said facing Mecca; for the cemetery of Uhud, which was now no more than a pile of stones enclosed by a rusty iron fence. They consoled me for having to visit all this in a rush, at the whim of a Hijazi taxi driver who was money hungry and obsessed by our female companions. Mosques: razed and rebuilt. The cemetery where the Prophet's companions were buried, having died for their faith: closed to meditation and surrounded by merchandise. Later, I thought of these dates when, wandering again along Medina's American-style avenues, contemplating the graceless neighborhoods where modern middle-class Arabs dwelled, I searched in vain for remainders of bygone eras, something that could stand in for origins and pathways. Wahhabi Medina was doing all it could to chase away my Medina and all those Medinas that had been. But these didn't wholly disappear. They hid in a place whence their celestial irony will no doubt come and strike the new Medina with lightning.

Medina, my home. Not the Athens of Pericles, not the Jerusalem of the Temple or of Constantine, not the Rome of plodding divinities and of Saint Peter, not the Paris of the Concorde's sacred square, where the sacrificed king was buried beneath an obelisk (in a grandiose ritual with revolutionary crowds gathered around the guillotine). None of these could displace Medina, my mythological home. It lived on in all of Islam's cities. It will find its way around the city that forbade me even from seeing the Prophet's tomb, that kept me from everything I wanted to see, touch, smell, everything that might have taken the prayer and the chanting of the Qur'an and connected them physically to the miracle of a tradition's birth. In the absence of streets, buildings, or sanctuaries, in the absence of old Yathrib, only palm trees and dates led to this place. Palm trees and dates gave me what Islam's charismatic community had seen and eaten, which I, too, in turn could see and eat. They also renewed the link with those who lived in these oases before my charismatic community: their language, religions, the tem-

ples, which I guessed at in reading the Qur'an and were returned to me as tangible objects by Ibn al-Kalbi, the famous
writer of early Islam, and modern archaeology. So I tasted
my dates, and now contemplated every palm tree I came
across. It was as if I were conversing with people who had savored this fruit once and calmed their soul at the sight of the
palm fronds atop the trunks, immobile, open, and stretching
toward the horizon.

As soon as the visit to the market was over, toward the end
of the evening, we returned to the mosque. It seemed to me
to be hesitating between the sublime and a film set, with its
Oriental minarets piercing the sky, its coppery domes, and
its Andalusian doors. Yet the immense, calm prayer seized it
and gave it a celestial beauty. I left it after the prayers, borne
on the soft clamor behind me that faded as I walked back
along the main avenue. I began to look distractedly for a
place to eat.

Thirty years or so earlier, I had watched, swallowing my
rage, as bulldozers gutted much of al Hufuf, once the Ot-
toman capital of eastern Arabia. This mostly Shiite city
stood in a beautiful oasis, in a small valley overlooked by
cliffs tinted gold and old rose. Its palm groves were irrigated
by abundant artesian springs, appearing and reappearing in
small pools. At the time, irrigation was being "modernized,"
and rapid destruction was underway in al Hufuf in the name
of "modernity." Whole neighborhoods were vanishing; well-
made adobe mud-brick houses and mosques were being
smashed to dust. A few people whispered that the operation
was meant to put the Shiite community in order—in other
words, to control it. If Qatif, the other Shiite town, escaped
this fate, the destruction mania did not spare Dammam, the
Sunni city in the east of the kingdom, some way to the south.
"Modernity" ravaged everything. There were only big highways, made for cars, and avenues which put on a grid the im-

mense new cities separated from one another. Neighbor-hoods with new housing sprang up everywhere, like those in modern Arab cities, with clinics, supermarkets, restaurants, and hotels. Dhahran, with its American base hunkered down behind impenetrable barriers, watched over all this. It was a concentration of military might and petroleum management, a representation of the "American way of life" that men and women from the Saudi elite came to savor, decked out in their Western clothes; for these jaunts, the couples doffed their veils, long white shirts, and keffiyehs.

In Dammam, I had the chance to meet a good number of women studying at the University of Petroleum and Miner-als. Most were Sunni, as were most people in Saudi Arabia who had key positions and enjoyed privileged access to high-level technical education at the time. Shiites came to work in Dammam and at night went home to "their city," Qatif. Sometimes I exchanged information and opinions with a group of students who were working under my direction. Some of them, when saying the word "Shia," even in the presence of a colleague who belonged to that group of Mus-lims, almost always added a canonical formula of damnation. Deep upheavals were sweeping through all the societies of the "Arab Middle East," which the consequences of the 1973 war between Israel and Egypt and Syria had probably accel-erated. The Greater Persia of Iran's Shah Mohammed Reza Pahlavi was undergoing even quicker changes. In this cli-mate, a linguistic habitus of this sort came across as a delib-erate habit, maintained and relearned.

Most of the young people I met, very tough in business and interested in sports, prayed "out of duty" or, as they would say with a smile, "because otherwise you can't get any-where . . . and . . . the religious police . . ." Indeed, the police were always around, and showed exceptional perseverance at prayer times, pistols at their hips, knocking on shop doors

with sticks and shouting: "Prayer! Prayer!" The students did
not ask me much about my own country, except about its
politics and women. "Is it true that where you come from
male and female students can have fun together?" "Yes, of
course, it happens," I answered. "Without paying, the boy
can . . ." "Yes, that happens, too," I went on. "Oh! I've
wanted to go to Morocco for ages! You know . . . here it's
very difficult, you have to get married!" I had ritual, secret
exchanges with a few adults—a little alcohol, a few meals of
hamburgers and fries, and always the same comments: "Each
country has its traditions, and we are not like the others.
Here, you have to do as others do; in Morocco, you're too
French." Or, as a high-ranking government employee remarked to me, "In Morocco, democracy has corrupted you.
Get rid of it!" I was stunned. At the time, Morocco was in
crisis: special measures were in full swing; parliament had
been suspended; and repression was rampant.

Generalized surveillance, doublespeak, "hidden refusals,"
conformism—yet I would forget all these evasions, all this
suffering, when, from time to time, unexpectedly a heaven-
sent encounter occurred. That was the case one lovely afternoon I spent with the *qadi* of Dammam: a man in his sixties,
a Sunni, who received me according to the rule of strict gender separation; a cultivated, sweet, familiar, discreetly good-
natured man, like many traditional scholars in my own
country. For the mid-afternoon prayer, he went into a corner
of the room without asking me anything and, his duty fulfilled, immediately returned to our conversation over a nice
cup of coffee. We discussed religion and Shari'a, but also
belles-lettres. He encouraged me to come back and, the second time we met, gave me the books he had written and
asked me to "submit them," as he said in the same tone of serious benevolence, "to the opinion of the *'alem* of Fez." I
found the same haven of peace and refinement at a lunch

given by a Shiite man of letters from Qatif in a large adobe house with several floors. We talked for a long while, just he and I, in the coolness of the breeze channeled through horizontal slits in the walls of his enormous drawing room/ library. Well-proportioned shelves held a rich collection of books, among them translations of Karl Marx, as well as Indian and Chinese bibelots. The part of Qatif had long lived off pearl diving and trade with Iran, India, and beyond. My host preached tolerance and complained of Wahhabi religious policy. I left the city wondering whether anything would remain of it once the ports had been extended and the ham-handed official urbanization was completed.

These memories of the fairly long spell I had spent working in the Gulf came back to me with singular vigor during these last days in Medina. The Hijaz had always had the great hajj resources; and the Gulf region as a whole, for the past half century, has had immense petroleum resources. Despite this difference, the disappearance of old Medina testified to the same deliberate desire to erase the past systematically that had eliminated al Hufuf before my eyes thirty-odd years before. Major Arab, European, and other corporations had made big profits in these raids on the "cities of salt." I had long attributed this to hunger for profits, the historic incompetence of bureaucracy, and the nonsensical behavior of people trying to prove something to someone: a compensatory, unreflective imitation of modernity, draped in *abaya* and keffiyeh, steering in the direction of long beards or well-clipped goatees and mustaches. Maybe there was some truth to that, but wandering in Medina showed me something else: I had forgotten that this was actually a form of modern totalitarianism, far closer to the defunct Soviet system than to the constitution of Medina or to Bedouin informality. A merciless formula managed by technocrats with sophisticated means of communication and espionage, techniques for daily intimidation, and a propaganda force that could recycle traditions and social pressures to its own benefit. In Medina, as elsewhere, it served us its exclusive version of the holy city and of the city. Its version and no other.

During the first days of my stay in Medina, I could not rid myself of the feeling that I was alone in refusing to give in to this Wahhabi city and in my pursuit of the dream "radiant city." Yet with time, I began to perceive that I was not alone. I am thinking of the mullah I met near the cemetery and of other Iranian pilgrims. These men mourned the imams who, according to them, had given their lives to the cause of absolute knowledge and justice on earth, who knew secrets inaccessible to common mortals; their radiant city was the city where the grace of the Prophet had interceded with God. Their holy city was one where this regenerative grace was a living presence among us. *Ziyara*, prayer, panegyric, and confession—all these called for and commemorated the certain return of the Hidden savior.

The indifference the Iranians showed to the other Medina, the city that sought to deny their existence, helped me slowly understand how other pilgrims sustained their indifference to this urban landscape where they carried out the rituals and essential functions of life. "Each of us is here to render unto God what is God's," I was told, and the rest didn't count. People were mainly concerned with following, as accurately as they could, the rules of a pilgrimage that would prove acceptable to God. Behavior that might invalidate it or diminish its merit (quarrels, selfishness, gossip, immodesty for men and women) was the topic of many conversations. The men constantly denounced "immodest bearing," feared only in the case of women. This was a daily obsession, as was the need for strict gender segregation. Our neighbors politely but insistently reproached us for our coed

living arrangements. Under the surveillance of a technician—I had met him a few years earlier and knew he had embraced the Wahhabi reforms—they made sure "their women"
were kept in "their own space."

I realized then this fairly generalized indifference resulted
from people having made certain choices: for instance, to de-
tach themselves from Saudi Medina or, on the contrary, to
adhere perfectly to its ethos. In one case, one simply went
through it, taking refuge in the light of the Prophet; in the
other, one lived in this new concrete city of prohibitions with
such certitude that even the prophetic light no longer lit the
soul's perilous paths. The men and women who were ready
to wear such redoubtable armor were many. An artisan I
knew urged me to cover a knee I had bared in a sudden
movement. An Egyptian pilgrim, taking a drag on his cigarette, pointed his index finger at my belly: a shirt button—at
the navel!—had come undone. I was wearing an undershirt,
but, he said, "That doesn't matter. You have to do up your
shirt!" Medina the Radiant thus faded behind the Medina
belonging to those who had discovered their mission as
God's agents on earth. Pilgrims heading for the source of life
went on their way, heedless of this cartography of surveillance. Others were content just to be there, free from responsibility and concern, enjoying a country fair, a short
holiday, or happy with a foretaste of paradise.

In this way, religion created quite contradictory currents
while arranging for them to flow together in a sort of mutually accepted ignorance. Each of us could move in his city.
My neighbor Haj Mbarek, who drove a pickup truck for a
government office, spent most of his time praying, smoking,
and making ironic asides about "this country's greed." One
day he said to me, "If God is One, why do we need to go
here and there to meet him? Why do they take us to several
places? Isn't it just because they want to do more business?"

I, too, felt distressed in this borrowed Chicago, with streets named after famous early companions of the prophet, such as Abu Darr al-Ghifari or Umar ibn al-Khattab, its shops and hotels given names like Piety Intercontinental.

The mosque only turned us back on ourselves, ensuring that we all obeyed even the most unacceptable constraints, all the while escaping them. Nothing kept the men and women here from approaching God and the Prophet with the most diverse intimate convictions: not the military presence near the sanctuary or the civilian police who crisscrossed the sacred space of prayer and guarded its doors. The Wahhabi preachers vainly insisted as often and as loudly as they pleased that men came first, and vainly repeated the order for women to stay at the back; they could believe if they liked that they were imposing absolute purity by separating with high, padlocked fences the spaces for men and women to pray. But the men and women were protected by their faith and existed in a fourth dimension, that of prayer, free from this administration of religion with its power to imprison.

I found this diversity of approach even at the very heart of questions about one's relation to God. Among Moroccans and Algerians I met, Wahhabi opinions regarding the oneness of God were very controversial. One day at the end of our stay in Medina, after the mid-afternoon prayers, we settled in for the sermon and the question-and-answer session. A small group of us followed this session on the roof of the mosque—the heat was stifling and it was easier to breathe in the open air. A young Moroccan boy—one could tell his country of origin by his voice and accent, carried by the loudspeaker—asked whether it was permissible to carry out the hajj for deceased parents and to ask God to forgive them for certain practices, like visiting the tombs of saints. The question was a thorny one, often discussed among North

Africans, since Wahhabi propaganda was relentlessly vitu-
perative about "visits and sacrifices at sanctuaries." The answer fell like a whiplash: "If these parents received the
doctrine of the oneness of God and continued nonetheless to
visit sanctuaries and offer this sort of sacrifice, it is useless to
undertake the pilgrimage on their behalf. They were polytheists. Their conduct was illicit, ignominious. Those who
committed such deeds are wood for the fires of hell!" That
evening I told Mbarek about an elderly man who had been
deeply shocked by the session and had said to me after it that
we were "all lost, we Moroccans who worship idols!" I tried
to explain to him that Wahhabism was just one interpretation of Islam among many. He didn't understand. Then I
asked him, "When Moroccans offer sacrifices at the shrines
of saints, do or don't they say the name of God before slitting the animal's throat?" "They do," he said hesitantly. "So
don't they put God first, before the holy man?" He fell
silent, a little reassured. Another man addressed him a few
minutes later: "What do they know, these *'alem*? Are they really ulema? Yes, we can see their beards and the towels on
their heads. But what's underneath?"

6

DENYING THE SELF TO THE SELF, OR THE ROAD TO MECCA

THE "VISIT," WE KNEW, WAS NOT THE PILGRIMAGE. OUR TIME in Medina was coming to an end. On Friday, 24 Dhu'l-Qa'dah 1419 (12 March 1999), we went to the last communal prayers. We stopped at a ticket booth on the square to pay for our sacrificial offerings. A charitable works corporation would acquire a lamb for each of us and sacrifice it at Mina.

Nothing made this solemn Friday office any different from those we had participated in during the previous week. The sermons were trenchant and brief. The first underlined the "need to move away from any practice that associates something with God, the only One, such as sacrifices to beings other than Him, such as visiting sanctuaries and seeking refuge among soothsayers and sorcerers . . . The punishment for all this is fire." The preacher's voice struck like a blade. The second sermon thankfully dispelled this vision. A more serene paternal voice urged us to avoid associating other creatures with God, to show our sincerity, to do good, and to devote ourselves to justice. The conclusion was a classical prayer for the success of all Muslim leaders, a solemn communal prayer closing the cycle begun with our arrival in Medina, with the achievement of the exact number of prayers that Muslim tradition says opens the gates of paradise. The sermon ceaselessly affirmed God's absolute oneness, repeating it almost maniacally. But no doubt because of the close proximity of the sanctuary, the hope for the intercession of the Prophet suffused the crowds, despite the Wahhabi curse upon any intervention between God and the believer by a third party. The sanctuary was there, having by a miracle escaped the demolition plan the Wahhabi Brotherhood had once advocated, for a time, arousing emotional concern throughout the Muslim world.

Last-minute purchases obliged us to plunge back into the busy crowd and elbow our way through it. Many people were preparing for "departure": "There is no god but God!" Abbas the artisan griped, "Wherever you go, they give you a punch. Punch you for everything . . . And these Egyptians are so messy!" But he also grumbled about Moroccans and their inability to wait their turn, stand in line, and obey the rules. Elevators especially had become death traps; there was no way of getting our compatriots not to pile in more people than allowed. Early that morning, on the Friday when we left for Mecca, eleven pilgrims had been stuck in an overloaded elevator and escaped death only thanks to the speedy intervention of the Saudi emergency squad. "How can you understand people who go along with their old parents' demands and bring them here, sometimes in wheelchairs . . . to visit these holy places, which are one big marketplace!" muttered Haj Mbarek, the driver whom the Moroccan Ministry of Health had sent on pilgrimage. His friends quietly disagreed and carried on without arguing.

For both my companions and myself it was *ihram* that

made the real transition from simple visit to pilgrimage. We helped each other don the two white cloths, the first tight around the hips and reaching the calves, the second thrown over the torso, leaving the right shoulder and arm free. The others helped me fasten mine with a wide belt, also white, with pockets for keys, money, and papers. My head had to remain bare. On my feet, as prescribed, I put lightweight sandals with neither laces nor buckles. After a major ablution of the body (not the one done before prayers, but the one that cleanses radical impurities, such as the emission of sperm), I thus entered the state of *ihram*. A purified self, three-quarters covered in draped cloths with not a single stitch allowed. Most of the men in our group did the same, although in theory this was not required until after our arrival at the place called Ali's Wells, about a half-hour drive south of Medina. To receive the maximum grace, we had decided to change in the neighborhood of "God's Messenger," even if that meant having to do it all over again later.

We left Medina after the last evening prayer and the prayers for the day's many dead. Our preparations delayed the departure until late at night. I had gotten sick two days before, and my fever, despite a few remedies, was not subsiding. I felt cold all the time in the lightweight ritual garb with its gaping openings. I could appreciate as I shivered that I was no longer being allowed to dress according to the exigencies of normal comfort. *Ihram*, donning *ihram*, entering the state of *ihram*: that was the point. The "visit" had not required this treatment of my body and my self—surely better to say my body-self. Praying and going to mosque, sanctuary, and cemetery had required ablutions, but one could wear ordinary dress, although white was recommended and almost universally worn (the only exceptions being, as I have noted, the Iranian women in black and the Turkish men in khaki). The visit, *ziyara*: this was a search for grace and blessings, the hope of success in this world and salvation in the next. And the intercession of the Prophet was its supreme and long-awaited outcome. Here was no obligation, no contract. The visitors made the effort to benefit from contact with the Prophet, his mosque, and the Radiant City he had bequeathed to Islam. Many hoped to encounter God's apostle in a dream. But discretion required each of us to make a secret of any exceptional favors we might receive. Our daily religious duties were the same here as elsewhere, but their extreme intensification in Medina altered their nature and tone.

"*Ihram*": a noun of action, the root, *h-r-m*, usually translated as "sacred." But it contains the sacred and the forbidden simultaneously. By shedding my ordinary clothes, I was entering into a state of forbidden sanctity, into the inviolable enclosure of a contract, into an alliance that made certain things illicit which were not so elsewhere or before. Things that remained necessary or desirable or both—copulating, reproducing, perfuming oneself, hunting, cutting one's hair, shaving, clipping one's nails, leaving the state of *ihram* and wearing ordinary clothes during the required time (and designated places) of the pilgrimage—we had to forsake throughout the entire ritual. This meant renouncing ordinary daily life and even inverting it—a common practice at the beginning of a ritual, as anthropologists have observed: abandoning the pleasures of sexuality and beauty, as well as things that prepare for or signify them (perfume, foreplay, coupling); denying oneself reproduction through procreation; forgoing subsistence work and drawing resources from nature (coupling, commerce, hunting); depriving oneself of other pleasures like games and physical exercise (hunting). No shaving, haircutting, or nail clipping suggested the same meaning as the other sacrifices and renunciations. But beyond that, perhaps these last three prohibitions also make us lie fallow: in ordinary life, we cultivate our self, our body, our social and cultural identity; and these prohibitions go against the grain of our inclinations. Also, this temporary return to an uncultivated state brings us closer to the state of Adam and Hawwa (Eve), even if not exactly. Their state, before the Fall, was not a state of nature, since the lives of our two ancestor-heroes expressed the creative Word and in a sense extended it; they did not know work, nor did they know reproduction, hunting, or desire. They were unaware of their nakedness (or seminudity, if you judge from the pictures we have made of them), and they likely knew nothing of haircuts, shaving, or manicures. In short, they simply lived within their virtual fall into culture, and just as that potential was in suspension within them, ours, too, had to be suspended during *ihram*. Subjected to these rules and modified by these sacrifices, the body was endowed with a new identity, shared with places and with other bodies.

What, then, was this enclosure I had entered and could not violate by leaving, lest I fail to do what was expected? The enclosure took shape in rules, laws, and specific changes in appearance that ordered its approach, that prepared me for harmony with the "sacred-forbidden" territory and mosque of Mecca.

The mosque of Mecca, called a Haram, a sanctuary, shares with the one in Medina this unique quality. The body— when it forgoes its limits, the clear configuration bestowed on it by tailored clothing—projects itself into a transforming time and space. I could feel it becoming a shifting territory of sacredness even before arriving at the limits of Mecca's sacred-forbidden spaces. I felt once again that I was approaching the unknown, and I struggled against the old feeling of fear. Perhaps Mecca's Haram waiting for me at the end of the road would take me over in a way I could not predict. My body, divested of its habitual contours, might be ab-

sorbed in bits and pieces, or dissolve as if sucked in by the
Holy Mosque. The malaise grew sharper and sharper. Was
this the delirium of a feverish man? Or was it that the delirium, already known in another setting, was feeding the
fever?

I was beginning to glimpse a destination that Medina and
Mecca constantly covered up. It appeared, then faded away
as it wished, and it was not within my power to evoke or re-
tain it; it flowed forth freely, like a spill of color in the light,
never all at once but always like something that was already
there. If one is attentive to the singularity of language, it
gives quite a precise idea of this: every word that comes up
has already said a great deal, so it resonates in an unexpected,
blurry way, as if in each usage it both retains something from
past uses and is ready to include all its future meanings. The
painter's gesture summons colors to reveal their metamorphoses in the light. I realized, only after the fact, that I was
seeing the vibrations and brushstrokes of Monet, Gauguin,
Cézanne, and Matisse; hearing, quite clearly, Debussy's velvet undulations. Medina spread through me as I left it, in
outlines and calligraphies of light.

The hour of departure put an end to my rambling
thoughts when I was told to get on the bus. The thousand
and one suitcases, the fruits of our Medina transactions,
made up a sort of mountain solidly anchored by nets and
ropes to the vehicle's roof and held down by a cover of gray
canvas. Piled in, jammed into our narrow seats, sweating despite the fans (the Saudi company specializing in "hajj product" had advertised the buses as "air-conditioned"), we
finally started on the road to Mecca.

Block after block of squat, featureless buildings passed by
the windows. Concrete: nothing but mediocre concrete
houses slapped together with no real skill. I cannot escape
this familiar vision of the "new" Arab city, with its aggressive

forms devoid of attraction or spirit. Thirty years earlier I had
seen this "modernism"—from Casablanca to Cairo, Kenitra
to Benghazi, the suburbs of Fez to those of Cairo—reach
Arabia's capital, Riyadh, and all the cities on the eastern coast
of the Saudi kingdom, "cradle" of Islam. Sorrowing and
helpless, I now found its crowning achievement around the
Prophet's tomb. Only the Great Mosque displayed its forms
in the light. Its minarets softly, patiently rose into celestial
space, plunged in night, raising upward this heap of walls
and chaotic building sites. It loomed from time to time as we
turned a corner, depending on the maneuvers of the bus,
which was taking forever to get out of Medina.

Abbas, who had chosen to sit next to me after putting his
wife next to a lady we had met, jumped and strained every
time the mosque appeared. He would exclaim loudly, then
burst into tears which quickly turned to sobs, "There it is, O
my brother, the mosque! There it is, your mosque, O
Prophet, O my love! I can't accept this separation, separation
from the Prophet . . . O my love, O Messenger of God!" Abbas wept anew each time he glimpsed a wall or minaret of
the mosque. "There it is, O my brother, there it is, there it
is." He was inconsolable and called on me forcefully. He
could see I was not weeping with him, but apparently this
didn't matter much, for he was giving himself to me with his
emotions. Maybe I should rectify this statement, because
Abbas was also crying out, "Here I am!" and not only to me.
To everyone and to himself, he said: "Here I am! I can't bear
this parting! How about you, how is it for you?" It was that
he had been in the loving company of the Prophet, had
united with him in the brilliance of his mosque: this is what
made him say this. Soon both women and men were weeping
like Abbas, calling the Prophet, addressing him, bidding him
farewell.

Abbas's repeated calls stirred me and brought me closer to

him. At that instant, I could neither repel his proximity nor respond to it appropriately. Then, as we got away from Medina and he calmed down, I was overwhelmed by a sadness that caught me in the throat. I could measure its power by my damp eyes, although I wasn't crying. The separation had certainly caught up with me in the end, because what we call union with the Prophet is in fact a *re*union. A line of demarcation was appearing, and becoming clearer; it marked the fracture that separation consecrated. The event, which I rediscovered through the traces it left behind, moved about within me through particular signs: fever, swollen throat, eyelids that were damp yet tearless. Weeping—I had learned this over and over at my own expense—is a power that not everyone can attain. Longing and loss brought me close to Abbas, just as, during a farewell celebration in the mountains, they had revived my twenty-year friendship with Haj Muhammad, now a seventy-year-old man.

At a *sadaqa* similar to the one my friend Lahcen had invited me to, on the eve of his own departure for Islam's holy sites, Muhammad and I had embraced. It was after the meal and the invocations, in a village of the High Atlas not far from where Lahcen lived. Many of the people there could not hold back their feelings, and soon the room had rung with sobbing, and with tears shed in silence. Haj Muhammad, like everyone else, had fallen prey to "nostalgia" and the "desire for reunion"—an irresistible feeling over which you have no control. To weep from such nostalgia means to burn with a desire for a return. But weeping from a desire for reunion with the Kaaba? Burning with desire to meet it again after time spent apart? What can that mean? Obviously, there had been no separation in the usual sense of the word. Haj Muhammad and his companions were going to Mecca for the first time—only the language seemed to be saying otherwise. Of course, the experience of a strong will,

acute yearning, burning desire, provokes emotions and upheavals. But to cry, to cry with nothing holding you back, to
give yourself over to tears because something has frustrated
your will or craving: we all know that only children are allowed to do this. For adults like us, in these circumstances,
what can this "rediscovery" or "reunion" mean? Had there
been a separation that had not implied departure after union
(as it usually does)? There was no other way to explain the
tears we attributed to the desire for union and reunion.

So we must define this paradoxical separation. When a
child weeps, tears and sobs gradually replace the thing desired until the pain of the loss disappears. This does not
mean the loss is forgotten; but the child suffers less or even
not at all. The lost object takes on the life of a known thing
among the other familiar objects that make up a person's
world. Tears—of mourning, in fact—have transformed it. It
becomes an indispensable fetish, which agrees to be placed,
like a god, in a familiar location that one visits from time to
time, "for memory's sake." The "reality principle" is nothing
more than a biography made of parchments superimposed
on one another, on which are transcribed the various mourning periods that transform something wanted into something
past, each transformation affecting subsequent desires and
each desire awakening old longings. Tears recall the replacement of things by tears and of objects by pain. In this very
reminder, it recovers them, which means they were already
there, that they had produced, in various forms, our "child-
birth in pain"—a cycle of separations begun with a decisive
tearing asunder and continuing in our transformations and
our death. For all of us, as we fell into each other's arms, departure placed the Kaaba—a future object—in the line of
separations that had already taken place in history, of a continually premeditated departure.

I couldn't feel Abbas's pain any more than I had that of haj

Muhammad. But in both situations, I felt my own pain, expressed in the spasms in my throat, the tender stiffness of my movements, the rasping of my voice, the thirst. Just as I could not have felt another person's fever or suffering, I couldn't experience the emotions of the two pilgrims, yet I was moved to see them seized by pain. In that sense I recognized their condition, and this recognition worked upon my own humors. The words we exchanged, and indeed language itself, were an extension and aspect of that communication.

In the silence and torpor, Abbas kept on exclaiming and weeping at the sight of the illuminated minarets each time they appeared beyond the buildings. He would cry out, "The parting! O my brother, the parting!" Then, as if that lament had exhausted itself, he replaced it with "There it is! O my brother, there it is! There, there it is!" This "it," in our dialect a masculine nominative, designated both mosque and Prophet. Nothing could have been clearer. There was no ambiguity. It was perfectly obvious: "it" was mosque, sanctuary, tomb, and Prophet all at once.

And yet this "it" sprang forth to greet every random detail of the mosque: one minaret or several, a slice of the facade, the domes. Abbas's cry didn't change. So "it" floated free from its references. Its antecedent scattered, avoiding discourse, slipping away from the powers that tried to circumscribe it. Like the tears and sobs that were, Abbas said, "something that happens without your having anything to do with it." Like the tears that had overcome haj Muhammad's resistance, like the spasms in my throat. "Nothing can stop it," Abbas added for my benefit. That the parting could cause such sorrow was easy to understand. We were leaving a place charged with the life and actions of a man, an event which we Muslims placed at the origin of the community from which we received our lives. To be there, then to leave it, was a separation, especially since we were starting a new stage in the pilgrimage, with its own fears and uncertainties.

"There it is, O my brother," repeated Abbas, who obviously had only this sentence left to him. Or rather, it was the only sentence that could cross the threshold of speech, could take charge of language as a whole and sum it up, condense it. What was it these illuminated minarets—their fleeting, brief appearances in the sky over Medina, like giant, world-sized candles—touched in Abbas? No doubt a memory, a series of superimposed archives that are carved into language, into each person's language. A memory that transformed a hope for the future into a past, that localized what one could not situate in either the body or the spirit, or in language. Memories of omission, the work of all that is human in the present, having already been there. Each subsequent memory would omit something while it drew the contours of something else. The key to drawing, as Paul Klee said, is knowing what to leave out.

The motor's monotonous drone in the night silence made me realize that what had happened to Abbas had left him. After a short whir the vehicle stopped and the pilgrims wrenched themselves awake. We were at Abar Ali: Ali's Wells. There, we knew, we had to perform our ablutions again. Getting off the bus into the midst of the crowd of pilgrims and itinerant vendors, I saw the huge mosque with its high crenellated walls. Its massive volume in the glare of the floodlights, dominating a round minaret with its balustrade, stood out against the velvet jewel box of night. I could just make out the surrounding palm trees. The sight was one of a building that seemed to have fallen from the sky. The white-clad crowd was moving to and fro ceaselessly in prayer and invocation. It was a strange medley: buses; displays of merchandise; the enormous mosque, surrounded by the crowds in *ihram* who had relinquished their ordinary garb; drivers and vendors hawking biscuits, seeds, drinks, and cheap junk imbued with the miraculous presence; and the pilgrims, who were camping on a borderline. A people in sandals without buckles, their bodies half-covered in pieces of seamless cloth, were set out along a line of contact with and separation from a people of merchants. Nothing linked the two groups but brief commercial exchanges carried out almost wordlessly.

After ablutions in the building's toilets-cum-showers, we went to pray two prostrations in the peace of the mosque and the cool night of the Arabian desert. I was shivering all over and my fever was rising. I looked at the mosque again before getting back on the bus. We waited for the other passengers, which took quite a long time, since everyone wanted to respect the rules of what was done at Ali's Wells.

Coming after the city and mosque of Medina, this was the place where we visited the memory of Ali, cousin and "companion" of God's Messenger—both of them from the aristocracy of Quraysh. Ali: the guide, "God's sword," hero of many single combats, great mystic and writer, master of eloquence. The wise Caliph . . . "The wells of our lord, Ali, may God honor his face!" Salah reminded me. Everyone knew Ali on his intrepid black horse: at the gates of Khaybar, with a stroke of his sword, he had cut off the leg of the "tyrant" who ruled the city. It was Ali, too, who vanquished the ogre in a one-on-one battle, cleaving the monster's head between its two hideous horns. His sword, named Dhul-Fiqar, a special privilege remembered in Muslim traditions, was always depicted as lying before him, even when he was seated, and he was always flanked by Hasan and Husayn, his two sons, jewels in Islam's triumphant advance.

Yes, Abbas and I knew this lord and knew his name, bestowed on these wells and this site of ultimate purification which opened the doors of the hajj. We had often contemplated Ali respectfully, inspired by the beauty of his eyes and his thick jet-black beard; and (in our youthful lives) we had admired Hasan and Husayn, who stood like schoolchildren, their arms crossed, almost at attention on either side of their father's pyramidal stature (I almost said statue) in their short pants, tight at the knee, their tunics and keffiyehs— marvelous costumes in which only later (and with no regrets) I saw the mixed Arab-Turkish influence. This was Islam's most prestigious family; its portraits peopled the walls of the homes where we grew up, and the stories of the miracles it performed animated our public squares after the afternoon prayers.

Abar Ali: When not so long ago Abbas and I were adolescents, strolling in the dusty squares of our old medinas, not a single one of the hero's words or strokes of his sword had been lost on us. Now we received further benefits from his actions: the water from his wells was purifying us. We were at his *miqat*, the meeting place for people from Medina, as the Rabat jurist had explained to us during the training for the pilgrimage, the prescribed time-space for our entry into *ihram*.

It was past midnight when we arrived at the appointed place. Really, though, the time didn't matter. It was the place that counted, whenever one got there. Yet the root of the word *"miqat"* designates time. Arabic has a root and a rich vocabulary to signify space, location, a place, a site. Time and space are juxtaposed and opposed in Arabic as in so many other languages. Perhaps I had simply rediscovered an illustration of the well-known phenomenon whereby the same root can express opposite meanings, a secret of their language the Arabs themselves call the "language of opposites." This place, because of what happened here, was the time of a meeting. Nothing stayed here forever. Purposes met here, and that was what made it into a time, *the* time.

The decisive moment could only take place here, al-

though we were still far from Mecca's sacred-forbidden territory. God gives us time, all the time in the world, but we
were already at the meeting place: "I answer thy call, O
God." An American Orientalist of somewhat shaky learning
had found it appropriate to translate this: "At your orders,
O . . . !" Faithful to the tradition of crusading by the pen—a
tradition that is alive and well in America as elsewhere—this
scholar, like many of his colleagues, probably thought he was
rediscovering the warlike roots of the "Mohammedan"
faith—a cliché that straddled the Enlightenment. But if this
refrain, which we repeated ceaselessly from the moment we
entered *ihram*, involved anything related to war and surrender, it was war against the self and a surrender of the self—
both calm and serene.

Our new "costume" had nothing martial about it. The activities we carried out before wrapping these two pieces of
white cloth around our stripped bodies sent militarism back
to its partisans. We cleansed ourselves meticulously, washing
away any impurity caused by sexuality or menstruation, any
contamination by air, urine, fecal matter, or contact with
other impure materials: a corpse, blood, pork, a dog . . .
Purity thus restored consisted above all of readying us to fulfill a religious duty, the cleanliness being simply a consequence of this. We thus established the radical distinction
between us and the others, whoever they might be, by renouncing life: our white clothes closely resembled shrouds,
while the bared head and right arm directed us and testified
to a transition.

We were far from having bellicose inclinations. Busy mastering and denying signs of our vital functions, we also had
to forgo productive and destructive activities. At the late-
night hour marking our leap into *ihram*, we crossed a line
cutting us off from life's intermediate manifestations. The
rule suggested that rather than staying with the continuities

of repeated everyday life, we should keep up the new momentum that led to a path and a narrative, toward an attainment and an end: it meant denying oneself, and so denying oneself to others. Indeed, it was to realize the world as an end.

All these prohibitions, which seemed to bear on things outside the self, in fact touched equally, if not more so, on the uses and representations of the body. Since I eat and drink and, in normal time, have a sex life, I secrete matter. These secretions cross the surface of my skin, their channels starting and ending mostly on the face. But because something has to reach the mouth, nose, ear, eye, skin, starting point for excitation, the very ideas of arrival and departure prove to be relative. In any case, the usage of the world is the usage of the body, and nothing escapes its coordinates. Thus by this progression, the entire universe gets mapped out, returning to the body the matters and forms appropriate to its usages.

After entering *ihram*, the rules for purification became stricter and extended to other manifestations of life: personal relations, transactions, intimate thoughts, visual contact, and laughter. The limits on laughter marked the joy of the encounter with gravity, contrition, and solemnity, so that the regulated use of my body allowed me to enter life and defer my death even as it proclaimed it. The body, my body, showed itself for what it was, image of the world and anchorage of it. It's an old intuition, and it's naive for modernity to believe it out-of-date. The ordering of *ihram* offers a place for everything: up, down; right, left; in front, behind; face front, profile; horizontal, vertical; before, after; soft, hard; raw, cooked; salt, sweet; fragrant, nauseating. It does more: the oppositions create a hierarchy. "Before" also means "old people first!" or "nobility first!" or, as I too often heard in the mosque at Medina, "men first!" Before was superior to

what came after. The moment of revelation was the apex of
the pyramid, starting from a breaking point: the beginnings
set the standard. We were following the trace of these beginnings that had occurred "before us." To do so, we had to act
as if we were forsaking what had followed.

In our lives as pilgrims, what came after had to recede into
the background. It couldn't be eliminated—that would be
impossible, since it would be to reject our own lives. Rather,
we were asked to subordinate "after" to "before," to the initial gesture which gave the first response: "I answer thy call."
The body, the self, clamored not for surrender but for return—a return so as to reinstate, in other words to institute,
this "first time" for us.

We had been taught that once we entered *ihram*, we had
to pronounce the formula immediately, followed by our intention, out loud or to ourselves. In our case, we intended to
carry out an *umra* first. According to the instructions given
us in Rabat, the appropriate pilgrimage for us was the one
called enjoyment, which included the *umra* followed by the
hajj proper. *Umra* is neither a "little pilgrimage" nor indeed
any kind of pilgrimage. Nor is it a "visit," as the trip to Medina is called. It's a rite of worship like the others, with its
own rules and stages—circumambulating the Kaaba, running
between Safa and Marwa, cutting one's hair, leaving *ihram*—
and we had learned the prayers and invocations that went
with each stage. *Umra* can be performed at any time of the
year, whenever one likes. It's optional, but they say it "washes
away" the year's sins. Its meaning also encompasses life, establishing something, permanent worship, arriving at the
center of life.

We had learned all the gestures and words. If there was a
sense to look for, it lay in carrying out a stated intention and
practicing what one knew correctly. As for efforts to inter-

pret or search for a meaning, that was a different endeavor. No one was obliged to engage in it. On the contrary, we were advised to listen to the experts and meditate on what they taught us. Ultimate truth, for us and them alike, was up to God. Words are deeds and, like other deeds, lead us to the master of the Holy Places. The declaration we made and the intention we stated were exactly like the profession of faith: both a path and an engagement.

In Rabat, during training, I had met people from every walk of life except high-ranking civil servants and the bourgeoisie. Some of them had long wanted to go on pilgrimage, but hadn't been able to because their work didn't allow for leave. Others had simply waited until they had accumulated the money for it. Technicians and civil servants tried to save up money to make the trip as early as they could, experiencing any delay as "a failure" in their "obligation toward God." Low-level employees seized the chance at going on hajj at their companies' expense. Yet others thought about it for a long time first, because they saw the hajj as a decisive return to religion and to the straight and narrow path.

My concerns were about the legitimacy of starting with the intention of approaching the pilgrimage from the point of view of an anthropologist shaped by Islam who would study it with the new identity "his" discipline gave him. I was privileging a particular means of gaining knowledge, even though I took as my starting point the words and writings of the Muslim tradition I claimed as my own. I was practicing a form of interpretation in conflict with the one I had learned at school from my Muslim teachers. More seriously in my own eyes, I was being unethical in not publicly announcing my research intentions, and I therefore felt my moral and personal aspirations were somewhat degraded. Still, a right I considered inalienable—the right to know and to question—

consoled me in this difficulty. And if this right were not acknowledged, I thought I'd give myself license to work without hiding anything. So I wasn't afraid of punishment,
especially not from humans.

Yet I paid dearly for my position with the malaise brought
on by my distance from my own society. Whatever people
may say about "indigenous" anthropologists, I was and am
suspicious of the false legitimacy this identity might offer
me; skeptical about declarations made by many anthropologists and others regarding their radical nomadisms, their
search for partial truths; skeptical of miraculous reflexivity.
Divisions, dispersions, and both interior and exterior exile
made it impossible for me to pretend that I "fit" my tradition, or to purport, without further ado, to express it with a
privileged voice. What I wanted above all was to keep a distance (among various possible ones) that might give me an
angle, a bias from which my world would appear to me anew
and, at this stage, in unexpected colors. After many attempts,
I was learning that this distance kept shifting and that it developed in the questions preoccupying me.

On the road to Mecca, my experience of this distance took
a more acute and painful turn. The more I described and
recorded what I saw and heard, the more it troubled me. The
customary places that men and women regularly occupied,
which varied according to their work and their immediate
aims, were quite familiar to me. I could thus move from em-
pathy with my companions or with religion to my writing.
Other people—like the guide from Beni Mellal who looked
after a group of women as their legal "guardian," in the absence of a father, husband, brother, or other close male relative—navigated between the intentions of pilgrimage and
those of commerce. He had several different intentions at the
same time: devotion, trade, and politics. Others added
tourism to the list, like Haj Mbarek, who, as he told me, was

"on the trip, but for the rest only God knows." Then there were people who had "just come to see," as a young executive from Casablanca, fond of philosophical discussions, told me.

The trials didn't end there. Something was hitting me harder: I lacked the serenity the people I talked to enjoyed, whether skeptics or believers. My existence itself seemed problematical, and I lacked that immediate presence of the invisible many pilgrims obviously rejoiced in. On the other hand, to describe their lives and their approach to the rituals as being devoid of reflection, and the very fact that I was often tempted to do this, said less about them than about me, and about my illusion of being privileged with a religious refinement that was also a social refinement. The trip was deepening the cracks in me, intensifying my frailties.

Skepticism was one type of therapy, and certain forms of irony gave me moments of real well-being. But irony, of the sort only the gods can manage, excluded any confidence in it that could have been other than episodic. In short, I was incapable of prolonged skepticism, since my life was a gift with which I was satisfied. But the singular irony of this plenitude presented itself as pain. It wasn't death, not even my own death, that was really the problem; it was the fact that the gift was a gift of death.

"I answer thy call," "To Thee," "Thou are One," "All praise, all grace to Thee." Of course one could think of surrender. But no philology in the world, no "restoring the historical context" (so dear to dull-witted historians), could keep me from choosing return and submission. Gift of oneself, irenic, and not a surrender while standing at attention. Despite my distance, something touched me. To try to circumscribe it completely was vain. But the gift of the other pilgrims moved me, the more so since it rushed into a presence, in the form of a void in me, the trace of which showed up as research.

I, however, was giving a gift when my life didn't require it, whereas my companions gave themselves to a being that wanted but did not need their gift, since in principle it was deroid of need. Yet the rule worked as if giving were the answer. No question of restitution, compensation, "counter-gift," or contract. Only trust, submission, faith. If giving had been the origin of the contract, giving would have fulfilled it. The contract was the result of need; the giving, "just as if," was a constant reminder that all the terms drew their power and duration from metaphor. My way of giving was no less ambiguous than the others'. But I was marked by the seal of unforeseeable futures, suspended from the morality of very real life, and I was navigating at sight.

The pilgrimage I was writing about was projected through these prisms, and since I could not predict their refractions, I had to resign myself to claiming them after the fact. Beyond reciprocity and contracts, the horizon slipped away from reason and re-formed again and again in the ethical sentiment that the advent of the human awakened: the unique unfolding of a world. The hajj experience was changing my horizons radically, and I was prepared to embrace what came.

Maybe my companions were giving me the gift of their faith. Everyone included me in their prayers for salvation, and perhaps I was thus receiving something that would help me out of my difficulty. Just as there were rules for the pilgrimage, there were rules for reception: hospitality without complacency, personal involvement in relationships. Beyond that, I could only navigate uncertainly, and my situation was all the more paradoxical inasmuch as people often asked for my help in matters related to ritual. I was educated, and I could read the synopses about the hajj. A man asked me one day if it was permissible to let his wife keep their money while he performed the circumambulation and vice versa, taking it in turns. Someone else asked me if a woman could carry out the ritual without a guardian being constantly present to accompany her. And what did "modest garb" imply for women, and what about the separation of women and men?

Abbas and Salah had anyway decided they would not be separated from their wives, and one woman in our group didn't have a real "guardian." There was an additional complication: I was without my wife yet was sharing a room with these couples and a "single" woman. This earned us direct and indirect comments, sometimes voiced out loud: "Worship requires separation"; it was necessary to forsake "Moroccan permissiveness"; as a neighbor in Medina said, "Here in Saudi Arabia, we're not in Morocco!" We also had to deal with our own differences: If worship was the priority, should the women do the cooking or not? And if so, up to what point? What should we think of the fact that some women on the hajj managed to do all the housework and still pray as much as, or even more than, the men and the women who didn't do any chores? Finally, how should I handle accomplishing the pilgrimage while preparing an anthropological book on the subject? Didn't science work by separating from religion? Could the elements for such a book come together when the anthropologist was in a state of *ihram*? No one ever asked me that question explicitly. Some of my companions were willing to discuss religion and the pilgrimage with me, and Abbas often told me incidents and anecdotes. I wound up writing my notes in front of everyone while the others talked on and militated in favor of "bringing Islam back into our societies."

Comments and questions I had already heard in Morocco recurred quite frequently here: "The hajj doesn't exist anymore; it's all about trade. Travel agencies and governments want a piece, and you'll see how materialistic our brothers in Mecca and Medina are!" Or, "Politics is involved. Everyone wants to promote their nation's interest." And, in response to these concerns: "The hajj is a duty. We do it for God . . . We have to forget all this and do it as God commanded!" And also, "All this"—pushing and shoving, altercations, cutting in line, getting an airline ticket by any means possible, including bribery if necessary, rushing to get better housing at the expense of other pilgrims—"all this is against hajj ethics."

The rules were variations on a global rule according to which the event had to take place so that everyone could derive the expected benefits. It had to take place "as usual," under "normal circumstances," or in "the best possible conditions." Everyone worked toward that. Nation-states coordinated their efforts to manage individuals and crowds. On our arrival in Arabia, we had gotten our badges showing our identity, address, title, and group membership. These were based on the "special passports" and other documents sent back and forth between the Moroccan hajj administration and the Saudi services, where we were represented by a national Mission force. Security measures were also based, alternatively or simultaneously, on trust and faith. Our destination was "the House of God"; the "God of this house" saved us "from hunger and fear." Ensuring the ritual meant ensuring that the pilgrims could approach God in complete security: a political economy of discourse was active day and night. It produced a pilgrimage free from worldly intent. Civil servants proclaimed that "the only goal is to worship God, the Almighty, leaving aside political disputes and narrow national interests." As if echoing these proclamations, the Saudi press and bureaucracy reminded us every day that we were "guests of the Merciful One." Individually and collectively, we belonged to the community. At the same time, each of us was an "ambassador" (!) for his country to the Saudi nation and to Islam's annual great gathering—"guests of the kingdom that guards the holy sites." Narrow national interests, according to this doctrine, were those impeding cooperation with "the kingdom." But many of us knew that Iran and Iraq challenged the legitimacy of the Wahhabi "appropriation" of the holy sites. Revolts, disorder, demonstrations, even bloody confrontations: these things occurred and could not be excluded.

To accomplish the hajj "normally," according to the rules, we tried to do the right thing in every circumstance. We followed the rules. Each time we had to choose one of several available options before moving on to the next. Success depended on knowing those rules and having a good sense of the game, of course, but it was only reached by adjusting more or less precisely to global, fluid conditions in which we had only a goal to guide us: that of an "excellent pilgrimage," the legal scholars' favorite expression. At this point, I was no longer really sure which was producing which: Did the political economy of discourse produce the pilgrimage, or did the pilgrimage, continually on the move, defy the economies by opening up our lives to loss?

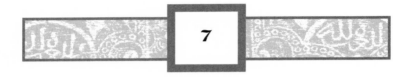

UNTITLED

WE HAD BEEN WAITING IN THE BUS FOR A LONG TIME, AND THE passengers started moving around out of impatience and to stretch their legs. I did the same, despite our Egyptian driver's injunctions to stay put. The cool desert night pierced my skin and I shook with fever. Abbas and I went to have a cup of tea. The vendor came from Bangladesh, as did the few others I met at Abar Ali.

We were back on the road to Mecca quite late at night, chanting the *talbiya*, the first time followed by the declaration of intent: "I answer Thy call, O God; I answer Thy call, *umra*!" Our instructors and the pilgrim manuals recommended psalmodies and chanting between prayers. Individual praise of God's grace, exalting his glory, took up the intervals in the collective chanting. Someone would always take the initiative and the others would soon follow. Our voices sought each other and rose together.

When emotions had reached a certain intensity, a few men, all quite young, got up to preach. Two of them especially struck me. The first, who taught at a lycée in a town not far from Rabat, began by speaking of "the meaning of true Islam," and then his presentation became harsh as he denounced the loss of faith, "hypocrisy," and corruption in Muslim societies. He cited several Qur'anic verses and sayings of the Prophet to revile the absence of justice and the "race for money." From this, he moved on to a condemnation of materialism and its "tyrants," clearly suggesting that Muslim governments, thus stigmatized, were illegitimate.

The second sermon was delivered by a fellow I knew in Morocco: a technician with a wife and children, comfortably settled in good middle-class quarters, a man who had gotten ahead in his career by the sweat of his brow and become fairly prosperous. I don't know if he and the other volunteer preacher had agreed on a plan of action or not, but the second one gave an even more energetic and menacing speech than the first. He exhorted us to "return to God" and to be modest as ordained in "divine law." "An Islamic life must avoid immodesty and the mingling of men and women," he said. The law, according to him, said that women's bodies must be covered—as was his wife's, no doubt; he kept her under close surveillance, along with a few sympathizers veiled from head to foot, their faces shrouded by scarves or hoods. This was the outfit that would keep us from taking fatally dangerous liberties! "Reserve" was also important, for it reduced contact between men and women to the minimum: no reaching out or taking a hand proffered in greeting, no eye contact. At every moment, we had to guard against sinning by sight or touch.

Immodesty was an unveiled woman, symbol of the neglect of Islam, "Islam abandoned by Muslims themselves . . ." It was easy to predict the next phrase: ". . . abandoned, and therefore decadent and underdeveloped." Evil was summed up as "imitating the ways of the infidels. And so it is necessary to return to our Islamic system in our ways of eating and dressing, in our way of life generally . . . A hadith says we must cultivate a rugged look. How, then? Well, by refusing to imitate the adornment the infidels indulge in."

I had read or heard all this before. When I was in high school, this message had clashed and mingled, somewhat confusedly, with Morocco's nationalist reformism of the time, with Baathism or Nasserism. And, no doubt because of my lack of experience, I had sometimes sought help in cheap editions of the works of Sayyid Qutb, the main thinker of the Egyptian Muslim Brotherhood, and Abbas Mahmud al-Aqqad, an Egyptian writer called, ploddingly, "thinker of the Arabs"! Egypt offered our young minds its mass-produced goods. Virile beauty was rugged and therefore rigorous: pure and clean. A wide, loose robe that hid the body's shape was finished off with a head covering and a beard. According to one's taste, one could put in practice this last tradition—attributed to the Prophet, of course—by growing a thick, preferably ungroomed beard or a small goatee and mustache (the Wahhabi fashion, universally followed in Saudi Arabia). For some, shaving was prohibited; for others, it was acceptable.

The two sermons went together like two parts of a single anthology. I knew anathema well. No doubt most of the pilgrims did, too—even those who hadn't learned to read and write. For a long time now, religious programs on radio and television had been adding their notes to the authority of Qur'anic schools and preachers, and of pamphlets that spilled out of shops and covered the sidewalks of Muslim cities. Everywhere, "Qur'an houses" and networks of activists condemned openness to others and indeed any historical experience of change, which was stigmatized, described as "servile imitation," "unbelief," "foreign domination," "the West."

Abbas and his wife, Zuhra, knew these pieces by heart. In Medina, they had kept us in line, with apt quotations whenever they thought the occasion called for it. The couple, both artisans, knew quite a lot—and in a way that escaped the logic of any system. They were militants keen on doing their "Islamic duty" whom the others regularly consulted. Everything was clearly set forth along two poles: desertion/return, authenticity/imitation, sincerity/hypocrisy, freedom/domination. Everything had been demonstrated, and so the freedom to speculate, to fumble, to prolong discussion and hesitation, to seek inspiration was excluded. Might this not risk ambiguity, deviation, indeed anything alive? If such were unfortunately to materialize, then one had to repeat the demonstration according to the proper method. These geometries invented an order. How close this order came to the structured orders our professors of anthropology had taught us!

As the night passed and our vessel glided through the darkness, the engine's hum drowned out the voices. The chanting became inaudible and more infrequent. Our preachers, like the others, succumbed to exhaustion. The traffic and immigration police stopped our vehicle once. In a daze, I forgot what I had done the previous day and where I was coming from. When I recovered my wits, realizing my head had been bobbing uncontrollably, it was dawn. My *ihram* was sticking to me, and I could feel the same dull stupor I saw on the faces of the others.

We stopped a second time somewhere on the road. The charter company served us breakfast: bread, milk, and orange juice. It was around five in the morning. I was in a pitiful state. Abbas helped me leave the bus and get back in. The sun was already high when we made our third halt, this time not far from Mecca, at a sort of station for the ultimate preparation. We performed our ordinary ablutions before

returning quickly to our seats. We drove on for a few moments and were almost immediately on a wide avenue. This
was Mecca. We began chanting the *talbiya* again, voices
ringing out in unison. Entering Mecca had renewed the pilgrims' ardor. It was past eleven in the morning on Saturday,
25 Dhu'l-Qa'dah, 1419 of the Hegira, 13 March 1999.

Medina had somewhat prepared me for what I was going
to see in Mecca, but it didn't cushion the blow entirely: highways, tunnels, white buildings four, five, ten stories high; intense traffic; and, as always and everywhere, a smell of
gasoline. We felt no particular curiosity as we went down the
streets. My companions, like the other passengers, had a goal
that seemed to make them indifferent to the city and its pollution. The point was for us to settle in as quickly as possible
so that we could go to the Holy Mosque.

"Adoration" and "acts of worship": this is how I translate
"*ibadat*" and "*manasik*," two key words. I tried the word
"*tuqus*" once or twice, but it didn't mean much to anyone.
Someone translated it as "the weather," as in the forecast on
a news bulletin. I wasn't surprised. "*Tuqus*" is a recent adap-
tation by Arab Christians to translate "rituals." Besides, I was
the only one using this word to describe what I was both
practicing and observing. "*Manasik*," a word I rarely heard
uttered by uneducated pilgrims, was often used in the hand-
books and sermons, yet even the most knowledgeable among
my companions didn't know its precise connotations. But
when they said, "Let's go to *manasik*," they meant the acts of
worship not only at the prescribed time—for instance, at
morning prayers—but also at the obligatory place here in
Mecca, acts done only once a year or once in a lifetime.

Our *umra* took half a day. After twelve hours of traveling,
coming and going to find our lodgings, we hastily performed
our ablutions again and headed for the Holy Mosque. We
went down a wide boulevard lined with more or less undis-

tinguished white buildings; the traffic was loud and heavy, the crowds very dense, becoming more and more compacted as we drew closer to the mosque. Then, halfway there, at a street corner, I saw two minarets dominating a large grayish white wall. I learned that this was the Gate of King Fahd ibn Abd al-Aziz. We went around it to the right to enter through the Gate of Peace. Taking advantage of a break in the ranks, we crossed the vast gallery covering the path between Safa and Marwa and reached the central court where the Kaaba stands. At last, I could contemplate it at leisure. Like everyone else, I paused instinctively. We were between noon and mid-afternoon prayers. There was the imposing cube, its unusual dimensions, garbed in black, the frieze of gold calligraphy running along its four sides. The surprise was complete—despite the immediate familiarity, despite the sense of being reunited with a Kaaba that had lived in our lives since childhood in Qur'an recitations, conversations, writing, drawing, painting, photographs, newspapers, television, cinema, poetry, songs, stories . . .

We began to pray—the two required prostrations to "salute the Mosque"—and then we joined the rotating circles. This first circumambulation into which we plunged was that "of the arrival." We started off, as planned, at the south-southwestern quadrant, called the Yemeni quadrant. Crying "God is great!" and saluting the edifice with our right arms raised, we set off counterclockwise, at a slow run for men, a quick walk for women, and were instantly pulled into the immense, perpetually moving human circles. Prayers, invocations, and laments rose from all sides to the sky. A golden light bathed everything against the dark backdrop of the arcades, rotating in the opposite direction. The kinesthetic impression I received with each movement was one of winding something up, following an outline in concentric circles. Vertigo. Now and again I would move left or right to make

room for formidable black workers who bore the elderly or
the infirm on stretchers hoisted above our heads. I pivoted as
I approached the Kaaba. On my seventh time around, I managed to touch the silk sheeting that "clothes" it. The crowd,
impressively oblivious, pressed toward the Black Stone. I
went around once more, hoping to touch the glass protect-
ing it, but was violently tossed away by the crowd. I didn't
try again but saluted it from afar and slowly left the moving
masses.

Men and women were relentlessly propelled, as if by a
magnetic force, toward the Black Stone, which was guarded
by apparently unarmed men. Others were plastered to the
building's walls, motionless and silent, under the sun's rays.
Supplications joined the prayers: for health, for the relief of
distress and misfortune. I withdrew little by little to the back,
where the arcaded galleries gave a little shade. I couldn't take
my eyes off the cube in silken black. Women around me
were praying, pleading, sobbing, and begging for forgiveness. Facing the Kaaba and surrounding it, we were tied to
each other, denied to ourselves by *ihram*, which modifies the
limits of bodies and identities. It was testimony to a condition I didn't comprehend. Emotion flooded through me.
Tears welled up in my eyes but didn't flow, putting me in
tune with the others. I will never know, I am sure, with what
these tears were associated, but I was experiencing something concrete and precise: I felt I had been stripped bare by
the sight of the "Ancient House," with no hesitation and
above all with no fear of the law. Religion communicated to
me its power above the law or perhaps beside, over, beyond
it. A plague on the courts' authority! The great Shari'a
courthouses that had crushed me in Medina shrank and disappeared behind the black cube. Now I understood the
meaning of certain statements I had often heard: "What happiness to be here! How good God's grace is . . . What joy one

feels at seeing all this." Or, "Seeing the Kaaba, I felt the most intense joy I had ever known." Without presuming to know what others felt, I realized these phrases now meant something to me.

Soon I left the covered galleries and rejoined the circumambulation. This time I went to visit the Hijr, the place where, according to tradition, Hajar and Ismail stood when Ibrahim exiled them. Sarah, according to the narratives I had read, could no longer tolerate her "servant," although it was Sarah, unable to bear children, who had suggested to the aging patriarch that he approach the Egyptian woman. A low porphyry wall encircled the place; two gold lamps framed the entrance. Many women—far surpassing the number of men—were prostrating themselves here. Our group gathered once more, and we went to pray at the station of Ibrahim, the founder of "original Islam," who, according to the same stories, came here to meet his family and, along with Ismail, built the Kaaba and founded Mecca, "mother of cities." We made two prostrations around a small pavilion, shaped like a sanctuary with a gold and crystal dome over a lighted lamp. I had read that "this is where Ibrahim first gave the call to prayer, turning in each of the four directions of the world." A few steps away, we went to the "well of Zamzam," at the place where Hajar had miraculously discovered a spring after running anxiously between Safa and Marwa. According to a fairly widespread version of the story, it was the archangel Gabriel who revealed this source of life to her. The child was thirsty, his life in danger. Hajar's efforts, her devotion, and her faith in God were rewarded.

Behind Salah, who spontaneously took the lead in reciting the invocations, we went quickly down to a hot, humid underground room. I drank from one of the glasses set out beneath the taps. One has to do this while invoking the miraculous water's virtue; I had already tasted it at the

mosque in Medina. Ultramodern machines pump out water
for the millions of pilgrims who come to Mecca. Abbas
spoke of the "joy" of bringing some of this water back to
Morocco, "like all the other pilgrims."

Then we went up the stairs to the gallery, a few hundred
meters long, that covers the path between Safa and Marwa.
Seven times we covered this obligatory distance between the
two rocks (which barely break the surface of the earth), men
running slowly, women walking. The path only started at a
certain distance from the rocks, and neon signs showed the
limits. We recited the obligatory Qur'anic verse that calls
this itinerary *sha'ira*—men out loud, women in low voices.
When the cycle was completed, a Moroccan woman didn't
hesitate to cut off a lock of my hair: this act is compulsory for
both sexes. I suddenly remembered that the word "*sha'ira*" is
also used for the mark identifying animals to be sacrificed. A
link was appearing: between marking, separation, sentiment,
and growing awareness.

Our *umra* was completed a little before the mid-afternoon
prayers. We made the four required prostrations in the
mosque's western galleries. Then we prayed for the dead. As
always, during prayers, gender separation reclaimed its prerogatives, and as usual, Abbas and Salah started to justify it,
this time with renewed energy. I pointed out that men and
women entered the mosque by the same gates and were together for the circumambulation, which my two companions
had not noticed. Our debate continued in front of the Gate
of King Fahd. Abbas observed that women prayed separately,
which I acknowledged, reminding him of the lacquered-
wood screen, too high to see over, that separated men from
women at the mosque in Medina, and I didn't miss the opportunity to remind them it had padlocked doors. My companions decided not to answer, and we pressed on through
the tightly packed crowd in the forecourt of the immense

mosque and in the adjacent streets. We went to meet the
women near a supermarket on the way back to the apartment
building where we were staying. The sun, crowds, traffic,
noise, and smells drained me. Dragging along like an au-
tomaton, I climbed the hill with the others in search of a
restaurant. We washed up in a long, narrow Pakistani place.
At the entrance, an electric barbecue was spinning the inevitable rows of industrial chickens. On the other side of the
door was a coal brazier. Inside, benches placed at right angles
to the walls left open a little passageway to the kitchen,
where we placed our orders. We waited in line for the veg-
etable stew and a little rice, which we wanted with a
charcoal-grilled chicken. The sauce—thick, oily, and red, a
concentrate of mixed spices and peppers—burned my lips
and throat. The heat of the kitchens and the grills became
suffocating. I had been feverish since leaving Medina, and
lunch finished me off. I left the infernal place quickly. A few
moments later, I staggered up the stairs and made it to our
common room, where I collapsed on my foam mat. The others arrived just behind me. Farida asked me a few questions
and gave me some more pills. As a woman physician, she
didn't offer to examine me.

Once I had rested and gathered my strength, I went back
to the mosque. I didn't want to lose one bit of the day's last
prayer or the nighttime circumambulation. I had taken off
my *ihram* and, after washing and shaving, put on a clean shirt
under my white cotton robe. With my white bonnet on my
head and slippers on my feet, I left the room. It was rela-
tively cool, which made this first night in Mecca sweet.
Crowds were everywhere—on the sidewalks, in the streets,
in between the buildings. Under the bright-as-daylight
neon, the scene appeared unreal. I went back to the rows of
people praying in the square dominated by the minarets,
monumental gates, and high marble wall. I glanced to the

left, at a building with reinforced-concrete foundation walls, its tinted bay windows towering above the mosque—the king's house leaning out over God's house.

I took refuge in the mosque and went to crouch at the foot of a marble pillar beneath the polychrome ceiling. We were arranged in compact rows, one behind the other, our still, motionless silhouettes stretching as far as the eye could see. Voices rose, echoing each other and then meeting in sentences, words, syllables, a hum that covered us like a dome of sound. When the muezzin called, silence prevailed in the vast mosque. We prayed at a moderate pace. After the prayers for the dead, I went back to the gallery overlooking the courtyard. Circumambulation had begun again. The stretchers on which disabled pilgrims were huddled, the men in *ihram* and the women veiled, glided through the air around the black cube, above the multitudes. Splashes of bright color dotted this sea of white silhouettes moving in concentric circles: black, green, pink, sometimes red or orange. I knew, since I had seen it in Medina, that the black robes were worn by Iranian women and the green scarves by Indonesians. Other splashes indicated Africans or Asians.

Soon enough, I realized I wasn't the only one watching the spectacle. Other pilgrims, both men and women, came here "just to see." "I can't take my eyes off it, what a vision!" repeated a young salesman from a city in southern Algeria. I exchanged a few words in English with a small group of Indonesians. They told me they often came back after evening prayers and went up on the terraces to "enjoy this extraordinary thing" and observe that "we're all here." For the Algerian fellow, this was "the great thing about Islam," with all its peoples. It was clear that this vision fascinated him just as it did me.

I left the mosque late in the evening, after glancing one last time at the moving circles, and crossed the path between

Safa and Marwa. The shuttles went back and forth seven times here, too, from left to right, like the circumambulation. In the long, brightly lit covered gallery of polychrome marble, wood, and stucco, the two-way path was constantly filled, a column of women on one side, men on the other. In between the two was a lane for the handicapped, the elderly, or the weak. They followed in Hajar's steps in wheelchairs pushed by employees from a special company.

On the way back, past the high floodlights that spilled raw light on the crowd, I stopped in front of twin towers standing on a single base and connected above ground level by glassed-in escalators. It was a bit of Saudi-style New York. Far away, on the hill, the old fortress of Ajyad watched over the sanctuary and the city. As I made my way—slowly, due to the crowds and because I was climbing the hill—I went back in my mind to the black cube. It had seemed to be floating on the surface of the human masses, but stopped as soon as one looked at the crowd instead. I thought to myself that I was under the spell of Noah's ark braving the flood with a pair from each species on board: here was hope and faith in a new life once the waters receded. But those who were weeping, pleading, and pushing through the crowd to throw themselves against the cube's walls, inert, arms spread like wings, wanted to cling to this house where they found faith enough to expose themselves to everything, even to an excess of life. And, as if everyone knew this, people passed without seeming to pay any attention to the bodies clutching the walls. Each of us was alone, our solitude reflected back at us by the black cube.

I was coming to see how important it was to repeat the circumambulation. And even on our first night in Mecca, I felt something surprising about the need to contemplate the same movement right after one had accomplished it. Evidently, it was futile to seek a single motive for this, which everybody felt. The only thing I was sure of was that an attraction kept pulling me back to the Kaaba, its angles projecting in the four directions that indicate the totality of the universe.

"In front of the Kaaba, facing the House of God, you forget everything." The sentence kept coming back. Far from the Black Stone, I heard it constantly. On the street, walking back to our lodgings, I could still see the circles revolving without haste; I could feel their imperious and peaceful strength. In its innocence, that strength could be as murderous as it was beneficial.

Abbas woke us the next day, as usual, around half past four in the morning. We had to get ready for dawn prayers. Now that we were in Mecca, my friends were trying to fit in as much as possible. Images from the previous night came back to me: the crowd, the dome of sound, the irresistible movement. But today, Sunday, 26 Dhu'l-Qa‘dah in the year 1419 of our era, I was too exhausted to move. The others insisted, but I stayed on my mat. My companions woke me when they came back. They told me it was very hot and that crowds had already filled the avenues, streets, courtyard, and interior of the mosque. In circumambulation or at prayers, "there's not even room for a pin." They discussed the possibility of saying our noon prayers in the room. Then, following the rhythm of our lives in Medina, they went to sleep. As a general rule, I would spend the rest of the morning writing, and then resume in the afternoon. Today, though, Abbas, awake before the others as usual, started talking about the circumambulation. "It's better at night," I remarked, "when it's not so hot." "Oh, circumambulation is a great thing!" I had heard him sobbing, praying, and pleading as we turned together. Now he was speaking in a calm, determined tone. "You have to prepare for the hajj!" he told me. "There will be trials, and fatigue . . . but it's for God! Your fever will go down, God willing."

We settled into Meccan life, having left *ihram* after the *umra*. We had time to enjoy a pious, free life before leaving for Mina. It was becoming clear that I wasn't sharing my writing project with the others. I talked about it from time to time with Salah, but he didn't try to go into detail or probe deeply. Besides, everyone acted as if we all had the same goals on the hajj. Abbas had asked me a second time, in the presence of Salah, if I normally prayed. "I stopped praying and performing the other rites when I was a teenager," I replied. "I do pray from time to time, and then it's like a soothing visit to a house where I was brought up. I redis-cover a natural way of relating to my community, which is that of Islam." The group let me paddle my own boat, while we shared the rituals and much of our daily activities. The pilgrimage proper was only eleven days away. We were set-tling into our Meccan rhythm, and we had left *ihram* after the *umra*. We had time to enjoy a devout, free existence be-fore leaving for Mina.

That Sunday was our first routine day in Mecca. After a morning of well-earned rest, we lined up to use the bath-room in the hallway so we could do our ablutions again. This time we didn't have to wait long, but what a trial! A putrid odor emerged from the toilets and the shower. We locked ourselves in, one after the other, the women before the men, and left quickly to head for the mosque. As usual, we had a very hard time making our way in the heavy, noisy traffic of trucks, pickups, taxis, buses, and private cars. Near the souk on the main boulevard, we several times had to force our way through. We were already sweating heavily in the city heat, and for the first time I could smell the sewers; this would be a daily experience of varying intensity. We also had to reckon

with the trash that pilgrims threw in the street. The sanitation department sometimes couldn't manage, though the
service was well funded and the men worked hard.

For the first time, I noticed a few black beggars, most of
them mutilated. Some moved along on one leg and one
hand; others showed the stump of an arm. Maybe the limbs
had been amputated following sentences passed in one of the
Saudi kingdom's courts. It was very difficult to broach this
subject, but when I asked a taxi driver about it a few days
later, he confirmed, somewhat reluctantly, that for some this
was indeed the case.

It was truly a relief to get to the mosque's gate. I followed
Salah and Abbas, letting the women enter first. I was surprised to find a woman entirely covered in black sitting on a
chair to the right: one of the armed guards. Her male colleagues were on the other side of the door, watching the human flood closely, intervening in case of doubt, directing
people to other doors when necessary, blocking the entrance
to avoid scuffles. Happy to be in the mosque at last, I
breathed in the cool air beneath the stucco and marble
arches. I was pleased to note once again that many women,
separate from us but visible, were moving confidently
through the beating heart of Islam.

We had some time before prayers. We traversed the
crowds to reach the upper galleries overlooking the courtyard, to watch the circumambulation. The vision had
lost none of its bewitching power. I could feel my legs trembling, and Abbas once again started to weep. I was overcome by a feeling of slight vertigo, similar to what I feel
when I look into bottomless water where one can guess at
deep, savage currents beneath the surface calm. I was shaking, and my heart was beating unsteadily. I recognized the
mounting anxiety, the feeling that gripped me at moments of
extreme attraction, which I knew was dangerous. Perhaps

this was the meaning, forgotten today, of the state of religious awe.

I decided to stay in the mosque to wait for the next prayers, at sunset. I went down to the ground floor and sat beneath one of the domes, having taken a Qur'an from the closest shelf. I stayed there reading the suras I knew well. I've always liked the ones entitled "the bees," "the cow," "women," "al-'Imran," and "the people of the cave with their dog," as well as the stories of Yusuf (Joseph), Sulayman (Solomon), Musa (Moses), and Pharaoh; the tales of ancient peoples like 'Ad and Thamud. The dark poetry of the suras telling of the end of the world and the afterlife fascinates me. The verses about the beauty of creation rendering unto each thing—earth, skies, mountains, night, moon, stars, planets—the enchantment of first times. I avoid the suras that threaten lukewarm believers and infidels with eternal hellfire, that detail the torments inflicted by the angel of death, that draw in a lightning gesture the fall of the damned through infinite space, ending in a bird's beak; or the suras that depict the blessed contemplating the suffering of the damned in Gehenna.

The reading tired me and I lay down for a while, closed my eyes, and, like many others, let myself slip into sleep. Like them, I'd open my eyes from time to time and resume reading silently. I rediscovered an unaccustomed calm in the murmured recitations. People were seated, reading or reciting, or stood in prayer, or performed a few prostrations before going back to the circumambulations. I returned to my reading for a moment, and it was my favorite, the Sura of Light, in which God is light and is portrayed not with attributes such as wrath or the power to administer exemplary punishment but simply as enveloping light, emanating from a lamp filled with oil from an olive tree that is "neither of the East nor of the West." Rapture.

These verses themselves refute certain modes of knowledge that all too often degenerate into trivial theological dis-
putation. I thought of a French translation of the Qur'an
which for decades was considered authoritative. The very
erudite Orientalist who wrote it compared this sura to a
somewhat similar passage from the Bible: the comparison, of
course, suggested that the Qur'anic passage was a derivative
one. But when one rereads the Sura of Light, it's quite easy
to realize that even if it derived from a passage in the Bible,
it reaches zeniths which the earlier versions don't even approach. As is so often the case with material of mythic inspiration, later versions go in previously unexplored directions
and toward new creative horizons. Historical and philologi-
cal criticism, while indispensable, reaches a limit here, and
the limit is all the more unforgiving in that the relevant science makes it impossible to detect.

A little before the last prayer of the evening, Abbas
and Salah came to find me, accompanied by the young
technician-preacher I knew. The man greeted me coldly, and
I him; I quickly returned to my reading. Then the prayer was
such a revelation that I forgot the very existence of this re-
sentful person. The reciter's voice caused each syllable to vi-
brate with secret nuances. It was clear and strong but not too
loud. It took me into worlds I hadn't yet frequented. I
walked lightly, unafraid, among wild beasts that went peace-
fully on their way, beneath a sun that shone without burning.
There were only tones and timbres, forms and movements,
perceptions and presences, gifts and acceptances, absences
and gratifications. Everything responded in a faultless
rhythm that had no exact symmetry. The world found its
double in a sort of felicitous blueprint.

I had no idea what my companions were experiencing
when they heard this voice. Abbas thought it was an "extraordinary recitation" but didn't say more. As for Salah, he

was embroiled in a discussion about "the greatness of Islam" with the pseudo-theologian whose company he sought. I left them to watch the circumambulation once again. It was already late. Moonlight brightened the atmosphere. The lights over the mosque and its vast forecourts radiated far into the sky above the city. A cloud of tiny birds appeared at regular intervals and dispersed quickly into the dark. Around the Kaaba, a dark shape dominating the indistinct, moving crowd, the same scenes still played out: people crying, pleading, touching and kissing the "garment," making desperate attempts to get closer to the stone by lifting parts of the black covering. Every time, guards intervened firmly but nonviolently.

I went home alone. The crowd had thinned except around the jammed underground toilets. People were preparing to spend the night around the mosque and nearby buildings. They lay down on makeshift beds: blankets, pieces of foam rubber or cardboard. I moved distractedly through this intense activity, for the images of prayer, the running between Safa and Marwa, and especially the circumambulation were still roiling through my mind. It wasn't just me; they aroused the interest of my friends and triggered discussions. The image of whirling water interested Abbas and Salah, who said it meant spontaneity and power. Salah especially wanted to see "the power, the glory, and the greatness of Islam," the power of a message whose miracle, according to him, was in the gathering of all these souls from "all the races rushing from all the regions of the planet."

Some time earlier, a man from the region of Taza, a big town in northeastern Morocco, had joined me. A rich peasant in his fifties, he sang the praises of God, "whose will can gather all these creatures around Ibrahim's Kaaba." He kept on repeating, "This vision makes you forget everything, and that is happiness." He fell silent, and then lamented the fact that three times before he had tried and failed to make the pilgrimage, foiled because of "crooked deals and corruption to get anything—a passport, registration on the lists." It was the same thing when it came to emigration, he added. "My children live in France. Everyone knows them, but every time the departments manage to register me too late." Then, without the slightest transition, he asked me for details about excess luggage. He explained he had made "marvelous purchases in Medina: four or five suitcases full, and bags." Listening to this man's preoccupations about his return home, his questions about the cost of excess luggage and number of bags, I heedlessly forgot my daydreams about the circumambulation. I was looking, but not seeing. I followed the story of how he and his wife had moved into a filthy building in Mecca where they had to "stand in line starting at one in the morning to get to the bathroom." Nor did he spare me his recriminations on the subject of bad food, an inconvenience that could be got around quickly thanks to women's work: they "cook at night for the next day, with things brought from home—olive oil, peas, paprika, dried prunes, tinned meat."

After these conversations, I decided I had to reconsider the questions that had guided me up till now—first of all, the ones I was asking myself, about the legitimacy of my project, the horizons or dead ends awaiting me that might defy my expectations and predictions. Since Medina, I had begun to accept (but still with a reluctance I didn't wholly confess to myself) that I should have been prepared for the reality I was seeing and experiencing. But in one sense I was prepared, because in fact I had always known what to ex-pect. But still I had to admit I was going from one surprise to another. Reality, then, was both familiar and a little "off." The longer I was in Medina, and now in Mecca, the component parts were coming together as if on a stage. True, the things I saw existed independently of being in a stage set. I could come and go in the buildings and shops, walk down the avenues, go to the mosque, and so forth, but still these pieces of reality seemed to exist only in trompe l'oeil. In Medina, I had been on the trail of the Prophet and his companions, and the Radiant City, which lived according to the rhythmic chanting of prayer, spread its halo over the Wahhabi city and its religious mechanics. I was in neither one nor the other, or, rather, I was in one and then the other, they were the same city. But the difference between the two was more acute in Mecca because of the pollution, heat, and crowds, and because of the city's site—planted in a crater of gray unforgiving mountains.

So things were not as they seemed, neither the sublime nor the common. I thought about having left the mosque the previous evening, with my companions, after the night service: the giant skyscraper, its many stories and escalators, the clouds of nocturnal birds, the markets, ice-cream parlors, and luxury hotels. I thought of Abbas's reprimands, his protests about the inequality between "us and the Rabat people, who are feared in high government circles, in Morocco, and got much better lodgings than we did." Our ordinary life in Mecca was not ordinary at all, and it was making everyone edgy. In my group, Abbas the artisan reproached us frequently for not paying attention to him, for rejecting his suggestions, for not listening to him on religious matters. Was he not as good a Muslim as we? Maybe, he began to suggest more and more often, he even knew more than we did, even if we only listened to him politely and didn't take his advice. Made up as our life was of both the spiritual and the trivial, and with all the trompe-l'oeil effects around and about us, we were cut adrift, and over and over again we had to find our moorings in the ethics of the hajj. The very word imposed order on our disorder.

Going back to our apartment, I was still thinking about the man from Taza and his preoccupations, the purchases he had made to satisfy the guests who would await him on his return home. I went down the hallway and crossed the big landing where the Nigerian cleaners slept along with an elderly man no one would share lodgings with. My companions were talking and drinking tea, and they greeted me amiably. I explained that I had lingered to look at the Kaaba. We talked about it for a while. Everyone knew the events of its founding, as tradition had them. The women joined in the conversation, though they were separated from us by the sheet hanging from a rope Abbas had rigged—a makeshift curtain that was pulled into place only when it was time to sleep.

We all agreed on the story of the exile of Hajar and Ismail, on the dangers facing mother and child, on the miracle of their survival in this arid, inhospitable basin, on the exemplary obedience and faith in God shown by father and son at the moment of sacrifice, on the divine mercy that saved Ismail both from torment and later from temptation by Satan (whom we were going to stone in Mina). We exchanged thoughts on the subject of the Black Stone and its origin. "It comes from paradise," Abbas reminded us, wanting to end our friendly controversy on this point. The rest of us apart from Abbas and his wife, Zuhra, knew that scientists had a hypothesis—the stone was a meteorite—but of course such thinking was inferior to divine omniscience.

One thing led to another, and we started talking about what I was writing and what I thought I might learn by studying the pilgrimage. This time my companions wanted to discuss the subject in depth. I told them again that I wanted to understand the actions we carried out each day according to the precise rules. My friends listened as they always did, with some interest but also perplexity. Maybe it was Salah, the scientific one, the engineer, who tried hardest to understand my project. Abbas simply gathered I was studying the hajj and seemed satisfied with that.

Salah knew a little about social sciences. But, like many scientists, especially engineers, he wanted to look for correlations among variables, establish chains of causality, make logical deductions. He wanted to use notions taught in biology or mathematics. He felt that what we had just carried out—actions coordinated by a prescribed order, with a beginning and an end—should have a clear, immutable meaning. In this way of thinking, going around the Kaaba was going back to the world's axis, where God made creation, and to the state of Adam and Eve before the Fall. Running between Safa and Marwa referred to the signs of God, in whom faith is necessary for salvation. "The reason for everything is that man needs to be guided by God. Otherwise, he follows his desires and lives in corruption and disorder, and that destroys him. The reason for all that resides in hidden wisdom." And the function? "Acts of worship turn humans away from their desires, which tend to be destructive, and toward a collective effort to perfect the world, until God decides that the universe must come to its inevitable end." To my questions about the number of actions and the repetition of them, he replied that these were commandments of which God had the secret; to carry them out as we did was simply to submit to his orders and testify that we had put our destinies in his hands. He was floating in metaphors, just like me, but he continued to insist he was formulating clear propositions.

Intuition of danger, feelings of solitude and uncertainty, fear, and suffering: these are known experiences. What do they have to do with the rituals of worship? The house of God, the Kaaba, is a sanctuary. According to a well-known Qur'anic verse, one finds there confidence and assurance against "hunger and fear"—in other words, against loss and death. No intuition or interpretation could give a meaning to the rituals as they were prescribed and practiced. Even with the clarity Salah claimed (by relying excessively on scientific idiom), they always led to God's mysterious ways.

If there was a meaning to be found, it was no doubt indistinguishable from a form of knowledge. My companions knew that the world was finished, death inevitable, resurrection and the Last Judgment foregone conclusions; that sin led to perdition. They used similar interpretations to understand dreams and recognize good deeds. There, too, there were procedures and rules to follow. Once learned, these became an immanent part of action and became clear in the practice of the right words and gestures. The meaning and full experience of action and of religious emotion were thus part of the flexible form and changing horizon of their manifestations. To have a sense of religious action, meditation, supplication, weeping, and prostration meant that one recognized the means of expressing them; you could only be mistaken if someone had premeditated plans to lead you astray.

The *umra*, which we had just carried out, washes away the previous year's sins. Its effects prompt some people to come back to Mecca every year. On the other hand, the pilgrimage proper, which is obligatory only once in a lifetime, washes away all past sins. "You come out of it as if newborn." And on the "enjoyment pilgrimage" we could benefit from certain freedoms regarding the ritual interdictions. We could stay in Mecca and enjoy the proximity of God's house. The actions of the *umra* took us along the path to the wellspring of life, but in the days separating the *umra* from the hajj, we would return to a life of leisure, profit, sexuality, and so forth. We knew that leaving *ihram* provisionally taught us not only how to return to a life in which one cannot absolutely separate purity and impurity, but also that this interval of freedom echoed the renunciations awaiting us in the accomplishment of the hajj—renunciations that were to guide our lives until death.

Another question was nagging at me. If there was meaning to all this, it came fleetingly, at such an angle that we could only see the parts nearest to us. At a young age I had learned how to accomplish my religious duties. I kept intact the memory of the profound sense of tranquillity that follows prayer. I felt the same kind of freedom when I managed to conform more or less to my ethical aspirations. And yet now, as I tried to observe and analyze the hajj, a project that set me apart from my companions, the question never left me: Was I betraying them? In one sense, yes, since I couldn't make them understand that I was looking for manifestations of existence in the elaboration of my own world, my own identity, still being formed yet already made. My companions didn't go along with the difference I made between the immanence in the world of the encounter with the other and the transcendent present that is Allah. Testing oneself, by taking every possible risk (to change one's life or to renounce it, to devote oneself wholly to Allah by returning to authorized "orthodox" practice and to its codified beliefs), was alien to my friends: for them, faith in God became real through worship, a rigorous succession of actions following the rules.

I had many intentions: one was to write a book that shed some light on religion and on what my academic discipline has taken to calling rituals. But, as always, my project was related to the question one asked oneself about how to exist. I approached worship as a participant, from my own point of view. And if I refused both constraint and salvation by this means, I liked the assertion of irrationality surrounding all the world's rational laws that it suggested to me. Awareness of this irrationality cut me off from rationalist critiques of religion whose message I was encountering. My attachment to Islam's life-forms had given me my only mythological home. I had never really had any other, although some— Greco-Roman, Jewish, Christian, Buddhist, African, or Amerindian—were familiar to me.

The pilgrims I met paid little attention to questions about their intentions and deepest convictions. They never asked me about mine. My companions were very discreet on this point, applying the well-known rule "To each his own intention." On that side, I wasn't hiding anything. The Muslim tradition of travel literature about the hajj may also have served to protect me against Wahhabi inquisition. I was quite calm as I filled my notebooks.

Still, while my companions thought they were putting their beliefs into practice, I wanted enlightenment on the possible links between the motive for religious action and the motive for the actions that go along with it, making it possible in daily life. Whatever risks I took in meshing my existence with that of practicing Muslims who were seeking eternal salvation, I couldn't narrow the gap that separated me from them. Learning justified my being at their side. But to the communion they offered me and I accepted, feeling that after all this was my home, I had no truly legitimate access. I was adrift—and had no title.

8

THE UNWELCOME ARCHIVE

ISLAM IS MY HOME. IN WHAT SENSE DO I HAVE THE RIGHT TO claim this? It has been, and still is, the source of nourishment and life; with time, it has become my sole refuge. In the past few years, some disgruntled souls—both Westerners and Easterners—have resuscitated a long-forgotten opposition between "the abode of Islam" and "the abode of War" (Muslim and Christian lands, respectively). But I learned of this dichotomy quite late in life. Legal scholars sometimes alluded to it without really believing in it; it was antiquated; in my early life, whether at primary school when Morocco was a French protectorate or as a barely decolonized high-school student, I never heard my teachers of Arabic or religious studies mention it. Nor did anyone allude to it at the university in Rabat where I received my higher education. Where had I encountered this famous opposition—which people purported to believe was an eternal one, a veritable obsession for Muslims?

In Europe and later in the United States especially, a

poorly grounded version of Orientalism spread inappropriate interpretations of this expression, according to which the
abode of Islam was carrying war into European and American territory. Yet in fact, none of the Muslim nations of the
earth, having only recently emerged from colonial occupation, were capable of defending themselves against the over-
armed European and American powers. By the 1960s and
1970s, all the major capitals of the Muslim Near East were
within reach of Israeli missiles, and none could obtain justice
for the Palestinian people—Muslim and Christian alike—
who were being despoiled by an unprecedented type of colonialism.

I went back to Morocco as often as I could so as to forget
the fury of war and the media's insanity a little. Every time I
returned to what remained of my village, I rediscovered Islam, my home. The steppe lay as far as the eye could see
around scattered clusters of low adobe houses. Jujube trees
with gnarled trunks cast their gentle shade on the animals.
People drew water from the wells early in the morning or at
mid-afternoon, when the herds came in to quench their
thirst. And at sunset, the light air carried the clear, sweet call
to prayer far into the distance. A small one-room building
surrounded by a low fence: this was the mosque. Here as
elsewhere—at the foot of the Atlas Mountains, on the Atlantic plains, in the Tunisian Sahel, the Nile Delta, the lands
and oases of the Fertile Crescent, the shade of the mosques
of Marrakech, Tunis, or Shiite al Hufuf—I could taste the
serenity of Islam. I could find its friendly signs in the very
heart of the shantytowns, and sometimes in the soulless
modernity of Arab cities. I kept hoping that one day one
might rediscover in it a life that was made to our measure.

For a long time—since the fall of Granada in 1492—Islam
had tended rather to protect a way of life that stopped at
the sea's (especially the Mediterranean's) coastlines. People

called the sites that were good for mooring "gaps," and for
two centuries or more lived on the defensive. This way of
life had its own dead ends. Ferocious conservatism, closely
guarding its power and privileges, gave rise to murderous
and incantatory manias that metamorphosed Islam's
prophetic inspiration into "the Word of God"; the Qur'an
became a dictionary of quotations or, worse, a mere toolbox.
Ancient edicts about women, non-Muslims, apostasy, and alcohol were elevated to the status of "divine law." Yet it wasn't
a prison but a world, and one capable of the greatest happiness. Islam's arts preserved their power, its people retained
their sensitivity about sharing, and its mystical paths led far
beyond the commonplace. The fiction that there was a political succession to the Prophet had shown its inevitable pit-
falls, but Islam's initial inspiration was still alive, and it
continued to nourish archaic forms which challenged des-
potism. This peaceful version of Islam still existed in daily
life, fracturing the structure of authoritarian colonial rule
and its later reinterpretations. Strident voices of hatred from
East and West tried to drown it out, but it hadn't disappeared.

The further I advanced in age—which is to say, the further back I went, since death, too, always comes before—this
house of Islam came back to me just as I returned to it. The
further I distanced myself from modernity's religious languages and their imprecations, devoid of testimony, the
more power of endurance I drew from this home. It thus became doubly mythological. In Islam I lived side by side with
perfectly identifiable characters with whom I could very naturally converse, argue, or disagree. It was crucial to me that
they stopped and listened to what I had to say, that I could
voice my recriminations, skepticism, and incredulity with
them. I was free to call on them at any time—and just sit
with them and have a conversation. We have shared the same

stories since childhood. When I was younger—they were, too, of course—their nonchalance and innocence were no less than mine. Now, all of us past fifty, we were surprised to find ourselves becoming more serious, with a hint of irony. When I realized—without any witness and with no one's death having anything to do with it—that my end was at hand, I welcomed it and put it away with my possessions. Allah several times claimed—with great vehemence—the life he had given me but I chose to ignore his insistence and to keep my life to myself.

I had refused Yahweh almost nothing—no more than Jesus and the Christian god in his trinitarian form. I read the stories of each and listened to their voices. But we had not grown up together, though Yahweh and Jesus were for a long time my neighbors. The first, very advanced in years, had a thick beard and bushy eyebrows; we were very close. But he was always discreet and never left his neighborhood. In my juvenile incarnation of him, Jesus didn't deserve the agony inflicted on him. Long ago, the French colonial church bore his crucifix throughout Morocco's towns and villages. Like Allah and Yahweh, he lived in many houses—with pitched red-tiled roofs, towers, and bells that rang at regular times, especially on Sunday. As for Yahweh and Allah, they occupied houses like our own, with terraced roofs; Yahweh's were smaller and lower than the others, entirely covered, whereas Allah's were big and had courtyards; from the minarets, which looked out over every landscape, the call to prayer rang out five times a day and at the end of the night.

I knew the Greek gods, too. They had taken for themselves, and to the detriment of humans, the sweetest perfumes and the choicest pieces, the self-destructive excesses and repeated reinventions of themselves, eternal beauty and eternal leisure. They had left humanity the chains and had feigned absentmindedness so the flesh eaters could steal a little fire for cooking. In fact, they abandoned the Greeks, their servants, to their tragic fate, not really being able to do much about it. These gods scarcely spoke; they only had the strength to send signs to a few oracles. Venerable men and women in the ancient world told their tale through the mediation of the image, and the tales of their transactions with humans.

Yahweh asked nothing of me, and at any rate he had a covenant only with his own people. The Greek gods didn't speak to me, and I didn't know the language of their stories. Jesus offered me his love, but I couldn't understand why he had taken love to such an extreme. The people who wrote the Gospels perhaps had some reason for affirming that his passion went to such lengths.

I had frequented these pantheons so assiduously and for so many years that they had become very familiar to me. Their denizens were like aunts and uncles or old friends. I loved them and needed their presence. They helped me, although I couldn't go along with their way of thinking or adopt their lifestyle as my own. They were settled in comfortably and led an easy life among tasteful furniture. I was pleased to accept their invitations, but I could only relax completely in my own home, which was Allah's.

If I kept my Muslim life for myself and for others, it was because I had entered it without having fully decided to. I was realizing this little by little as I accepted the pain and uncertainty inherent in interpreting my will. My imagination made the effort before reason or liberty did. Strictly speaking, I learned neither of these two at school. Rather, I learned how to use them both systematically—especially the freedom to make mistakes and start again instead of depending on ready-made recipes. That school in French Morocco produced us "from scratch." It limited the learning to which we were entitled, but it supported the seductive ideology of knowledge not limited by either revelation or reason. It of-

fered a way to reject the colonial situation itself. And one
could appropriate, all reasonable reasons notwithstanding,
the idea of following one's path with no limits other than
those of conversation and creation. I remembered a life free
of constraints until adolescence—or, rather, a life whose constraints did not deprive me of liberty. But as soon as I started
thinking about other ways of life, some of the rules that until
then had guided my actions became obstacles. No doubt
there had been, well before the drastic colonial transformation of my country, contexts and moments comparable to
those I was experiencing. Still, I was born during that transformation, when new contexts deprived me of freedom.

To enter my life and to accept the wounds made by my
own will was synonymous with feeling a multiplicity of the
self. To be sure, I was attached to Islam's acts of worship
(prayer, fasting, the profession of faith) but not to their regular practice, which was far less important to me than the
mystery of the commandment, and touched me far less
than the rule that gave no rationale for requiring them. Between the world's many manifestations and Islam's commandments, there was no link but will. For centuries, people
have tried to find the rationales and "secrets" of these acts of
worship, as the great twelfth-century scholar and religious
thinker al-Ghazali did, for instance. More recently, some
people have seen the hajj as a great annual Islamic congress,
and prayer as a form of sport! None of this accords with the
perceptible evidence. The commandment to worship must
be met with trust, confidence, and faith. The only link: salvation. Happiness that a form of life achieved by shaping itself
according to this evidence predicted the desired outcome.
This was done "in the name of God" and through this name,
which is the mystery revealed to humanity.

Among the three forms of monotheism born in the Se-
mitic Middle East, it was easy to find similarities and transfer-

ences, and just as easy to locate disjunctions and oppositions. There is no doubt that it was Islam that first called for communal solidarity in its acts of worship, and indeed explicitly enjoins believers to engage in it. A collective consciousness is in continuous gestation thanks to these practices, and not the inverse, if by consciousness we mean that together we are going beyond the assembling of rights and powers, in other words that we are engaged in creating a consensus for the sake of action, our testimony coming both before and after legal stipulations and the reports from the court clerks.

Pascal offers two propositions that have always interested me but ultimately are irreconcilable. On the one hand, the heart dictates, and reason either submits or recedes. On the other hand, reason eventually speaks for the wager on God's existence, which is always a winning bet; this is a rational decision, even though it contains an unknown element. My problem was different. I knew I received my life through a will to bring life about. I knew also that my community brought me up to move in that direction. And finally, I knew that my being, like all beings, went beyond itself—through the senses, language, dreams, passion, need, desire—the list goes on. To bet within this set of two terms didn't satisfy me, so I had simply stopped betting. Once again, I became almost what I had been before reading Pascal, but now I lived in fear that an invisible force would quickly punish me, guilty of wanting to deplete my reserves of life on my own, guilty of being sure of nothing and being unable to exclude anything.

That anguish faded over the past few years, but I felt it return in Medina and culminated in Mecca. I couldn't rid myself of the sense of imminent punishment, of a plague that would suddenly arise and defeat me. This fear tortured me, because it was more than just a representation. It paralyzed me, gave me shudders. Sometimes the phantasm came over me in the middle of a prostration. My frailty certainly derived from my extreme isolation in the midst of a crowd of people who were confirming their faith (or appearing to do so) while I was just as if "at home," approaching worship as a professional job and as a language opening out onto the mystery of my life's will, my will to live. I addressed and carried out the acts of worship respectfully. They bound me to others, to all the others. But because I was elsewhere at the same time, in a state beyond myself that many would not have accepted and that would have triggered hostility, repression, or execution, I felt isolated, faced with this endless succession of instances of punishment (community, father, name of the father, in the name of the father).

During the twelve days I spent out of *ihram* in Mecca, I sought moments of peace. Like the others, I didn't sleep much; more often than they, I suffered from insomnia. Being present in Meccan life, "close to the House of God," exhausted me. Many people found intense happiness in it. "You forget everything," as they said to me. I had heard the phrase before leaving from several people who had made the hajj: Mahdi, an Iranian diplomat from a powerful family of mullahs; Fata, a Ph.D. student at Princeton, originally from Indonesia; Mouh and Bajjou, close friends from among the Rheraya, in the western High Atlas. And this radical forgetfulness often featured prominently in pilgrimage accounts I had read. There were a few exceptions, perhaps the most noteworthy being that of the Iranian writer Ali Ahmad. The surprise was all the greater to hear some speak of "repose" and peace.

Si Larbi said the same thing. He was educated in theology and had taught at a mosque near Rabat before going into business. I ran into him on the second day of our sojourn in Mecca—Sunday (26 Dhu'l-Qa'dah 1419, 14 March 1999). He was as always well dressed in his white djellaba and turban, which he had donned again after having removed the seamless white cloths. He walked unsteadily and seemed tired; and his features, highlighted by a close-cut beard, were emaciated. He noted how surprised I was to hear that the pilgrimage could be restful and enjoyable. I told him he had lost a lot of weight. He advised me simply to "anchor" my faith and told me if I managed that, everything would change.

Like my friend Lahcen, Si Larbi had paid his debts, performed numerous acts of worship and piety, organized the farewell ceremony, and asked forgiveness for any offenses against his relatives or neighbors. He had cut any ties that might have bound him to sin. He had left his pious wife in his brother's care. "Nowadays it's better that way. Before, when the trip lasted for months or years, people had to get a divorce and remarry when they returned . . . When the pilgrimage lasted a long time, women were free to remarry to make a new family . . . Pilgrims had to be ready for anything, including death."

Si Larbi was staying in a building a little farther up Ajyad Boulevard. I met him by chance, after evening prayers. I had left the mosque late, after watching the circumambulation one last time. My reveries were interrupted by the sight of pilgrims preparing to sleep around the mosque—eating fruit, preparing some dinner, enjoying ice cream. The sanctuary was lit up like a stadium, and as animated as a great rally. Meeting Si Larbi thrust me back into the other scene; around the Kaaba, the circle continued to revolve, giving off its calm, imperious strength. In the night, the black cube sailed on as if cut from its moorings, while the humans clinging to the vessel moved on toward a port whose name was known but that was in a foreign land. Si Larbi was right: "Before coming here, you have to put everything in order, and anticipate meeting death."

As was often the case before we went to bed, the members of our group exchanged a few impressions. Haj Salah—we now addressed each other using the title of *haj*—agreed with the image I proposed of the "sailing ark." "I hadn't thought of it," he said, "but that's right." Haj Abbas preferred the idea of a link with paradise and, of the Black Stone, asserted again that "it comes from paradise." Once more I mentioned the theory that it might be a meteorite. "Even if it is a meteorite, God's science is God's science. We know very little," he said, and added, "Apparently it comes from paradise. It was white, and then became black." Someone else repeated the widespread story, recorded in some written works, that the change occurred when "a menstruating woman approached the stone." Our conversation ended at this point.

We returned to our routine: prayers and visits to the market gave our days their rhythm, although we bought less here. We had filled our suitcases in Medina, and the Quraysh merchants turned out to be just as everyone said: "more money-hungry and much less affable than the people in Medina." We could forget daily life in Morocco all the more easily as life in Mecca became more organized. I ran into Si Larbi again, and I found him even more exhausted. He was an elderly man, but I hadn't had the impression he had come here with the aim of dying near the sanctuary, a goal to which many pilgrims aspired. Many had their wish granted; and deaths were a frequent occurrence. I don't remember a single canonical prayer that wasn't followed by prayers for the dead. "To die near the House of God: what a happy end!" But the signs were now that Si Larbi was getting ready for just that. He was coming to carry out his duty, to cleanse himself of sin so that "God, in his mercy, would give [him] a happy death and take a soul that had obeyed his decrees." A successful pilgrimage was the decisive step for him, or the sign that such a conclusion was possible.

None of my companions wanted to die this way; they sought only forgiveness. This was a stage that confirmed their piety and guided them more firmly along the path they had chosen. They were all quite young, between thirty and fifty, with children still at school; they had acquired apartments or houses and were in the prime of life. For Si Larbi, my friends, and myself, the pilgrimage was a passage. But the next stage, which redefined the preceding ones after the fact, was not the same for everyone. One among us had not settled his debts before leaving; his creditors knew, as he did, that there was every likelihood of his returning safe and sound. "Forgetting everything" meant not having anything to worry about. "Everything is suspended . . . There's only worship." The hajj concluded one stage and was the passage to another, a path marked out and a guarantee for the future. It was like a story that one knows at the beginning will end well. Forgetting, then, summed up the first part in a single stage, the hajj. For was it not the fortunate realization of the past? And the retrospective, of course, was a prospective.

In my own itinerary, the hajj came at a time when my anthropological work was leading me very naturally to think about religion and when, after I turned fifty, I became less tolerant of the different types of spreading conformism. My academic research had motivated me to interrogate my own identity more and more acutely. Also, as I already mentioned, I approached the hajj with existential dilemmas I could no longer ignore. So the experience of the pilgrimage brought back into every fiber of my consciousness various still incandescent archives. The fantasy of imminent punishment turned out to be much harder to master than I would have thought. Was I, in this world, at least going to have a

death about which I could do something while awaiting it?
In a sense, we were all exploring this question. For me, the
path led to a door that was not in inhabited space and had no
inhabitants behind it. This absence was hardly a form of
transposed empirical knowledge. I had no image of absence,
not even in the silence of forests or the restless shimmering
of the sea.

Our itineraries were taking shape but, like sentences, became distinct only when articulated. They traced out their
meanderings, bifurcated, and came back anew to us. We welcomed them, more or less surprised. They intertwined, settled their differences, and defined each other. We became
attuned to each other in this way, or got on the wrong foot
with each other, or developed conflicts, or generated mutual
indifference. We became used to living as a group, and we
could respond correctly in any instance by insisting on the
pilgrimage rules. Soon, in this new life, each was left to his
own devices. Worship, the marketplace, visits, meals, sleep.
But all the rest—for instance, the question of sincerity,
which haunted me personally—had to be kept to oneself.
Regarding the difficulty in reconciling detachment with salvation, as orthodoxy and membership in the abode of Islam
suggested, I got few reactions. The others preferred to
change the subject, or told me, "No matter how much you
search, ask questions, copy European ideas, you'll end up returning to the path of Islam." Or, "In any case, the door to
repentance is wide open. God can guide whom he wishes
and abandon whom he wishes." Didn't my dread indicate a
question of genealogy, of belonging, that hadn't been dealt
with? A profound sentiment tied me to the House of Islam,
of that I was sure; but the nature of my connection to it escaped me. A missing link.

Haj Mbarek, with whom I chatted from time to time, said
he was in Mecca "by chance." The Ministry of Health had

paid for him to go on pilgrimage. He was willing to worship God but didn't believe anything else: the pilgrimage was just "a merchants' conspiracy." The hajj coincided with the end of his career as an ambulance driver. His children were out of trouble, and he planned to retire with his wife to the village where he had been born, "far from all the intrigues." It was Monday, our third day in Mecca. We were following the same path, progressing toward the pilgrimage's supreme moment, yet each of us was discovering himself separately. Not as one would solve an enigma; yet, as we went through what came to us, an outline was emerging which, as such, indeed showed its incompleteness.

I had finished morning prayers and had decided to stay in the room. I was still sick and not feeling strong enough to go to the noon prayers. Hajja Aisha and Hajja Zuhra also had fevers, and Hajja Farida was getting ready to leave Mecca for Jeddah. I had been on the balcony since 5:30 in the morning, writing in my diary. After breakfast and Farida's departure, Haj Abbas let loose with criticism. He confirmed that she had left clandestinely by car with a brother-in-law, a man well connected in Jeddah who worked for a supranational Islamic organization. Not everyone approved. Farida was "a girl from a big family; she does as she pleases, and now she's going to Jeddah for some fancy shopping." As Haj Abbas would have it, the big port city was overflowing with "crystal chandeliers, jewelry, and precious textiles at very good prices." He kept on making comments, but we refrained from reacting. "She can't even spend a full week near the House of God!" he expostulated in the silence.

Hajja Farida had always ignored Haj Abbas and Hajja Zuhra. She barely spoke to them. The state was paying for her trip, theoretically so that she could care for the health of other pilgrims. She had given me pills from time to time, and once she treated Haj Mbarek and his companions, but they saw her as a woman first and foremost, and while they wanted her to take care of them, they avoided all contact with her, though I suggested they speak to her directly. They were all in a group: Haj Mbarek, along with two lower-ranking technicians under the leadership of Haj Ma'ati, a well-to-do peasant from the Rabat region. I'd gotten to know them well since Medina. "All our family did the hajj scrupulously. It's our tradition to carry out this religious duty properly . . . My father did it several times!" Hajja Farida told me once. I understood her father, who had recently died, had taken her on *umra* when she was small and she felt great filial piety toward him. Islamic rigor and social class were apparently allied in her statement.

Thus did some people manage to escape from Mecca. We knew this, but we didn't feel like following suit. True, we didn't have friends or relatives comfortably settled in a posh situation and enjoying the satisfactions of the Red Sea metropolis. And we also had no papers: the company chartering our pilgrimage had taken our identification documents, and we would only get them back on the last day, when we left the Saudi kingdom. The border police were supposed to give them back to us at the airport.

"We still have a little time left, if anyone wants to perform ablutions," said Haj Ma'ati, offering me a Marlboro. Like the rest of us, he had been awake since four o'clock in the morning to get a place in line for the toilets and showers. The conversation went on. People asked me for details regarding the stages of the pilgrimage. Several of us had noticed how avid the merchants were. "Rain falls on the holy sites in the shape of banknotes!" said another young pilgrim, a health aide by profession. We carried on smoking, smiles on our faces. Religious questions gave way to other concerns. Some compared Morocco and Saudiya, as we called the host country. "A happy land!" said Haj Nasser, faithful as usual to his gentle brand of irony.

Then we moved on to the eagerly awaited topic of secrets, conspiracies, and machinations in Morocco. "Rich people," said Haj Nasser, "have plotted to defend each other and keep all the wealth for themselves." It was the end of King Hassan II's reign. Everyone knew the king was sick, and he had always been the focus of an intense mixture of love and hate, drawn by the figure of the merciless father; yet his regime had lost its credibility. These men (except for Haj Ma'ati) were from cities in the Rabat region where urban growth had metastasized, with shantytowns and informal housing springing up everywhere in the chaos, encouraged by manipulation of the real-property laws. Speculators were seizing land and, according to Haj Mbarek, dispossessing the poor— peasants had been washed up at the edges of the city by the tides of rural exodus. Plots were sold off even when their legal status was unclear. These were the first calamities besetting the poor in search of shelter. Families were allowed to put up huts made of wood, corrugated iron, and recycled plastic, but sooner or later these people needed papers, residence certificates, ID cards; neighborhood officials then demanded four or five thousand dirhams. Everyone knew the sum would be shared out between the authorities and the developers. Haj Abbas told us it was possible to sell land with a legal contract bearing the authorities' stamp and official certification but omitting the buyer's name and the date. In this way, the property could circulate from one buyer to the next until the last—the only one who had to pay property taxes. Haj Abbas made no bones about engaging in such practices himself: "Everybody does . . . That's all there is, God forgive us!" My friends concluded that "conspiracy is spreading everywhere like cancer."

Yet neither Haj Abbas nor they seemed to be trying to establish other ways of behaving. They said that as long as justice didn't reign, it was permissible to "do the same as everyone else." Thus, ideals had to be preserved so that each could then behave as he saw fit. Corruption and special privileges were practiced routinely by many Moroccan pilgrims, who didn't hesitate to buy favors from their national authorities. Collective denunciation in fact led to justification of such conduct. We were victims of the system, it wasn't our fault, this was a way of life. Perhaps they were more outspoken against excessive accumulation of wealth and the exploitation of the poor. Special privileges, on the other hand, seemed to be accepted.

We had a lot to say about our families. Most of us had left our native villages and towns to settle in cities. The common complaint was that relatives, especially the brothers who had "stayed," stripped those who had left of their rights. And again, toward the end of the morning, almost every single one of us had managed to feature in a story of corruption or dispossession, a tale about fighting for what was owed to us and showing ourselves to be generous. "You have to accept and forgive." This was everyday life, and it had its rules; one couldn't change them. Simply put: "This is not religion."

These stories and conversations brought us closer to each other, and we left the building together for noon prayers. Haj Abbas and I prayed under a dome we were particularly fond of. The mosque was a haven of peace where I often found refuge. Tired out by the city, its noise and its heat, I was becoming used to staying here in the shade, breathing the less polluted air, between the midday and the evening prayers. The smell of people's bodies diminished after the peak hours, and one could find a little space to meditate, read the Qur'an, or stretch out for a short nap. I had started reading the Qur'an again in Medina, and I was continuing in

Mecca. Despite the devastating urban growth and the disappearance of every vestige of the old city, Mecca's name, as well as the mosque and the Kaaba, influenced my reading. The words rang in my ears: the injunctions were imperious, and the immediate evidence of the narratives resumed their bewitching calls. The verses of the apocalypse with their sonorous scansion raised the mountains and moved the stars. The dome communicated its serenity to me; the voices and movements of people praying lent me a helping hand. But as soon as I recited the suras, with their injunctions, reminders, and threats, the rhythmic syllabic slap of the words struck me very hard.

I left the place after having marked the necessary pause before the circumambulation. Trembling a little, my step uncertain, I hoped to leave the paroxysms of this music behind me along with the prayers for the dead. At the end of the day, these prayers always invited me to wander off into the night. My night. Those who passed on had crossed a threshold that remained open, awaiting those who would follow. A door, like the one a great painter once drew, cut out of the clear night, often sprang into my imagination. But this time the black cube sent it back into nothingness. This time the circle, seen from above, looked like a gigantic white flower with innumerable petals. Around the cube, life affirmed its energy. And the cloth covering it revealed precisely what it purported to hide: the will to bring life about. The cloth clothed nothing.

Under the sign of the Kaaba, differences didn't disappear, as apologists never tired of claiming. On the contrary: they stood out clearly and gained strength. They were recognized and simultaneously subjected to the values of solidarity and justice. These values did not imply that conditions had to become equal. Around the black cube, the circle consecrated the equal dignity of all Muslims, but it did not eliminate differences in class or status. People accepted these differences; at the same time, they subordinated them to religion and to testimony, which placed them in the realm of contingency. Equality was expressed in contingent difference, not through measures that would impose it by a universal (and abstract) definition of humanity. I felt this intuition of contingency sharpen in my mind and others'. Injustice that threatened dignity was refused here more firmly than elsewhere.

When we first arrived in Mecca, we had been taken to a building, quite far away from the one to which we were later assigned, without anyone having consulted us. Our exhaustion, the walking about, and the bus going back and forth through the city had made us cranky. Yet we had promptly accepted the lodgings we were given, especially since they were very near the mosque, on Bir Balila Street. In any case, we had been ready to accept any shelter so we could escape from our cage on wheels. After a while, however, the building's shortcomings became apparent, and they became more scandalous each day: dirt; putrid odors emanating from overflowing sewers; water shortages due to irregularities in supply (in Mecca, the trucks that fill the cisterns crowd the streets with noise and fumes); the water bottles on each landing covered in dust. Nor did we have any water from Zamzam, the miraculous spring near the Kaaba, which shocked the other pilgrims.

One day, late in the afternoon, I ran into a small crowd kicking up a fuss in the street in front of the building. Men returning from prayers quickly joined in. Anger was rising. People were making protests against the owner, the Moroccan Hajj Mission, and the *mutawwif*—that is, the head of the charter company responsible for us.* The *mutawwif*, who de-

---

Mutawwif, from *tawaf*, meaning circumambulation, was originally the designation of the person who guides pilgrims in their circumambulations in return for money, and who may also provide other services.

spite his title had nothing to do with rituals, was an invisible man exploiting his product—transportation, lodging, food— like a fairly unscrupulous businessman. I went up to meet my friends from the fourth floor. The narrow staircase made me claustrophobic. I had to negotiate past crowds on the stairs and squeeze against the walls to get around the refrigerators that cluttered the narrow landings. "If there's a fire, God spare us! We'll go up in flames, the lot of us!" some people said. Haj Ma'ati and his friends welcomed me and told me that a small group had been trying to alert the authorities since that morning, and that the owner couldn't be found. On the ground floor, in the common room, the turmoil was coming to a head. Men were talking on phones. In the street, the crowd was fast growing larger, with people shouting and pointing at the sacks of garbage overflowing at the entrance. The Saudi police stood by, looking on. Some people were calling it a scandal, comparing our building in its deplorable state with that of our Algerian and Egyptian neighbors, who were much better off. "I paid three million! They know how to fleece you, all right. And they throw me here, no better than an animal!" a demonstrator was shouting.

The crowd pressed around an employee from the Moroccan Mission who had just arrived on-site. From the front steps, he gave a few explanations, which no one heard; his voice was drowned out by louder ones rising from the angry crowd. This anger could have been avoided had the young administrator chosen his words and used a vocabulary of understanding, restitution, and compromise. Instead, he lit a cigarette before starting in again.

"May God light your corpse with it!" The cry shot out from the crowd and provoked a moment of silence.

Then someone remembered: "We're on pilgrimage." In spite of that, the invectives continued. Clearly, they were not just targeting the fact that the man was smoking. Quite a few pilgrims were doing the same. My friends on the fourth floor, as I've mentioned, occasionally offered me a cigarette with tea, and in our street the Egyptians smoked to their hearts' content. Tobacco was cheap, like other goods in Arabia, since taxes were low. Still, the image struck me: the comment had associated the fire of a cigarette with that of a tomb (i.e., hell), the smell of tobacco and the perfume of burial. It didn't quite jibe with the mercy we had come to seek near the "noble sanctuary"; nor did it go with circumambulation or Hajar's running back and forth. Furthermore, we only had a few days left before returning to God: the station at Arafat.

But there it was. Verbal violence had exploded like thunder in reply to a clumsy gesture interpreted as an expression of contempt. Something blew up—related perhaps to a feeling of powerlessness, and expressed as a call for punishment in the afterlife. Still, the functionary, puffing away, showed he wasn't playing the game. He went on exhorting us to be understanding Muslims, invoking the mosque's proximity and the imminence of the pilgrimage's greatest moment. Bureaucracy's habits were stronger than those of religion. Lighting a cigarette, for him, had seemed appropriate, even expected, in the context of his office and the administration's power. But it had a different meaning in front of a crowd of less privileged pilgrims.

At any rate, we were in an extremely new situation. Not because we didn't know what to do or how to do it. We had learned all the actions we had to accomplish. We had rehearsed them, as if at the theater, under the supervision of instructors appointed by political and religious authorities. But this was the first time we were actually close to the sanctuary where we were going to succeed or fail in our trial.

This situation was new and risky—for me, too. We were all displaced, "guests of the Merciful One." This must have been visible in our actions and reactions. We had been told many times, and reminded of the fact in words exchanged with the police: we were untouchable, and at the same time we were obliged to act according to the rules of divine hospitality. In Rabat, we had learned some of these rules: no quarreling, no violence; seek compromise and don't insist on difference; avoid excess, especially in words and laughter; proscribe jokes. These obligations weighed on our relationships. In particular, they prevented conflicts with the Saudi people, "guardians of the holy sites." We and all other Muslims were their guests. We had no other identity than that of "guests of the Merciful One." But we had discovered for ourselves that the Saudis could be intractable and sometimes brutal.

The situation at our lodgings threatened to deteriorate. Someone said it might be possible to alert the Moroccan press, but the suggestion wasn't taken up. The Saudi services were obviously experienced in receiving and monitoring pilgrims, and the latter were quite willing, incidentally, to "show each other the right path." In many buildings, relationships were forged between certain pilgrims and members of the Hajj Mission—not to mention the officially appointed religious guides who trailed some of the groups. There were none with us, but if one happened to feel bewildered by the rituals' complex nature, or were looking for exemptions and solutions to an unexpected incident, it was easy to find people who were keen to enlighten others, answer questions, and talk about the problem. Despite all this, the explosion of anger couldn't be avoided, and in the end the Saudi authorities took care of things. The title "guests of the Merciful One," which everyone brandished relentlessly, could resolve even the most radical differences. When the crisis died down that night, we asked each other for forgiveness and begged for divine clemency on behalf of the two men implicated in the cigarette incident.

Still, to me, the image of a person being burned with a cigarette in his grave kept all its violence. Perhaps there was in it also the idea of incineration, but it was especially the association of words that struck me: "cigarette," "light," "God," and "tomb." In the context of the altercation, where the bureaucrat had indeed put a match to his Marlboro, didn't the phrase just mean fire—in other words, hell? Who was insane enough to think that the fact of lighting a cigarette could be one of God's punishments? Of course, God is violent sometimes: there are torments and eternal hellfire for the wicked. These punishments abound in the Qur'an, the traditions, exegeses, and sermons. Not to mention the literature on the afterlife, which discusses these horrors in minute detail.

The actual commerce that religion has with violence is often disregarded in favor of a few abstractions. Vengeance by fire and destruction, justice through plague or the sword, annihilation in floods or attacks carried out by birds—these represent reparation and compensation through violence. The motives for divine violence aren't always comprehensible. In the altercation I witnessed, God was called upon to use his fire against a man whose act had been perceived as a gesture of contempt. True, it was suffering, above all, that was being expressed. Yet no one was innocent here. The power to damn someone is a real power. Marx knew it well: religion is not ideology in the sense of the "German ideology." It takes root in the reality of suffering. But between "opium" and pain, he forgot that religion is not a placebo.

Does this explain this implacable determination, this forward movement of the pilgrim masses, despite the obstacles?

For many people, fatigue, disorientation, tension, and quarrels were insignificant in the face of this progress. For some, like me, there was a feeling of imminent danger. Was this because the source of the powers that moved us was not always religious?

9

RESURRECTION BEFORE DEATH

WE STONED THE FIRST PILLAR AND MADE THE SACRIFICE WHEN we returned from Arafat. As planned, it was the morning of 10 Dhu'l-Hijja 1419 (Saturday, 27 March 1999), the first day of the Feast of the Sacrifice. By now my sense of time had blurred, for moving to Mina and then to Arafat had been a long, chaotic process. What with the trips, the ritual activities, the visits to the souks, and the long afternoon naps, day and night were getting mixed up. Later, reading my notebooks, I understood the sleepwalking state I was slipping into more and more often:

Wednesday, 7 Dhu'l-Hijja 1419, 24 March 1999. At half past nine in the evening, a young man made a surprise visit to us. He stood on the front stoop and addressed our small group in front of the building: "O good pilgrims! Make ready! Departure for Mina is tonight at eleven o'clock!" He repeated this announcement several times, then spent quite a while telling it to the men and women entering and leaving the building. He flat re-

fused the idea of putting up a written sign on the door: "Moroc-
cans don't like written announcements; they prefer spoken
communication." Without insisting, I left to perform the major
ablutions before putting my ihram *back on; then, like many*
others, I spent a few moments in the street for distraction. In
front of the Pakistani tea shop, Egyptians were smoking and
enjoying the cool evening. Vigorous negotiations were under
way with the peddlers who spread their wares on the ground
every day in the late afternoon. I sat on the stairs for a mo-
ment; I drank some Coke to quench my thirst as I watched the
fever of activity over knickknacks, scarves, cheap silks, jewelry,
and all sorts of hardware. As usual, the police arrived out of the
blue, and the vendors quickly wrapped up their goods in bun-
dles and ran up the street, which ended far off at a steep slope.
They pretended to get lost there in the alleys and crossways
while watching out for the police. The scene played out several
times, as it usually did. The police almost always managed to
catch one poor wretch or two, whom I would hear making their
pleas in Egyptian or Yemeni Arabic or in languages I didn't
know.

After midnight, tired of waiting, people scattered and
passed the time going to and fro, asking each other the same
questions: "Do you know what's happened to the buses? Are
they on their way?" "Have you seen the company agents?" "Did
the man who made the announcement come back?" I gave up
and went to lie down in our room. When I opened my eyes,
around three in the morning, we were still waiting . . . I went to
a phone booth, a few minutes' walk from our street, to call my
wife and children. On the other end of the line, in Princeton,
they told me they loved me and couldn't wait for me to come
back home. In ihram, *in the booth, I was incapable of commu-*
nicating the state I was in, and simply told them about my
ever-imminent departure for Mina. When I hung up, I was
brought sharply back, once again, to the harsh reality of

Mecca's avarice. "A hundred and twenty riyals!" the clerk shouted at me. I vainly asked for a receipt and refused to pay. Then, as if giving in to my request, the man caressed his keyboard and got his printer going: he gave me what he called my fatura . . . *I protested a bit more. "It's not the normal rate!" I snapped. "Calm down!" he retorted in a menacing tone. I obeyed and went off, shaking with anger; as if struck blind, I collided with a group of women waiting their turn in front of a shop. "Respect women!" shouted a voice behind me. I didn't have the courage to turn around. I had to walk on without responding, taking with me this faceless cry, and soon met up with my companions in front of our building.*

At half past four in the morning on Thursday, 8 Dhu'l-Hijja, we finally accepted the fact that the bus wasn't going to come, and we decided to walk to Mina. We stopped to pray at the Holy Mosque before going, taking a few things with us in small bags and leaving most of our stuff in the room. We walked along the highway for a while just outside the holy city. The buses, bumper to bumper, idly revved their engines. We left the inferno rapidly, and found other roads by chance. We felt sure that we were headed in the right direction, but didn't know exactly where we were. Soon a small, half-full bus came up; when the doors opened, we hopped into the empty seats, relieved but with no idea of how long the trip would take. Within a quarter of an hour at most, going through a gap in the hills and then parallel to a chain of gray peaks, heading east, we found ourselves at the entrance of a campsite.

It wasn't ours, however. We spent two hours wandering about looking for the place reserved for the Moroccan contingent. Then, when we found it, we learned that there was no more room and that our *mutawwif* wasn't there. Almost everybody was of the same opinion about him: "Moroccan filth!" Saudi agents then took charge; we were divided into groups and settled in air-conditioned tents, men separate from women. We were out in the open, far from the noise and petrol fumes.

Thus did we leave Mecca for our quarters in Mina before going to the station of Arafat—an immense encampment that stretched all across a valley and up to the surrounding rugged hills, around a small urban center with a big mosque. Slightly to the west of this center and suspended over the road was the giant access ramp connecting the three pillars that in Muslim tradition mark the places where Satan appeared to Ismail. The ramp doubled the available access space and facilitated the circulation of the crowds during the stoning. Having gotten my bearings a few days earlier, I had no difficulty finding the main places of worship. The town was very simple, designed in a grid plan along the roadways, but pilgrims regularly got lost here. Their sense of time and space, like mine, had been weakened. Lack of sleep had a lot to do with it, too. Long siestas made up for the nocturnal activity but added to the confusion between day and night. Men or women often went off on roads that took them away from the encampments, and they would be found in the desert, or wandering in other built-up areas. People tried to stay together to offer each other support and keep from going astray.

We couldn't count on the pilgrimage charter company for help. The manager, a Moroccan long settled in Saudi Arabia, still hadn't turned up. We had paid quite a lot for his services, but he was content to send us his underlings, who would arrive at the most unexpected hours, only to vanish as soon as a pilgrim brought them a problem or demanded that the contract be honored. Since we no longer expected anything from either the company or the Islamic Affairs functionaries, we slept until late morning in Mina. When I awoke, my ears took a while to recognize the sounds of air-conditioning and helicopters. Security and the threat of fire were no doubt the reasons for these regular rounds, which were coordinated with teams of police, military guards, and firemen on the ground. The Saudi state claimed credit for keeping the peace and preserving security during the pilgrimage. Next to our camp were the Egyptian, Algerian, and Sudanese settlements, and so on. Every nation had its own space, with separate, guarded entrances. Ours, like the others, was protected by tall wrought-iron fences.

I went out in search of breakfast, which the company had not seen fit to provide. Walking along a street, I came to a small square teeming with people where there were shops and cafés. Pakistanis served me tea and a bit of bread. I also bought a grilled chicken before going back to settle in the tent. The sun was high and its rays penetrated the fabric; I had to protect myself with my parasol. As I was eating, someone put up an improvised curtain between the men and the women. I expressed surprise to my neighbor. His reply was prompt, and the tone brooked no further discussion: "*Ihram* doesn't cover men's nakedness completely!" We exchanged glances; I started eating again, and the man moved off a little way and began to pray.

It seemed clearer and clearer to me that these questions of nudity, clothing, and modesty, which people tried hard to regulate, in fact were unresolved. In the past, garments covered men's bodies just as they did women's, the essential difference being that men were not obliged to respect the additional rule of being veiled. Today, in Saudi Arabia, men still cover themselves and women do the same, but the women are kept out of public spaces and spend most of their time in their family homes; if they work, they must do so while respecting a strict gender segregation. In Morocco, most men and a lot of women wear European clothes—the problem being that the latter articulates the shape of the body and leave the hair uncovered. So the question of contact between women and men remains unresolved in two ways that fuel each other. Contact always threatens to lead toward seduction and sexuality. This well-known risk is an old one, but it has become more urgent. In the past, clothing and partial or total seclusion made it more remote, gave specific, hidden forms to any transgressions; today, all sorts of new activities as well as changes in clothing styles put men and women into constant contact—contact that Muslim societies have not yet learned to ritualize, that is, to make commonplace. For this reason, men and often enough women, too, almost never let their guard down, because, in the absence of mediation, they must anticipate every possible risk.

Gender segregation is indeed an ancient practice, but it has never been absolute. In certain countries and certain social milieux, though, we see an unprecedented obsession with it, giving rise to an uncommon vigilance. In Medina and Mecca, as in Mina on that first morning, the compromises and half measures I was accustomed to had disappeared completely. People constantly invoked the need for absolute worship of God as a reason for insisting on gender separation. But because the risk was still not entirely eliminated and lapses occurred, the order had to be repeated constantly. Daily life, like religious life, had to conform—as if any relaxation of the rules, no matter how innocuous, might trigger the system's collapse. In this wrought context, with its anxiety about having to master a difficult transformation, religion appeared to me in a new light: as the sanctification of the responses human beings make to the risks associated with their own vital impulses, impulses that are a source of continuity but also of merciless dangers and conflicts. I had no other explanation for the particular forms these responses took in the ethical-religious totality of Islamized Arab societies.

By a kind of inspiration common to all foundational myths, gender relations were always carefully monitored. With an infallible sense, Muhammad's prophecy rediscovered the deep furrow that human society always plowed to ensure it would last and flourish. The act of union and, therefore, of separation was privileged over all others; Islam's message elaborated on it in minute detail; and its jurists became its constant, jealous guardians. Still, to keep the Messenger's infallible intuition credible and unbroken, Islam would have to put it back on its own ground: the sincerity and authenticity of the calling, forever confirmed by the transformation in Muhammad ibn Abd Allah's own life and in the billions of lives that his experience and inspiration transformed so radically. To reposition infallibility according to this criterion would be to recognize that the other faculties of the Prophet, of all prophets, were human; that they therefore gave humanity grace within the limits of a historical world, of internal and external tensions, and of interchange with the religious heritage of other peoples. Among the latter there were many who recognized prophecies of their own, even if the prophets of Near Eastern monotheism knew nothing of them or denied their authenticity. And all the men and women who went to the source of life returned with a radically new gospel, which they spread. Prophetic grace, in all cases, coexisted with the faculty of reason, with the ability to love and cease loving, to copulate, procreate, work for gain—in other words, with all the faculties and endeavors that remained purely human.

The new situation that Islam created for women broke with certain pre-Islamic customs. It firmly recognized their right to own property independently of their fathers, husbands, or brothers. It assured them of housing, food, clothing, and maintenance by making all these the husband's responsibility. On the other hand, it gave them only half the inheritance that a brother would receive. It eliminated polyandry and placed a woman's reproductive capacity unambiguously under the authority of the husband and his male relatives. Finally, it limited women's legal responsibility by making their rights conditional on their being represented by their husbands and his relatives. As a consequence, the family unit and lineage held a monopoly on reproduction and love, a monopoly protected by violence and exercised by men. It is understandable that in this situation women came to be perceived as an external threat to the group, that they became the "other." And at the same time in women were invested the central values that differentiated the Muslim group from others: Jews, Christians, and "pagans" of course, and naturally all those excluded from the circle of close relatives as defined in the Muslim community—in short, and to simplify, all those whom it was forbidden to marry. Thus did women become the symbol of differentiation between self (Muslims) and other (non-Muslims). The idiom of differentiation, and of power, was an efficient tool of domination perhaps quite early on. Muslims were induced to unite beneath the banner of powers claiming to defend the faith, now transformed into a universal identity; non-Muslims were put in their place, under the authority of these same powers. Revelation, then, opened the way to an organization of daily life which had its success but, like any organization, evolved in its own way and encountered other human constructs. And there it differed from the other path that revelation opens, the path of metaphysical renewal, which continues to invest human life with the feeling that it is more than itself. In the conjunction of the two, and with the subordination of this second source of inspiration, religion was transformed into an oppressive force.

In the tents at Mina, this conjunction showed itself in particular ways. Prayers and psalmodies rose from all sides, and they led into the canonical noon prayers, conducted by a zealous young technician who thrust himself forward without asking anyone's permission. A taciturn, reticent man, he was with his wife, whom he watched constantly to make sure she was behaving properly. I had once known him well, in his workplace in Rabat. He put as much energy into practicing religion as he did into making a living: he ran a nursery school in the building where he lived (violating municipal bylaws). He belonged to a network of circumspect but active preachers—engineers, technicians, students, and civil servants—whose influence increased steadily after the 1970s, uniting piety, militancy, and worldly interests. Its members profited from this network in their career advancement, gaining powerful jobs and positions. A few dozen of us prayed with this man, though his religious training was rudimentary. The members of the congregation he took over, with the exception of one man in his early sixties, were in their forties, and the scientific and religious expertise of at least a few of us was far more advanced than his.

The prayer was short, since in Mina and Arafat there are only two prostrations for each four-prostration prayer. It was already past two o'clock when we were called to lunch. We went to line up in front of a big ticket window. Company employees gave each of us a tray like the ones you get on airplanes—meat with vegetables, bread, water, and dessert. Nothing was missing, not even the little packets of salt and pepper, the ketchup, or the moistened tissues to wipe our fingers. These caused a moment's hesitation: Was the perfume light or could it penetrate the skin, in which case it was disallowed?

The psalms, sermon, and prayer drained what strength remained to us after the nighttime trip we had made to get here. We gave in to sleep very quickly—a time of rest and calm that was welcome in the heat, before the mid-afternoon prayers. When they approached, the sound of people coming and going woke me. I got up and headed for the toilets and showers to perform my ablutions, my head covered with a piece of *ihram* cloth. Someone stopped me: "The head must remain uncovered when you are in the state of *ihram!*"

I went back to my place in the tent after ablutions and hurriedly jotted down notes on the day's events. Someone turned toward me and asked if I was in a state of ritual purity. I stopped writing to answer that he should worry about his own ablutions and not bother with mine. He wasn't easily convinced, pointing out that he was only reminding me of my duties because it was almost time to pray. Another neighbor told him I had performed my ablutions as well as a two-prostration prayer before sitting down to write. In the meantime, activity had started up again in the camp, with Qur'anic chants as well as invocations and pleas ringing out on all sides. Strong young voices gave the call, and we got up to stand in rows behind the imam—none other than the technician, assisted this time by Abbas. The latter made us wait because, he said, "there's still someone missing from the community." It was the high-ranking technician from our group, who was probably obeying his subordinates' orders in this case (the three men worked in the same institution and had known each other a long time). The prayer began with the assessor doing a preliminary inspection to make sure the ranks were closed and the women were all behind the men.

I left the camp with a few men after the prayer, and we walked down wide streets bustling with people: men in *ihram*, women in ordinary white clothes. The order of masculine-feminine difference still prevailed, but the traffic, bargaining, and strolling made it become more flexible. We bought tea and water before turning back toward the camp. Thousands of pilgrims, especially men and women from Africa and Asia, were camping by the wayside on mats, bits of cloth, bundles, or scraps of cardboard.

Now we had to get ready to meet Arafat. Everywhere— walking about, sitting under the tent—people were talking animatedly. Prayers, invocations, and reading the Qur'an and hajj digests took up every moment between sleep and meals. We knew the decisive juncture was approaching: the station at Arafat. The preachers kept going over what we read in the digests: "Surely, the pilgrimage is Arafat!" The discussions and arguments were free and lively, due evidently to a new spirit born in the atmosphere of companionship and fervor. A sustained rhythm set bodies and souls in motion, moving freely toward the horizon of hope and liberation, beyond consciousness. Religion muted its legalisms, thus quite natu- rally recovering its transcendence in relation to the society that perpetuated it. So much so that the coexistence of in- junction, conformity, and free expression no longer surprised me. Altercations between partisans of Wahhabism and of the Malikites were intense. The Saudi propaganda services were winning over many Moroccans to rigorous gender segrega- tion, to the condemnation of sacrifices and festivals at sanc- tuaries ("saint worship," they called these), and to the total rejection of ideas, institutions, and lifestyles current in the West. The way the body was treated was a powerful index: shaving off one's beard and wearing a mustache in the Arab nationalist fashion, baring one's head, cutting and grooming one's hair, and wearing European clothes all had to be re- jected; growing a vigorous beard, covering one's head (espe- cially with a keffiyeh), and wearing flowing robes showed that one had made the break with European bourgeois dress. According to advocates of the so-called Islamic style, this demonstrated "sincere Islam." Praying with one's arms down along the body in the Maliki way triggered violent contro- versies. Many young Moroccan pilgrims advised us to abandon these "bad habits and beliefs" and rally to Islam—that is, to the religion of the Saudi state. They encountered indifference, however, or sharp rebuffs. Some people went so far as to argue that Arab potentates encouraged these differences, and to hurl invectives at the "emirs of money" and "the corrupt state."

Thus does the body—which on entering *ihram* signals its rupture with ordinary life and, by rejecting impurity and strictly respecting all the prohibitions (about food and other matters), preserves its boundaries—turn out to be also an image of what is at stake in the definition of relations among Muslims, and between Muslims and everyone else, first and foremost those called Westerners. Constituting a political body out of a sacred body is, of course, a very old phenomenon. But the unprecedented density of contact and cohabitation today, the intensity of circulation and the difficulty in mastering it, the new forms of violence and domination—all these factors of current globalization give urgency to the creation and re-creation of corporal identities.

I was finding in the defense of Wahhabism—as a religion, a way of life, a means of regulating "deviance" and gaining strength against other religions and societies—some universal motifs that were more or less emphasized in the thought and behavior of many Muslims. One could see these motifs in multiple images and formulas—authenticity; native and original versus foreign; pure versus mixed; identity and clarity versus ambiguity and division; in other words, what is ours versus what is other—motifs endlessly ramified to extremes of contrast and exclusion. Saudi Arabia's religion propagates these formulas by means that have not yet been appreciated or measured. Its political success as the nation of pilgrimage and petroleum has enabled it to propel an obscure sect onto the Muslim world stage and beyond.

The requirement of absolute gender segregation in Wahhabi doctrine and practice, as well as the marked differences imposed by other trends in Islam's new radical reform movement, was a prerequisite—according to these zealots—for the vital reconstruction of Muslim identity and being. The responsibility for maintaining this identity was shared by men and women, but it was up to the former, who have the authority, to defend it. In the "complementarity of men and women" (the terms being hierarchized) the whole group was mobilized to patrol the dividing line, which, the preachers insisted, must be a line of vigilance. In polemical attacks on Western societies, differences in belief and practice were no longer emphasized, as they once had been. That case had gone to trial and been settled long ago, on both sides. The new fortified line dividing the trenches was that of gender separation or, put the other way, integration. In the "civilized world," as I often heard in the United States, one called this "women's liberation." The new Islamic sectarians called it "licentiousness," "animality," "corruption," "disorder," "decadence." Through connected themes about the codification of the female body, the family, and society, contempt was heaped on capitalism and Euro-American liberalism. To the "civilized world's" insistent denial of the values of Islam, the reply was the rejection of everything borrowed from "Westerners."

In their response to the negation of self by colonial and imperial power, and to globalization, which only sharpened these two negations, the new reformers preaching their sermons about lifestyles did not necessarily "envy" the "Westerners" they decried. The politicians, intellectuals, "experts on Islam," and journalists in the United States and Europe who believe this may be alone in their obsession with envy and competition. Meanwhile, radical critiques, deconstructionist or other, of the imperial world's habits and ideas have gained support among those who have already distanced themselves—in diverse and often contradictory ways—from the most widespread forms of religiosity. One can call the sort of lives women and men build for themselves, in multiple creative efforts, "Islamic" or otherwise—that is not the decisive distinction; rather, the feeling that one is creating one's existence oneself is what matters.

For the future depends on having or not having the freedom to lead the life one wants—not on some deconstructive critique which can easily switch allegiance as it crosses borders. This freedom will arise only when we reject the totalitarian propositions of symmetrical, inverse absolutisms. At the heart of these absolutist structures are forms of modernity that feed off each other. Islamicized modernity is certainly one such form—a single and absolute mode of reasoning that works to grip human communities in its tentacles. The two societies in this respect supposedly incarnating "true Islam," Saudi Arabia and Iran, resemble the Soviet formula far more closely than they do any new solution. Like other options chosen by different Arab societies, they substantiate and prolong some of the abuses and dead ends once experienced in colonial nationalism. The lessons of accommodation, and the fluid nature of precolonial practices relating to identity, have been travestied and placed in the service of authoritarian states, as incapable of motivating renewal as they are efficient in repressing their people. The usual categories—woman, man, God, religion, family, legitimacy, salvation—have been recast for the "project" of community, nation, and state: phantasmagorical realities with autonomous machinery that is above and apart from the experience of people themselves. This sui generis apparatus has learned to exploit every nook and cranny of the archaic world.

Yet all the cogs, all the warps and wefts of government, all its knowledge and know-how, have in the end exposed the formidable power of the archaic world's blurred relics, which always gave those various categories initiatives with real meaning. The archaic may be an invention of modernity, but it beats modernity at its own game when it shows its frequently unexpected faces. Is this why an overwhelming majority of pilgrims didn't fall in line behind the minority who wanted to "remind women of their place"? I strongly presumed so. In any case, this majority took up the archaism of the moment, giving themselves over to their quest for salvation, ignoring the sermons and slogans spread about by the networks of dogmatic militants.

The archaic that moved in and through ritual turned out to be irreducible. It was a space without space, where initiative was beyond reach. This specific archaism, as in Medina, was now frustrating Wahhabi modernity in Mina and would do so again, with even more tranquil brilliance, at the decisive point of Arafat. The serene crowd's prayer flowed out to the horizons. Nothing could touch it—not the urban security grid around it, not the incessant buzz of surveillance and rescue helicopters circling above, not the media propaganda, not the squads of clamorous preachers, not even the exploitation of the pilgrims for business and as political pawns. My sense of this was only to grow stronger at Arafat; for now, it motivated me to think back on the feelings of surprise, incongruity, and unease I had sometimes been reluctant to acknowledge earlier, even to myself.

I had visited the plain of Arafat at the beginning of my stay in Mecca, after the *umra* rites. I had been somewhat disheartened by the sight of eucalyptus plantations and a female camel, harnessed and adorned for a photo op. She reminded me of the animals decked out for tourists to ride in Morocco and elsewhere. Climbing the Mount of Mercy, which is actually a small hill, I had been deeply disappointed to see the greasy bits of paper, pieces of cardboard, and empty yogurt containers abandoned there. I took refuge in the sight of the dazzling white stele at the summit that pulled the peak of the hill toward the sky. The modest dimensions of both "mount" and stele restored something whole and untouched to me with which my body took up a familiar, unplanned conversation— with messages going back and forth that kept their integrity because completeness didn't matter with them, nor intellectuality either. Going down, I posed with the camel—a perfect chance to mock the garbage and myself simultaneously. An ersatz voyage toward happiness, no doubt? I was convinced I was forbidden to aspire to anything else: a perception of integrity and a pastiche of it. But I knew that the comfort the religious experience gave some of my companions was inaccessible to me.

I had forgotten about this first contact in the meantime, and now we were in Mina preparing for another encounter. A government functionary came to tell us we would leave Mina late that night for Arafat. Predictably, the news spread confusion in our camp. Over and over we asked each other the same questions: "Do you know what time we're leaving?" "What about the bus, will it be here?" "Where are the company agents?" The latter reappeared briefly to throw us our dinner boxes. Between the poorly organized services and the vicious competition among the pilgrims—everyone wanted to be first, get in before the others, cut in line, take as much as possible—we were caught in the brawls and quarrels which accompanied every distribution of food. It was the eve of the station at Arafat, the station of pardon, the height of submission to God; we were all in *ihram*. And yet our solemn prayers were followed by these blind struggles. Although we ran no risk of dying of hunger or thirst, many pilgrims, in their floating consecrated cloth, fought over food rations, shouted, pushed at each other, and helped themselves with no concern for anyone else. The women stood aside while the mostly young men energetically jostled each other to get the most they could. If Darwin's theories had been verifiable, the scene would have provided proof of them. One could see millions of years of history condensed in a few gestures.

Seeing this didn't particularly shock me, since in my own country a great many men and women give in to this strange freedom, which eventually pulls into its wake those (equally numerous) who oppose it. Worse: here, people were fighting not for their lives but for mere advantages. I didn't recognize the same type of atavism that I immediately felt in the presence of animals: a fact of axiomatic violence, which, like pain, had no limits but those of its own expression. No, the struggle over food rations used highly developed representations and technologies, echoing an archaic pattern that had turned into a fantasy of need. The competition was fierce enough, but, given this degree of sophistication, it was thankfully limited to clever ploys, maneuvers, and jostling, and people avoided insults, punches, and death threats in this holy place. Enough remained of language and religion so that violence could be expressed in signs that substituted for signals. And pilgrims frequently redistributed the very things they had worked so hard to grab ahead of the others. I was regularly looked after by a companion with well-honed skills at getting food, and I wasn't the only one: another man went around the tent to make sure that "all the brothers and sisters" had something to eat. We are definitely less beautiful— but also, perhaps luckily, less pure—than animals. If there is such a thing as nature, it is not they, the natural beings, that she has made most dangerous. We, in the gods' image, awake each day as different species that take form in the dissolution of preceding forms. I was only half-surprised that on the road toward this meeting with a death that had already taken place, we had so much appetite.

We left Mina around midnight, having learned it was imperative to get to Arafat as soon as possible in order to find a place to sleep. We were exhausted, chronically sleep-deprived, and we had to ready ourselves for the next step to take place on the morrow, Friday, 9 Dhu'l-Hijja 1419 (26 March 1999). In unspeakable disorder we fought for seats on the bus, then traveled five or six kilometers down a very large highway cluttered with campers and people sleep-ing outdoors. "Lots of Indians, Pakistanis, and Bangla-deshis," said the Egyptian driver and our Yemeni guide. It was hard to locate our camp in the night, given all the crowds and traffic. The buses, packed beyond capacity, with travelers on the roofs, hanging off the steps and rear fenders, moved very slowly. There were pilgrims on foot every-where. It was late when we got to the tents reserved for us, very close to the Mount of Mercy. I lay down at once to sleep. Other men were next to me, and women occupied the edges of the tent, my companions' wives not far from their men.

It was four o'clock in the morning when I opened my eyes. I left my improvised bed, made my ablutions, and went out for some fresh air. I took a short stroll in the direction of the Mount of Mercy outlined in the first light of dawn, then returned to lie down and wait for the others to awake. Men and women emerged from sleep slowly, and then the familiar bustle of activity began. We did our dawn prayers separately; then, a little after five o'clock, we performed the morning prayers together, in our vast shelter. The crowd swelled with fresh arrivals of pilgrims. Volunteers were already monitor-ing the organization of prayers. Abbas fretted about the ranks, which were poorly formed and not close enough, ac-cording to him. Another man demanded that the women be sent back behind the men. "Our neighbors"—he pointed at another group—"prayed behind our women. Their prayer is invalid." Without a word, my companions' wives and the other women went to join the "neighbors' women." The two groups thus united in the correct order, "women behind men," we prayed under the guidance of an Arab tribesman from the countryside south of Rabat, discreet and very pious, educated in Qur'anic matters. From all sides, the clamor of invocations, prayers, and sobs arose, even though the station, as we knew, only began with the Friday communal prayer at midday.

People kept arriving in an uproar that spread over everything: the landscape, the crowds both standing still and moving, the highways, the scrawny trees—all drowned in white from the streetlamps, and the fine mist diffused by gigantic sprinklers. This diaphanous artificial rain, like the air-conditioning in the tents at Mina, was supposed to temper the sun's burning heat; people spoke of it as yet another achievement "of modernity, placed in the service of our values." I walked for a while in this rain toward the Mount of Mercy, crossing streets and impromptu markets. I stopped in front of a stall set up by a Bangladeshi woman and had a glass of tea and some biscuits for breakfast. All around, huge trucks were distributing alms: drinks, fruits, cartons of milk, donated by industrial and commercial firms whose names were emblazoned on the sides of the vehicles. Perched at the loading doors, employees threw this largesse to the swarming crowd. I scarcely managed to avoid a milk carton when an Egyptian pilgrim flung himself at me to seize it. We raced, dodging and feinting. I barely won, by pure chance, and moved away as my opponent plunged back into the fray. Clusters of people kept swarming around, shifting according to where the projectiles were coming from.

The Mount of Mercy was now nothing more than a mountain of white silhouettes. I guessed at where the stele was without seeing it, then turned back toward our tent. Men and women were gazing at the place in tears. Some were praying silently or calling to God. The fervor was spreading everywhere. Nothing seemed to dampen it—neither the markets set up all along the camps, nor the charities' advertising campaigns, nor the souvenir photographs (a specialty of young black African men), nor the supplicants and beggars. Back at the shelter, I found this same mixture of the spiritual and the mundane:

During the night, two men I don't know came to sleep next to me. After prayers, I speak to one of them. I discover he is from Tafilalet and, since he has a brother living in Temara, goes back and forth (regularly, from what he tells me) between Temara and Rissani. He asks me questions about "the pillars," about the duties and proper behavior expected on the pilgrimage. He is very scared of doing something incorrectly and invalidating his pilgrimage, so he wants to do not only everything that is prescribed but also everything that is recommended . . . He tells me that when he saw the Mount of Mercy he was overcome by tears and had to look away. I ask him about Tafilalet. He says the region has become like a city, that the state has put in electricity and the villagers now have power day and night . . . Then he turns to a woman whom a friend has placed temporarily in his care. "You want to go to the Mount of Mercy?" he asks her. "No, I don't need to walk around, because I don't want to buy anything here. I'll do all my shopping in the Radiant City. But if I can, I don't mind having my picture taken near the Mount of Mercy." Behind us, women are discussing whether or not they have to climb the mountain. One of them tells another: "If you don't, you won't have accomplished anything!" A young woman, knowledgeable about religious matters, intervenes to explain that "climbing isn't one of the obligations; it's only recommended for young people who are physically able to do it." One of my neighbors, fairly young, and a friend of the first, complains of fatigue and lack of sleep. He is not inter-

ested in seeing the place or in performing the rituals, despite
the insistence of a pilgrim who is exhorting him to go to the
Mount of Mercy. He leaves for a while and, when he returns, tells
me he went to wash: "They say major ablutions aren't allowed
during ihram. *But God forgive me, I had a shower. I can't help it;*
I had a shower." "God forgive you," I reply. After this exchange,
he lies down and falls asleep. Other pilgrims leave the shelter in
search of something to eat. They come back with bottles of wa-
ter, complaining bitterly about the lack of food.

I went out again for some air. All along a wide road leading to the mountain, the handouts to the crowd were still going on. Recitations and sermons were emanating via
loudspeakers from the mosque of Namira, of which I could
see only the upper walls and minarets, the voices floating
over the crowd and spreading out all the way to the black silhouettes of craggy peaks surrounding the immense basin.
They mingled with the *talbiya* chanting, supplications, and
prayers. This sky of prayer, this vault of piety, covered us all,
those wanting salvation and those in pursuit of more earthly
aims. Beggars approached me again: Pakistanis, Afghans,
Bangladeshis, and others. Here and there, I thought I saw
the elements of well-practiced scams: "I'm a pilgrim. I col-
lected the amount necessary to fulfill my duty . . . but I lost
everything." Or, "We Afghans are fighting for the faith."

I returned quickly to our shelter. Prayer and supplication
absorbed everyone, collectively and out loud, or individually
and in silence. Then I saw the same young imam step forward and begin the *talbiya* chant. All of us soon joined
in. The chanting lasted a good quarter of an hour, led by
other young men, some of whom wore cropped beards;
meanwhile, many men- and womenfolk not well versed in
theological debates clustered around country *tolbas* whose
presence inspired a certain discretion in our devotions. Soon

enough the chanting stopped; we knew that the hour of the Friday service was approaching. Some people performed their ablutions again, while others began walking toward the mosque of Namira. I stayed where I was, along with most of the men and almost all the women. Some of the latter had insisted on going with their husbands, who invariably gave them the same line: "It's too hot and crowded." Pilgrims pointed out that men were obliged to brave the heat and discomfort in their "jihad on the path of God." I myself and others—the majority—stayed put in the name of a different, widespread interpretation of Islam: "Don't go to extremes. Do what you can and tell yourself that God never asks a believer to accomplish something that is beyond him." Besides, were we not "the people of the middle ground"? Despite it all, the bearded young men carried on preaching a daily holy war, a new form of religiosity to which we opposed the sweet torpor of tradition.

We got up as soon as we heard the call to prayer. Volunteers summoned us to form in close ranks. Others shouted: "Women to the back! You, women, go to the back! We're here for worship and not for laughing and gossiping with our women!" I was sure this last remark was aimed at some of us, including myself. In point of fact, after prayers and during meals, we did return to the women's company, and this earned us a few reprimands, not always friendly. We quickly obeyed. I could only hear bits and pieces of the sermons coming from the mosque, without really knowing how we should perform this prayer, the most solemn one I had participated in. Then I saw a young man step forward and motion to our imam to fall back into the ranks behind him. The imam obeyed, but all at once there was a stir in the ranks. People asked what was going on. A few pilgrims intervened—some to support the imam who had been sent back and others in favor of the one who had taken over. This first

disagreement led to a second: one party wanted to group this
service with the mid-afternoon prayers and abbreviate the
two; another insisted on keeping them separate; a third recommended that we follow the prayer led by the official imam
at the mosque, while the other two maintained this wasn't really necessary. Each party stood its ground but avoided quarreling. In the end, a few men put the mistreated imam back in
charge and ordered the pushy young man to give up his claim.
So we prayed behind the first *taleb*, who kept a bit apart, staying in the background, and tended to say his individual
prayers in a soft voice. By his manner, he was confirming
what he had said to me when I had spoken with him briefly a
little earlier: "Religion is for God, not for human beings . . .
And that's the only way religion can improve people!"

The station immediately followed prayers. I couldn't see
beyond the camp, but, standing up, like everyone else, I
could feel deep within me the astonishing energy of a worshipping people: dedicated, devout, devoted. The shouts and
cries came in endless waves, followed by spells of silence.
Collective invocations alternated with individual prayers and
supplications, murmured and inaudible, when we sat down.
These were moments of rest, moments of meditation that
returned us to ourselves and turned us inward.

Unfortunately, this rhythm, which I liked so much, was
interrupted. A new difficulty arose, this time about the invocations. A large group of young men came to join a Moroccan preacher who had begun to lead the service. They had
brought their own list of prayers and invocations. We had to
repeat these "selections" word for word, the officiant accepting no pause and no individual supplications. Sweating pro-
fusely, we repeated dutifully, stifled in our canvas shelter. We
even repeated our guide's linguistic mistakes. Then people
couldn't bear it any more, began to exchange glances, and
even took the liberty of sitting down. The "guide" stopped;

then, in a vehement tone, and backed up by his companions, he enjoined us to resume "the collective prayer, out loud and standing." A terse response came back: "No! Would you kindly finish? People need time to say prayers for personal salvation, for the health and prosperity of their loved ones, for their leaders, and for the Muslim governments! No, sir! After the collective prayers, out loud, there is a time for contemplation, a review of our past actions, of our mistakes!" It was becoming clear that the texts he was trying to make us repeat did not come from the Maliki manual placed at our disposal by the Moroccan Ministry of Islamic Affairs. No: this was certainly not our official vulgate. It was fairly easy for some of us to recognize Wahhabi propaganda. The preacher retorted, "The Prophet pronounced invocations collectively, with his companions, and he led them!" "No!" a voice replied. "Sometimes they prayed as a group and out loud, and sometimes he let people withdraw and pray alone!" Most people wanted the young sectarians to withdraw, and eventually they did, making way once again for our country *taleb*, who returned unhurriedly to the center of things. We calmly resumed our binary rhythm, which dispelled the differences of opinion. For a long time, we alternated between prayers and silent, individual requests, phrased in the words each of us wanted to say to God. We stood for a long, long time . . . until the end of time.

We had been seated for only a moment when our imam signaled to us to rise once more. The afternoon was drawing to a close. After a long series of invocations and humble pleas, we remained standing in silence. Then, at a final signal, we broke ranks. Lunch was handed out, and we were told that we would leave right afterward. We ate quickly and, like everyone else, launched an assault on the buses. It was a quarter past five when our long battle to get seats began. After two hours of pushing and shoving, I managed to find a seat for myself and Farida, the young doctor whose husband wasn't with her. Through a wall of bodies separating us, I extended my hand to help her climb in. A few minutes later, an elderly woman planted herself in front of me. Leaning on her cane, she ordered us to leave the two seats, claiming that she had reserved them shortly before my arrival. Amazed by her implausible argument, I didn't know what to say. Then insults rained down: "Satan! God will punish you! You didn't come here for the pilgrimage; you came for women! And you brazenly hold out your hand . . . Satan, you display your sins for all to see. I'm going to call the police, they'll kick you off the bus!" This went on for quite a few minutes. I was stunned. Someone took the woman away, although I would gladly have given her my seat had she asked for it. I found it difficult to imagine what might have motivated her: her wanting the seat, or wanting to keep me from sitting there because she saw me as a demon and because, by berating me and simultaneously taking what was mine, she would have accomplished two pious acts? The second hypothesis would certainly prepare her well for the stoning of Satan, scheduled for the following day.

Around eight o'clock in the evening we left Arafat for Muzdalifah. We did so quite quickly, at a rate described as "overflow"—as if we were spreading like a flood. Millions of people on foot turned their backs on Arafat and ran toward Muzdalifah like a great river that had flooded its banks to spread through the neighboring valleys and ravines. Nothing could compare to this spectacle, which we watched through the windows of our boiler on wheels, moving in twenty-meter spurts, then stopping, interminably it seemed, in an uproar of motors, heat, and exhaust fumes.

When at midnight we arrived at Muzdalifah—the "halt" between Arafat and Mina—we were held hostage by our driver, who turned off the engine, closed the doors, and went off to have dinner, forgetting he had turned off our ventilation as well. All but fainting, we managed to shout loudly enough to alert people to go and get him—I don't know how in the middle of the night—reminding him of our existence. He came and opened the doors, not seeming excessively perturbed, and we threw ourselves off the bus. We performed the prescribed prayers for this halt and, in the dark, gathered pebbles for the stoning. It was not permitted to gather them elsewhere or at any other time.

We got on the bus again. For the time being, our exhaustion and the unbearable circumstances of the trip—six or seven hours to travel eight kilometers or so—preoccupied everyone. Standing, because I hadn't found a seat this time, I clung to a seat with one hand and, with the other, clutched a little bag (which I watched over night and day) wedged under my arm. Wearing *ihram*, I had had to remove everything I normally wore. I had taken off my wedding ring, which I kept in an inside pocket of the bag. It was five o'clock in the morning when we were unloaded at our campsite, which we discovered was already occupied. Pilgrims were guarding the empty tents for people from their own tribe or neighborhood, or for new acquaintances made on the pilgrimage. I wandered in the alleyways for a long time before finding a free corner at the edge of a large communal tent that served as a prayer space, where I unrolled my blanket and transferred my wedding ring to my belt pocket. I soon discovered that I was near the lavatories. I had neighbors, whom I didn't know and who were well sheltered at the inside edge of this habitation. There was no time to lose. After a long wait, I performed my ablutions and left the odors and dirt to carry out my morning prayers before heading to the pillar of Aqaba for the first stoning.

I was truly on the path of an elliptical return. This feeling grew in importance. The emotion I felt had something new

about it, and it swamped my efforts to identify ideas and images and my means of analyzing them. The images kept
coming, taking possession of my mind; I was at the mercy of
their whim. With my body immobile, prostrate, I was somehow sinking into a boundless inventory of images. The elliptical returns came free—in images that stood out from other
images which followed them, surrounded them, covered
them, or appeared in a fade-out detail. The rule invented itself after the fact, as if language had preserved magical formulas of association that it shared with image association:
contemporary traces which surrendered their meaning only
when read backward.

So by preparing to stone Satan and offer up a sacrifice,
was I not going, precisely, backward along the road? I was
coming from the station at Arafat, where I had "stood before
God." The image of the "Last Judgment," returning constantly to my mind, was not of my own making but a phrase
the pilgrims used among themselves; at every moment it
made what we saw visible, what we did feasible, what we
said, shouted, prayed, chanted, and murmured audible. It
was associated with every gesture and every word. And
thanks to its inexhaustible power of association, it lent itself
as easily to the politics of religion as to religions of politics.
It set very diverse strategies in motion; it embraced all types
of economy and means of accumulation. It did not require
that these be either symbolic or spiritual. Obviously one had
to admit that since it had moved generations, it could be the
source of conflict, conquest, indifference, or withdrawal and
retreats such as took place on that memorable day. On this
image of the Last Judgment, and on the image I had of myself—lost in the first—were engraved scenes and profiles
whose irony seemed pitiless. The defeat of the Wahhabi sermon thus testified in its way to the renewing power of this
station.

I returned to the uproar of the traffic jams. I was returning from the Last Judgment. I had been on trial before God,
with the others. We had all learned, early on, that we would
be judged at the other last judgment of which the station at
Arafat was but a preview; we knew that at the court where we
had just been, we would beg for salvation and hope to leave
with a favorable sentence. There were many images: body and
soul awakening after the long sleep of death; the razor's edge
between forgiveness, intercession, salvation, and hell. An image I hadn't known surprised me nevertheless with its "scriptural" overtones. A merchant from Rabat gave it to us, in
the presence of his wife and daughter, under the tent at Mina:

> All these rites are the traces of our father, Ibrahim. He
> abandoned his son and his wife in a deserted valley, with
> nothing. But he knew how God's mercy worked. One day,
> he spoke to God: "Give me another sign!" And God
> replied: "Do you not believe, O Ibrahim?" "So that my
> faith can grow stronger, O God!" said Ibrahim. So the
> Almighty said: "Get four birds and cut them in four, each
> bird in four [quarters]. And put a quarter of each bird at the
> top of one of the mountains, making sure to mix the quar-
> ters." Ibrahim did all that. Then He [God] said: "Pray and
> call the birds." So the birds came and circled his tent. Each
> quarter had returned to its origin and each bird with its
> body and soul.

Arafat: the site of absolute knowledge. Of mercy. Of the
return to one's original state after dispersion. What an enchantment! Muslim commentators support this view of its
meaning by reference to the root *a-r-f*: to know, to know
oneself; they say that on this mountain, Eve met Adam, after
they had been expelled from paradise, and told him, "I know
you." Arafat is the place of cognition and recognition, of mu-

tual acknowledgment among Muslims; and according to well-known versions those who meet at Arafat in fact have renewed the knowledge they had of each other as souls, before they came to earth.

At Arafat, in an initial elliptical revolution, in the knowledge and mutual awareness of the station before God, I rediscovered the learning that I knew as a soul. This occurred thanks to the characteristic virtue of an ellipse: I rediscovered a symmetrical counterpoint to my point of departure by following the curve opposite the one I had traveled between my existence as a soul and my incarnation: in other words, the advent of a person, with all the accumulated accidents that make up a biography until its final point on the pilgrimage. A philosopher once remarked that an ellipse is not a circle transformed. An elliptical revolution carries its origin and transforms it. In the other direction, there is only the result, which establishes this origin in the form of an invocation— that is, of the image projected without a screen. An elliptical revolution, like a linguistic ellipsis, forms experience into shapes trimmed to an extreme, owing their density to a ruthless reduction.

On these circuits, the first came last. One returned to Mina, as one did elsewhere, by a symmetrical path that reversed the previous one. Salvation—or, at the very least, the transformation of hope into knowledge (reinforced by the mutual testimony given by "standing together before God")—came before the sacrifice. And yet in the foundation myth, victory over uncertainty and the sacrifice came first, in the interval that provisionally separated the protagonists from death, resurrection, and the Last Judgment. So the ritual changed the sequence of events that came after, and resurrection came before death. We hadn't yet carried out the stoning and the sacrifice when we went on to the ultimate, final station. On the contrary, we went to the furthest point of the life span and crossed the threshold of death, before coming back to sacrifice. We thus confirmed both our reprieve and the end of the reprieve.

Everyone knows that stopping at Arafat "is like stopping at resurrection and the Last Judgment." The analogy continues naturally, concluding with intercession, ultimate forgiveness, and "eternal happiness." At that point, it touches primordial innocence: birth. The pilgrimage washes away all sin; one emerges from it purified, "just like a newborn baby." I could no longer avoid the question that this "just like" always poses. Of course I wasn't the first person haunted by it. It has always been there for anthropologists and also in religious, philosophical, and artistic thought, not to mention science, technology, and political experimentation. Every day, in the most ordinary situations, we behave "as if" we were more than . . . matter, spirit, a waiter, a billionaire. But the question bothered me personally; it appeared increasingly as a basic consequence of my attitude to it: if I faced it so often, it was simply to avoid it. Choice and action always freed me momentarily from the anxiety the question aroused. Or was it the anxiety that brought back the "just like": the something that was put on stage?

Ritual pretended to reassure me by setting me firmly on, and before, that stage. But this repeated assurance was undermined by the simulacrum itself, a figure of anxiety that knowledge tried to outwit. In my way of proceeding, I sought in fact other assurances: verifications, well-regulated successions of events, a world whose reality could be understood by laws that were mine, too, a reality that allowed my mind to recognize these laws as its own signs. A miracle. Either I had to be natural, or nature would recognize itself in me. But the ritual denied me the conquest of this happiness, holding me suspended, alive in a language that pretended tomorrow happened last night, acting as if the actions sealing my destiny had taken place in reverse order.

The ritual ellipse is made up of a departure, a stop, and a return to the starting point. It is repetition and memory: memory of time's starting point, of history's narrative body, and of the end of the story. It unfolds the story and ends it. It repeats the unfolding. It unfurls it once again, in a few days, each proceeding from the one before, to trace the ellipse's curves, one nestled inside the other, in disregard of the ordinary succession of night and day. It is not, thus, simply putting "recovered time" onstage.

People, living in the world, go on leafing through the world's pages as if these were future lives they had been given before; they go on welcoming these lives, which haunt them even though they arose only in what was in the process of becoming. Only possibilities, ellipses, and simulacra form them in repetition as a misuse and abuse of language: "cube," "House of God," "race," "stoning Satan," "sacrifice," "stopping before God," "standing before God," "Mount of Mercy," "cleansing one's sins." The very real emotion that brought me into close proximity with pilgrims, all absorbed in accomplishing a spiritual project, resulted from a promised reunion "between thought and motion." Perhaps it gained its strength by awakening in me archaic architectonics in the forms of the halt, the departure, and the times in between. I could feel the ancient sedimentation at work here. The masks transported me. They motioned to me, always making sure to move away. They condemned me to abuse language, to speak in metaphors.

10

MEMORY OF FINITUDE

I CAN'T FORGET THE SCENT OF ANIMAL BLOOD AND SWEAT. IT has lingered with me for a long time now. It came back forcefully on the evening breeze the night we returned from Arafat. We were heading to Mina on the crowded bus to which we had been assigned in Mecca. As usual, we were stifling in our narrow seats. Men, women, and suitcases took up all the seats, aisles, and space near the doors. I was hanging on to the handrail that ran down the center of the bus, my rucksack on my back. We had prayed and relaxed at Muzdalifah in the middle of the night, and now we were all struggling against sleep as best we could, holding close the forty-nine pebbles we each had gathered for the stoning. We had only four or five kilometers to go to reach our camp at Mina, but every time the bus started up, it stopped again only a few dozen meters farther on. The traffic was so bad that we spent most of our time at a standstill.

As we went along, I began to smell the sheep. Then I saw the first enclosures. The scent grew stronger as livestock sheds paraded interminably before our eyes, at the foot of mountains whose sharp peaks I could just barely see. A little way from the road, the animals were spending their last night, immobile under dim electric light. One could see serried rows of round whitish shapes stretching off into the distance. Sheep raised their heads as we passed, looking at us with that resigned anxiety which domestic animals show when humans approach.

I still had a few memories of the forms my life had taken in my youth—like buds that were fulfilled burgeonings. Those old times were times of cracked earth, of shoots working through the crust of soil with silent, incredible perseverance, of barley rising, of golden crops soon cut down by robust young arms, of animals frolicking, drunk with life. So I knew the gaze of these penned-in beasts all too well. I could remember the flight, the panic, the questing eye of animals seized for the slaughter at the abattoirs I had seen in my youth. I could hear the heartrending bleats, the pleas rising to the sky with the steam and swell of hot blood. These same scenes would be repeated the next day, the day of sacrifice; millions of living creatures were waiting to be put to death.

In Mina, the sheds looked like a giant concentration camp for animals: two, three, four million heads or more. An immense crowd of pilgrims was preparing to sacrifice them as an "offertory," along with the sacrifices of expiation or alms. No matter how many times I reminded myself of what differentiates us from animals domestic and wild, no matter how I widened this distance by thinking about faceless, speechless species, incapable—as we imagine it—of expressing emotion, still the mingled scent of blood, excrement, and sweat once again gripped me by the throat. We were gathered here to save our own lives, a salvation requiring that we kill these animals. The mass of pilgrims, who had reached

the peak of renunciation—after the station at Arafat, the
prayer at Muzdalifah, and the stoning at Mina—was about to
snuff out millions of lives. Maybe it's true that when I saw an
animal I saw first a generic type. Yet each act of immolation
put an end to a life as singular as any human life; it was an act
of violence—murder, in a word.

The sight of these millions of sheep, held for a brief stay
of execution, awoke other scenes. I saw again the animals
suffering in the abattoirs, the animals whose throats were slit
for the great Feast of the Sacrifice, a joyous family celebration. Slowly, the horror that always seized me when I heard a
beast's final death rattle came back. Once again, something
familiar was catching up with me in a new, unbearable guise.
Its source was there; I could see what flowed from it; but the
closer I got, the more it eluded me. My father slit the animal's throat in the name of God, for all of us, for our happiness. His hands, dealing death, came back to me—male
child, a man one day, with a sure promise of the bond, order,
continuity. Was this what they call tradition? A palace that
belonged to me but on its own terms, not because of a right
I might have claimed, that opened its enchanted apartments
but only unexpectedly and as a chance occurrence.

This return of the familiar in the guise of the strange left
me feeling divided. Everything became hesitant: my gait, my
voice, the tone of my conversations with others. The sight of
those millions of animals herded together for destruction
forever contaminated the image of the lone patriarch offering up his own son as victim to obey the divine command. It
introduced misfortune into the miraculous replacement of
lamb for child. Modernization of the hajj certainly had
something to do with it: the optimal-productivity animal
pens, closed-off areas, grid-like arrangements of space, fail-
safe security and surveillance systems. Each domain had its
own camp: the masses of animals in their sheds and, not far

off, the masses of humans in their camps surrounded by high
chain-link fences stretching ad infinitum along the straight
streets. Nothing could escape this rationality. Police vehicles
on the ground and helicopters constantly circling overhead
completed the picture. This order would allow the human
masses to annihilate the animal masses in the name of God.
At first glance, modernity did not seem to have changed the
objective, but this might be only an appearance, for in modifying the scale and rhythm, the timings and the systems, increasing the administration, it perhaps affected the ways of
practicing the faith.

In this framework of a nation-state draping itself in piety,
the silent, stubborn pilgrims went on with the ritual. I got
only snatches of answers to my questions or, more often, tac-
tical retreat: "We're here to worship," or "You have to accept
adversity as a sacrifice on the path of God." But there was
criticism, and quite sharp: acknowledging the Saudi efforts to
increase security, improve the installations, mitigate the shortages in supplies and the quality of certain infrastructure, many
pilgrims nonetheless complained they suffered from the con-
gestion, from the brutality of the Saudi civil and military per-
sonnel, from the drastic restrictions put on their freedom of
speech and movement, and from the constant surveillance.
But few men or women would voice these opinions. Although
I had known some of my companions for a long time, even
they didn't, really, want to go into "these difficulties." Everything that happened was part of the hajj and we had to accept
it, just as we accepted our religious obligations. "We're here
for the hajj, and each of us should be concerned about saving
his soul": this was the leitmotif. In this way they expressed a
form of detachment from the world—from the Wahhabi
modernities that had transformed our ways of bearing witness. This was not an escape into an inwardness one might set
against the external conformism required by the state appara-

tus. It was the creation of a new condition, a new way of life when on pilgrimage.

"We're on the path of Ibrahim," said Salim, a shopkeeper from Taza, Morocco, still young and fairly prosperous. I was walking with him on the morning of the Feast of the Sacrifice, toward the place where he planned to have a lamb slaughtered. He knew that in Medina I had given money to a charity to carry out the sacrifice in my name, so I didn't have to go, but he suggested I accompany him. We had grown closer over the previous days as we slept side by side in the big tent that also served as a prayer space. Salim told me he had saved up a lot of money (almost seventy thousand dirhams) to meet his expenses, especially for presents and the homecoming party. As we walked, he kept repeating, "We're going where Ibrahim went. We're walking in his blessed footsteps and imitating our Prophet, who followed the path traced by Ibrahim, the Friend of God. We're imitating them both—may God accept our sacrifice!" No doubt he intended this litany of prayer and invocation as much for himself as for me. I had learned all about following for oneself in the footsteps of the prophets at Qur'an school. We all had to bear witness to their action through an action of our own. By bearing witness, the moving crowd was activating the repeated dawning of a world. Our daily life would from now on be only like this: as if it were unfolding in the footsteps of the prophets!

At the foot of the arid black mountains in the defile of Mina, which we went through as we would have walked toward the gates of the hereafter, trade was brisk. Bedouins were tough businessmen, and the Moroccan pilgrims didn't give them an inch. I was contemplating the sinister animal pens we had driven past the previous night when my companion asked what I thought of a fine ram he had just chosen. We were in a very large slaughterhouse, where the

animals were waiting to be seized and handed over to sacrifi-
cers dressed in green. Without really hearing my answer, my
friend clinched the deal and handed the victim over to two
men, who grabbed it and laid it on its side facing Mecca. After pronouncing a brief invocation and the *takbir*, "God is
great," they slit its throat with one swift, sure stroke before
suspending it from a moving rod that would take it down the
line to be cut up. Carcasses hung from these rods as far as
the eye could see. As usual, I was stunned by the spectacle of
such violence at the heart of this sacred ritual—all the more
so in that it is meant to bring us peaceably back to God. As
the victim gradually became an inert thing, I was better able
to pay attention to what followed. The carcass was quickly
skinned, gutted, and cut up. Salim took a few pieces, as well
as the tail; he scattered salt on the meat, put it in a plastic
bag, and, before heading back, asked if I wanted some of the
carcass (most of it would be given to charity). When I de-
clined, he turned his back on me with a show of irritation.

We went back to the camp in silence. Suddenly Salim
stopped, made me do the same, and stared hard at me. "See,
I take this home, with the water from Zamzam. It's better
than all the gifts, all the goods of the world: the *baruk* of the
hajj. May God grant us the Prophet's *baraka*, to us and to all
Muslims!" I simply said, "Amen," and started walking again,
looking around at the rugged landscape, the hills standing
out sharply in the transparent morning light. Far off, the
peak where the angel had come to tear the familiar veil of
the world sprang up toward the sky. It was there, on Mount
Nour, that a vision had stunned a member of the Quraysh
tribe, that an angel had ordered him to read, write, recite; it
was from there that he had gone so precipitously, fleeing the
place in "fear and trembling."

The sun was already high as we neared the camp. We
walked silently in the midst of the crowd. Was it because

Salim knew that in Medina I had paid for a sheep to be sacrificed in my name that he asked again before we parted if I
was sure I didn't want a little of the "pilgrim's *baraka*"? I answered that the important thing, for me, was to perform the
rite, to reflect on my beliefs, and, as I had told him, to write
my book. I felt that for the first time Salim really understood
what my project was. He didn't try to conceal his astonishment: "To reflect . . . But don't you have the same faith as us?
Anyway, each to his own intention." How many times I was
asked that question!

We had done everything at top speed, since the sacrifice
and the stoning that preceded it were only valid if carried out
in the morning, so as to return to Mecca for the circumambulation and be back in Mina again in time for sunset
prayers. My friend left at once. Like many others, I chose
the other option: to spend two more days in Mina and finish
the stoning before returning to Mecca. In the tent, I found a
young civil servant from Settat who had already cut his hair,
as prescribed, after the sacrifice.

I decided to rest for a while. Along with a few neighbors I
had met up with again, I stretched out, and we spoke nostal-
gically about this same feast in Morocco. "There," said a
young peasant from Benguérir, "it's just *shukh! shukh!*" He
repeated the onomatopoeic sound, running his index finger
along his throat to mime slitting it. We all started longing
for kebabs, whole roast sheep, *tajines*, and steamed mutton
head. "Oh, steamed head of lamb, with just enough salt and
cumin . . . Satan be damned! It's time for prayer!" We immediately scattered to perform our ablutions and join the
prayer ranks. It was early afternoon.

My fever had gone but had drained my strength. The
emotion aroused by the sacrifice had followed hard on the
turmoil of the first stoning, which I had undertaken immediately after morning prayers. I had left the camp alone. The

five people I had joined, not without some reservations, on
my departure from Morocco had turned out to be a motley
crew, with no other aim than a narrow observance of the rite,
which for some of them meant a release of almost all their
ambitions and a liberation of their acquisitive instincts. Medina and Mecca had offered commercial displays that catered
to this materialism cushioned by a good conscience. The
mercantile formalism of the bourgeois women who spent
their time in either prayer, chitchat, or shopping, and the
domineering behavior of their husbands, with their school-
book religiosity, had alienated me from their company. I felt
greater affinity with a couple of prosperous artisans I got to
know in Mina. They seemed to understand what sober practice of one's faith could bring to a person's life, and they were
far more tolerant.

Since I was no longer performing the rites with my old
group, there I was in the streets of Mina, walking alone toward the pillar of Aqaba, on the road to Mecca, for the first
stoning. I strolled in the midst of a dense crowd that moved
along between markets, taxis, buses, and impromptu camp-
sites set up in the streets. When I reached the entrance of
the causeway leading to the pillar, I stopped suddenly,
gripped by fear and an all but irresistible desire to turn
around and go back. Shaking and bathed in sweat, I paused
for a few seconds, and then suddenly launched myself into
the crowd. No one had pushed me. My own body had made
the decision. My mind was a blank as I slid into the human
tide thickening about me, carrying me forward, tossing me
left and right. I felt the current bearing me off like a wisp of
straw. In the chaos, I tried as best I could not to trip and
barely managed to dodge collisions. I also had to watch out
for groups of people going against the flow, in complete violation of the safety guidelines. The closer I got to the goal,
the more the crowd swallowed me up, squeezing me so

tightly my feet were scarcely touching the ground. I looked for and found, not far from me, a young and very strong man, and I threw myself in his direction. Saddiq—that was his name—reassured me: "Stay with me, don't be afraid . . . Where are you from? I'm Sudanese. Come on!" He took me by the hand. We sank into the crowd spinning, like an enormous whirlpool, around the cylindrical wall that protected the obelisk-shaped pillar. Behind Saddiq, I tried to aim for the pillar. I sent my seven little pebbles flying in its direction, one by one, to the cry of "God is great!" With an uninterrupted, sinister pattering, the pebbles piled up around it. On my last attempt, I tripped and fell. Sadiq's helping hand swept me in a rush, panting, out of the tornado. I embraced him and threw myself against the ramp's low wall to catch my breath. Slowly regaining my wits, I realized that I had lost my parasol, my *ihram* clothes were in shreds, my sandals were gone, and my feet were bleeding. On the way back, at the foot of the giant causeway, vendors had piled sandals. Like me, many pilgrims bought a pair to replace the ones they had lost in the whirling crowd.

We all knew we were on the path of Ibrahim and Ismail, following the way traced out by Muhammad, the Prophet of Islam who, according to tradition, had taken up the patriarch's teachings. Our religion, we had always been taught, was thus one of return and recovery after a long period of decadence for monotheism: *jahiliya*, as it is called, the era of heathendom and ignorance. When we perform these rites, we fall into step with the Prophet as he fell into step with his predecessors. Centuries had elapsed between them and him, between him and us. We were heirs of this practice, despite our divergent goals and despite differences in age, sex, race, nationality, language, and class. During this day of sacrifice, the chain of the dead was extended to those men and women who came here to learn again that the substitution was only temporary. I could also imagine this chain as a human column coiling in circles around a starting point suspended from the black cube.

We were acting, then, as the prophets did. There is no way around the "as," because we were not those prophets. It would be sacrilege to think or act otherwise than by following their example. Foreseeing our weaknesses, the hajj rules specified the failings likely to taint it, failings we had to repair through sacrifice, fasting, or giving alms. We knew there was no identity between our heroes and us even as we followed their example; all our efforts were to bring us closer to them and yet reaffirm the irreducible difference. Besides, we—Moroccans, followers of the Sunni Maliki doctrine— knew that our observances were not exactly the same as those of other Muslims who follow other schools. We were, then, on the same path, but we didn't tread it in quite the same way. The model itself, too, did not appear with the same features; even if the differences were sometimes very slight, the pilgrims adhered to the doctrines prevailing in their communities. Like a script taken from a performance, those doctrines organized the ritual process through a second interpretation.

In what we did, we tried to shape our actions to an example and a model. We acted in conformity with the model. But on the one hand it was inexhaustible, and on the other our actions were its only concrete realization. The model was unattainable, then, moving away from us as we moved toward it. So model and action configured each other mutually or, rather, constantly exchanged with each other in a reciprocity that only underlined their separateness. In that back-and-forth, each presented only an excess of itself. The real could not coincide with the limits of empirical configurations any more than the ideal. From one end to the other, the sets of actions that led to the conclusion of the pilgrimage, after the station at Arafat, were silhouetted in this halo of excess, anticipating the elaborations to come: an unceasing "redescription" of the order of things.

Everything thrust us into this dynamism: the coming together with no other objective than the rite, the sites with their eschatological charge, the dramas superimposed on them day and night, the prayers, the circumambulations, the strolls in the markets, the departure for Mina in the middle of the night, the nighttime return from Arafat, the gathering of pebbles at Muzdalifah after the night prayer and the return to Mina at dawn, the going off again for the stoning, then the sacrifice; last, the race to the final circumambulation; the frequent deaths, regularly announced, the news of pilgrims who lost their bearings and disappeared, sometimes found again only thanks to the efforts of specialized search teams—all this meant there was always more to hear in what was said, more to see in what was seen, more to contemplate in what was thought.

Everyone could read the section of our manual on "stoning the pillar of Aqaba." Still, people quite often said, "Stoning Satan." I could write, or read, "Stoning the pillar = stoning Satan," or " 'Stoning the pillar' counts as 'stoning Satan,' " or "They say stoning Satan when they mean stoning the pillar, and vice versa." So I knew the usual meaning of "stoning Satan." Still, one had to admit that "stoning" and "pillar" didn't always go together in that usual way. And what about "stoning Satan"? That was more difficult. People also said, "Gathering pebbles to stone Satan"—a common expression.

During a discussion one evening with a group of pilgrims from the Marrakech High Atlas, Haj Ali told me: "You can say stoning the pillar. In fact, you're stoning Satan at that point. It's Satan we're defeating, in ourselves as well." This exegete works as a notary public. He was educated at a

Qur'an school before attending a traditional institute teaching Islamic sciences. We had met through my friend Lahcen. Two or three times I went to see them both in Mecca, and naturally we took the opportunity to exchange impressions. Haj Ali told the story of the sacrifice yet again: the vision and the command that Ibrahim was given to sacrifice Ismail, the son's acceptance, the journey to the killing place, Satan appearing three times and using "all the seductions of life" to incite the child to disobey and abandon the plan. And then the response by stoning. The pillar wasn't Satan, but it was Satan we were stoning when we stoned the pillar.

Pillar and Satan unfold in an endless multiplicity of meanings. Satan can appear through doppelgängers, look-alikes, masks, ambiguities as limitless as they are terrible. "Pillar" might be a generic word, but "Satan" is usually a proper name. Yet the name also occurs in plural form, and it can refer to a group of individuals, like the name of a genus. The other name, "Iblis," is also used, though more rarely in the plural. It, too, functions equally well as a proper noun, in which case it marks a category only insofar as the name "God" does, too. "Satan-Iblis" shares a classificatory virtue with the noun "pillar," while simultaneously referring to a single figure—much like the name "God." In common usage, however, there is no difference between "pillar," "Satan," "stoning," or "stone the size of a bean" with which we must arm ourselves according to the rule. Nor is the difference or relation between the visible and the invisible—more generally, between what can and cannot be perceived—in question. It goes without saying that Satan is always present and active. I knew the signs and symptoms by which he could be identified; there was a relative consensus on this among the people I talked to. On the other hand, they were responding to an action whose reality they established as being-by-act, whereas I was content with its being understood through experience and a certain form of knowledge.

What, then, was the act that consisted in stoning the pillar, stoning Satan? My interlocutors and I had no disagreement on this point: we threw "pebbles the size of beans" at a pillar. We knew that the interpreters of the holy book had decided on the size. Stoning Satan by stoning this pillar therefore had to be understood as doing one by doing the other. More precisely, in this context, we were putting our will in accord with the will of those who, according to the story, had to vanquish Satan. In such a process, it was understandable that our projectiles had to be no bigger than beans: the small size made them easy to gather and carry, besides inflicting minimal damage if they missed their target and hit other pilgrims. In other words, all these acts were "as if." The pilgrims were acting *as if* they were Ismail—not by throwing pebbles at a pillar, since the ancestor of the Arabs, the son of Ibrahim, didn't attack a pillar. His stones—their size, unlike ours, wasn't specified—were meant to strike Satan himself. Given this, it became possible to attune one's will to his, or at least—in doubt and in existential quest (as was my case)—to recognize the gesture and attune one's will to it in solidarity.

It is always the case that to do one thing by doing another is to act metaphorically. It is an unfolding, unfurling: a development in the sense that something gets going through drafts and dodges, risks taken, good and bad luck, uncertainties along the way. At the site where the pillar of Aqaba stands, there was at least shared knowledge: Satan had appeared to Ismail to abort the projected sacrifice by inciting him to rebellion. This face-off left its mark, which called forth a commandment written in my pilgrimage manual:

On the day of the feast, once you have done your morning prayer and the sun has risen, you must go to Jamrat al-

Aqaba, the tallest and last pillar on the road to Mecca, and stone it with seven pebbles the size of beans. You have to make sure that each pebble hits the pillar and does not go beyond or beside it.

Before throwing each pebble, we had to shout, "God is great!"—the cry of sacrifice, of martyrdom on the battlefield, and of slaughter. The morning prayer had sealed the consecration of this act; the time between it and noon prayers was the time for going toward the goal. We were on the path of the Prophet. Our pebbles therefore had to strike the pillar just as Ismail's had struck Satan. Only ours were counted: seven for the first day's stoning and seven at each of the three pillars on the second and third days, between sunrise and noon prayers.

"Striking in the same way" gave us an order of ideas, parameters whose shape, proportion, and measure we had to discover. How would one find pebbles the size of beans in the middle of the night? We had to have an idea of both the size of a bean and the size of a stone. Two million believers set themselves to making this comparison in the dark, in a state of exhaustion brought on by ceaseless motion, going against the tide of ordinary life, in which night and day bled into each other. Each of us therefore created our own beans and bean-sized stones. Then again, how was one supposed to understand that while the story mentioned three stonings in one apparently uninterrupted action, we had to stone for either two or three days (according to choice)? Of course, the story and the law were not mutually determinative. Rather, one had to see them as evoking each other—so that what we were doing certainly had something in common with what Ibrahim and Ismail had done and yet could never claim to equal their actions.

Ismail had stoned Satan himself. We were stoning a pillar.

He was alone with his father. Millions of us were converging on this object, pelting it with pebbles, and shouting, "God is great!" Yes, this was the cry of supreme sacrifice, and it was as if we were attacking an invisible enemy. The cry was addressed to him, defiantly: the cry of a martyr accepting death to keep the enemy confounded. Like Ismail, we were chasing Satan away so that we could receive the death God had ordained for us. Satan wasn't gone; he was defeated and chased away. This victory was met with jubilation, readily expressed in tears of joy. We exchanged the feeling of profound satisfaction experienced in the success of the enterprise. No one wanted to miss out. Elderly women with no strength left paid young men to stone Satan in their name. They sang God's praises for allowing them to discharge their obligation in this way.

First *effroi*, then a frenzied attack, jubilation, triumph, a feeling of liberation: finally the end of the ritual was approaching, and the relief was real. Yet at the second and third stonings, on 11 and 12 Dhu'l-Hijja, the emotion was just as intense. When Haj Abbas and I, on either side of his wife, approached the three pillars in succession, we had to lift up Hajja Zuhra several times to tear her from the crowd. We were exhausted after this effort and quickly escaped from the crowd to catch our breath. "What a day, what a beautiful day!" Hajja Zuhra kept saying, in tears, a lovely smile lighting her face. "I stoned Satan! I stoned him! I beat him! May God let me continue in this way!" And yet we could still remember the muffled, steady pattering of the pebbles, rising above the crowd like a thick, formless voice. "But that's the voice of the tomb!" Haj Lahcen told me later, when I described the deep anxiety the noise had aroused in me.

Since Medina, I had been walking in the places of death. Not in the Prophet's mosque, or in Mecca's Holy Mosque, not at Arafat or Mina, either—no, those places radiated with

life. The places that so absorbed me I could no longer hear
my footsteps were ones that opened and closed as they
pleased. When they were open, I knew that death was ahead,
that it was my future; when they closed, it was my past, and
it was desired. I could never say that this returning past had
occurred. Conjugated in the present and future tense, it was
a past that could only be told as a story. With a sort of un-
wonted power, it transformed every life story into buds ready
to blossom. In the places of prayer, I knew I was moving toward it and—which came to the same—it was coming toward me. In the other places, the past followed me, caught
up with me only to release me into a sort of ironic indecision
that was both provisional and definitive. I was discovering
my existence anew—not for the first time, certainly. But this
fresh discovery, which grew clearer with each of the hajj's
walks and stations, showed me myself in an utterly new light:
the novel silhouette of a concrete self set against the wide, as
yet virtually unexplored horizon of its doubles. We pilgrims
in a crowd of pilgrims featured in these scenes, with their
contours constantly redrawn. I gained no depth by introspection or by a kind of intensified lucidity, though I worked
regularly to achieve both. Rather, we took on profiles, pilgrims in a crowd of pilgrims, because this process of rediscovery made a projection of introspection, and an
assumption of image from reflexivity.

"Let's go stone Satan!" "What a beautiful day! . . . I beat
him!" "You must go to Jamrat al-Aqaba, . . . and stone it with
seven pebbles the size of beans." "But that's the voice of the
tomb!" "The stoning is dangerous, with us all aiming at the
same thing; sometimes you get a pebble on the head . . . I accept everything on the path to God, you have to see the
good side; any difficulty on the path to God is welcome . . .
The Saudis do what they can, but a lot of people cause disorder." "This whole crowd has to go to the same place between

sunrise and noon and aim at the same pillars. That's dangerous, and people die—sometimes in the hundreds. The '*alem*
can't agree about widening the circle [around the pillars] . . .
They really should. In religion, God smooths the path, God
always eases things for us, so why can't they . . . I don't
know."

   In these fragments, one can recognize the injunctions
taken from a pilgrimage manual. Clearly, Hajja Zuhra had
derived immense satisfaction from defeating Satan. Her
words, tears, and smile surprised no one. Her husband expressed the same feelings, as did many others around us. We
understood what it was about. After the stoning, I, too, felt
relaxed and happy. I had successfully taken part in a powerful
collective bombardment, and I was safe and sound. My character and resolve had been put severely to the test, but I was
happy to have been able to leap into the human torrent and
perform the actions. For me, Satan could be certain forms of
the negative—evil. Outside the hajj my daily thoughts and
deeds made the efforts to fight this negative each time I
could identify it, in whatever context. Still, there's a big difference between these daily efforts and the effort crowned
with success at Mina. In the cosmic order of gesture, we
were on the same wavelength. A well-regulated gesture
obeyed the injunction "you must." The pebbles could not go
beyond or to the side, or they would be invalid. A gesture of
assumption and presumption. Assuming and assumed: re-
sponsibilities for duties, knowledge and acceptance of danger, sacrifice on the path to God; performing and finding
oneself despite (and with) the disagreements of authorized
interpreters and jurists, despite (and with) the challenge to
textual authority. Presuming and presumed: that the stoning
of the pillar was the stoning and vanquishing of Satan; that
the sound of the pebbles was the "voice of the tomb"; that
the noise was a "path."

At the place the pillar marked, we presumed a presence: Satan's. A presence both distant and actual. The pillar was associated with the place where he had appeared, but he was always there, in this place where the pillar rose high above the crowd. It and he were never parted, never left the place. When we arrived, he was already there, since that was the place to which we assigned him. The pillar was therefore a relationship, which threw me into a confusion about doubles while it also invited me to skip over the uncertainties and perform an act of will. How else to explain the fact that I preserved, intact, the memory of the stoning and the sense of well-being I felt afterward? Something manifested itself, and in sharing it, we savored a recognition and an identification. First, there was Satan, or his proper name, these pebbles, these pillars, these rings of people let loose around them, and, finally, this gathering which put an end to everything. Nothing could be more concrete than this scene, and yet nothing more concretely unreal: suspended between the inescapable laws that govern our empirical existence and the illusion that constituted it. Beyond were signs addressed to each of us that pulled us toward the outer limits of meaning.

At those limits, the tangible objects we had recently learned to call symbols produced emotion at the very point where meaning was exhausted. This was their primary vocation. The aim was not so much to bring to light or to recognize a dilemma, to offer abundant sentiments and definite intentions, which would have intoxicated that crowd at Mina or induced moods in each of us; it was, rather, to show us the known and dangerously mobile face of the Sphinx and the Gorgon. Symbols bring human beings back to one another. If these objects indeed had "a certain human substance," I couldn't help thinking it came from this reference to humanity and that therefore their attempt at substitution would always be imperfect, always be outflanked.

From now on, I had to accept these outflankings of the self. The midnight prayer was, as always, a moment of peace, and nothing disturbed the return to Allah. The psalmodies and silences re-created the universe, as they did each time. Their features were familiar, but they presented themselves with a newness that only appeared once—as if, in such novelty, time were folding back on itself. This prayer, gathering the pebbles, and the following confrontation with death—all these events mutated into a mimesis of effort. The morning prayer opening the last acts of the cycle raised the curtain, in peace and quiet, on the world: always the same and always told anew. Here it was, our world, fabulation restoring it to its first existence: as fable.

The fable unveiled itself, of its own accord, in ritual. Or rather, fable and ritual accepted the transmutation into a story line, which commanded: "Do as Ismail did. Gather your stones, attack Satan, and give yourself a sacrifice, give yourself for sacrifice. This is a commandment about which God alone knows the secret." A plot. At the same time, it told me, "To do as Ismail did, gather your pebbles and go stone the pillars. But unlike Ismail, you are not unaware of the outcome of your action today. On the path of sacrifice, unlike Ismail, you already know it is an animal you will be sacrificing!" A story line, an imitation, then, whose outcome was set in advance. In short, I wasn't like Ismail, and the ritual told me that clearly, but did it not also order me, in the next moment, to be like him all the same? For a long time I suspected I might be on the path of another plot. Each time the idea came to mind, I quickly pushed it away, consigning it to the realm of conjecture. And yet little by little I became reconciled to the paradox: that the origin myth which each human life carries with it appeared at the horizon of its finitude.

11

MEMORY OF VIOLENCE

A HAPPY EVENT CONCLUDES ISMAIL'S ADVENTURE. THE SUCCESS of the stoning and sacrifice repeats the ending of a story which, in the rite, was made ours. Yet the evidence was that the drama anticipated another conclusion. However, if I ended up accepting this in regards to my personal destiny, the distance between the convictions of others and my own kept me from going forward. The interpretation of this distance now seemed inadequate. The anguish was insuperable for all of us, although it didn't come from the same sources for the others as for me. Because, indeed, uncertainty coexisted with hope of salvation—the other side of dramas about death and the hereafter. If I'd had the sense of rediscovering an existence, in fact it was in that of my companions. In the ongoing world that was being configured in ever fresh compositions, it wouldn't be right to think I was alone in feeling that we kept seeing the fable of our life recurring. Of course, it was neither the time nor the place to discuss this, since we were still in thrall to the plot. The success of the stoning and sacrifice was certainly an anticipation of salvation, but it hardly eliminated suspense or guaranteed a good end identical with the one that capped the founding heroes' deeds. Putting Ismail to death shed a brutal light on the ending for us all, which had already been played out and which nevertheless we kept catching up to. The happy ending to Ismail's sacrifice was just Act One. It led merely to an intermission.

Stoning. The violence it unleashed was only an imitation of an original violence. But the movement back and forth between the two was perceptible. Once the initial moment of fear or hesitation passed, we threw ourselves into it ever more enthusiastically, our zeal increasing with the shout of "God is great!"—so much so that the mimetic violence became real, and the two intermingled, the one covering and recovering the other, each giving its efficacy, which came from time immemorial, to the other.

The calm and relaxation the violence produced after it was spent betrayed one of its directions: it turned inward to the self and its myriad sparklings with others—others' bodies and faces, first and foremost. Each cry, each drop of sweat, each contraction and release, each smile or grimace, each blink of the eye, each contact, each time that voices joined or eyes met—everything arose as a hint, a tentative call and response from one to another, to the Other.

Qur'anic exegesis and the stories of the prophets amply express this: Satan is part of each of us, another self, a double whom it is vitally important to keep in check. He is the "I" who leads us astray. Permanent, salutary violence must therefore neutralize this double, overcome him, and exact his respect. At the same time, we must accept the harsh reality of his presence. Never annihilated, this intimate enemy is always at the ready. There are means to defend oneself against Satan, but there is no way to kill him.

Now, by shunting him aside, all the father and son did was

clear the way leading to their foreordained deaths, which they accepted contrary to their most legitimate desires. More dangerously, they accepted a double violation, if one may put it that way, of the law given to humanity by revelation: the murder of a son along with the murder of an innocent creature. When we heed the fact that the slaughter was justified because it was sacrifice, it becomes still more horrifying: the violation of a taboo presenting itself as an exemplary sacrifice, and doubled by its radical cruelty. The use of violence against Satan opened up violence against the self—unbelievable, abnormal. But the first was justified as obedience to God, through the father—who chose to carry out the commandment received in a dream—while the second forced both father and son to behave in violation of all norms. This violence was absolute, justified only by itself; showing great power, it did not come from feelings such as hatred or envy (unlike Abel's murder by his brother Cain).

The image of father and son going, as one, to the utmost limit of the obligation to submit is saying that the double violence of the sacrifice is also singular. At this point of origin, which can be confused with no other, there was a violence that each human being wrought against himself, and everyone bore witness to it. The throngs of people absorbed in the public worship at Mina knew that the long-awaited son had been a gift, later reclaimed. They also knew that this whole maneuver was a test; that from this ordeal, once endured, came grace and a replacement: permission to sacrifice and to eat domestic animals. They knew that the patriarch could not but believe in a dream in which God himself had made his will manifest.

That initial violence was what was talked about most often: the son being offered up by his own father's hand. That was the image constantly called to mind during the pilgrimage. It had always touched me deeply, and in truth I experienced a double reminder of it. Its regular recurrence was an ordinary thing. At the holy sites, it came back to my memory just as, today, it comes back while I write this book. In Mina, though, it transcended its limits; then, instead of being reassuring, the image drew me beyond itself. What confusion! Henceforth nothing would protect me. Things that had always been mute clung to me or rashly made themselves known, as if my merely looking at them engulfed them in a shapeless consciousness. This is why the millions of pebbles and the pattering noise from beyond the grave had so struck me that I could no longer make out orders, words, light, heat. Everything happened in an immense thundering roar, and my normal hold on the world gave way.

Ismail came back, like a rock hit by lightning. The raised blade came back, the blade falling on the throat. "Ismail": a proper noun like other nouns—"vision," "reverie," "dream," "slaughter," "sacrifice," "patience," "God," "substitution." The words themselves came back, things among things—or, rather, they returned to their violence as things, so much so that the image having ceased to make this scene reassuring, this return to the violence of things was revealed in its truth as reunion. "Knight of the *faith*," he was called: Ibrahim came back, having dipped the cutting edge of his blade in the afterlife of the image. And this title was his alone—not by right, but owing to a fact to which I and others could testify.

But how could one testify to another reality of things without the privilege of faith? The contingency, therefore exorbitance, of grace required me to remake the world with other signs, to create, in scarcity, my own myth of origin. But, as always, beginning is—beginnings are—difficult. Where and with what should I start? Each initial scene disappeared into another. With so many comings and goings, so many illusory anchors, the sacrificial scene at Mina, on 10 Dhu'l-Hijja 1419 of the Hegira, had every semblance of

being a present moment. One could rise above these sem-
blances, anticipate them, precede them, or radiate around
them. Absent a legitimate choice, which in every instance
would have been too singular, the story and its crucial hall-
marks compelled this freedom. In the manner of a fairy-tale
hero traveling through unknown, enchanted landscapes, I
discovered that the entrance I had taken at the beginning
was also a back door.

The horror I always felt at the sight of a man slitting a
beast's throat had grown stronger during the sacrifice in
Mina—so strong it lost its name, led that name to defeat,
and thrust me into that defeat. An unnameable thing: carrying out the required sacrifice of the son fractured all meaning. It filled every vacuum. A landscape that was familiar yet
had no bond of reciprocity with a language. A landscape of
silence. Loss of the name affected more than emotion: in this
landscape, the sacrifice was the only landscape. A landscape
of silence to which we belonged. Far more than a paradox
that would have allowed one to rediscover a world God inhabited in his own way, projecting human words without
sharing them, this landscape invited me to contemplate its
limitless transparencies, which were as one with the regres-
sive opacity of words.

The image of the sacrificial son, of human sacrifice, of a
male sacrifice carried out far from women, this image whose
outlines were so clear was constantly shrouded in darkness.
As if painting, its techniques forgotten, was unable to show
chiaroscuro; like the moment at the end of a day when twi-
light gives way to night. The evidence was there and at the
same time distanced itself: the Almighty designated Ibrahim
for this trial in and through a vision or dream. The rest was
well known. The vision occurred in broad daylight, while
daily activities and concerns were suspended. No surprise in
this turn of events. A suspension less radical than that which

night effects. In any case, Ibrahim had a vision, and between it and meaning a certain ambiguity arose. The patriarch announced he had seen himself sacrificing his son. The authenticity of the vision was certain; this was God's friend, and he could not be the victim of a satanic plot. But it was the son who spoke of a command, while the father had merely recounted a vision. And neither of them hesitated to act according to what they thought the meaning of the vision was. The vision was something that happened to Ibrahim; it changed his life; now it would be composed of events foretold, but whose consequences he could not know. And although faith drained them of meaning, the unfolding events depended on the will of father and son; this was a formidable responsibility for them. For in effect they were on the right path only if the son's legitimate desire and love were experienced as lived agony and passion. It was the hour of maximum danger, when completed actions sought their identity in a future that had already taken place.

This singular progression met the one in the dream; but whereas the Freudian dream required interpretation and meaning deciphered by someone else in order to have value in an ongoing life, Ibrahim's dream required, first, an act carried out in faith so as to advance from one event to the next, thus building a life in which an interpretation could be made only of what would have been. The enigma of God's commandment animated the plot that led to the outcome we know. The son and father were saved by the substitution of the ram. But this regained time of salvation was going to carry in itself the indelible mark of a delay, a suspension. "Father," "son," "God," "vision," "Satan," "stoning," "sacrifice"—all these nouns repeated the suspension indefinitely, and time became its repetition. Not only did the world pass from before to after, but time was also the manifestation, in this world, of the worlds of which one must always take cog-

nizance. Or, rather, belief that must be preserved against all
odds, since Ibrahim's example shows that will and action at-
test to its preservation, that Ibrahim "believed" in his dream,
as God pointed out to him in the Qur'an, addressing him in
perhaps ironic and approving tones.

Thus ritual appeared to me as language through and
through. I had learned the Qur'an at a tender age, and now
was merely retrieving the spoken memory of it—a memory
that troubled my memory. But what kind of retrieval was
this? How to formulate it? How and why did this Word return, like a field plowed with furrows, with both fractures
and joints? These questions would no doubt return more
than once. I couldn't get the better of them; the best I could
hope for was a few moments of respite from them. My Babel
was the colonial Babel; to this day it multiplied collages, passageways, Escher's perpetual staircases, and the floors I
climbed and climbed, feeling I was close to a destination I
never reached. In this Babel, which lived in my home, languages pulled me into their mutual transparencies and lines
of perspective. At the end of these courses, there were thick
forests one had to clear and clear again to reconquer their
territory.

I had long known that my colonial Babel brought about
the return of landscapes striped with this Word, of fault lines
running across this woven material. I took intense pleasure
in this, pleasure in mastering practices with unforeseen results, in repeated meditations. With, as a bonus, the enjoyment of the dangerous, semi-clandestine activity that the
energies unleashed by perversity made possible—the back-
and-forths, the instability of features, the maps of mountains
that became mountains, the perspectives that suggested
depth only to become once again mere splashes of color on a
flat surface. Other Babels arose and vanished, shadowing
each other. All of them came or went, however, with a "there

is," third person or neuter, which I had the power to conjugate in the first person. I took delight in applying my hearing, smell, and other senses to them.

Instead of "I," perhaps it was possible to use "there is." Strange as it might sound, the form came close to a conjunction of space and being, a conjugation of space to being—that is, in a time that placed one in the other and by the other. It was about learning how to rediscover the lines that joined and separated Babel. Ritual, language through and through, would enable me to see the erased points of a delicate outline. But none of this would happen unless I grew accustomed to reabsorbing symbols and their interpretations in the excess and loss of nouns, unless I learned to walk backward, to construct emotions through symbols!

As language through and through, then, the rite spoke to each of us—to the others and to me, because we spoke it to each other. In this place, Mina (and at all the others—Medina, Mecca, Arafat), we spoke in every genre and style: from poems to "accounts," exegesis to dialectic, law to anecdote, analysis to panegyric, conversation to silence. We spoke in psalms, chants, seated, standing, in rhythmic prostrations, in circles—tight, strong, and calm around the cube, wild and fearsome around the pillars. We spoke in steps and words along the path to the sacrifice; we spoke in brandished blades and gifts of death: in blood. These words sought out no future for themselves in "original" tongues, still less in superimposed statements elaborated by some unconscious cogito. The rite, I remembered, "addresses someone," is for someone. It takes that person into account as one would take into account the questions he asks or addresses to himself, his aspirations and suffering—with the ambiguity one can discern in the well-known expression "terms of address," the words one uses to address parents, neighbors, and others, men and women, superiors and subordinates. In that sense, during the ritual, we called on someone using a name that doubled his name, with the risk of discovering, after the fact, that we should have used another term. When we spoke during the rite, we were addressing not an "*absent term*," as good heirs to the Enlightenment such as Lévi-Strauss would have us believe, but an actual person; we "cared for him," him as a question, as one, as "he who," when he was. "Unity," "identity," "time": to these words all interrogations returned.

Whom was the ritual for? For whom did it care? For whom were we caring? Whom was it aimed at, and whom were we aiming at? Who was aiming at us? We were no longer alone; the entire crowd was no longer alone. Yet it was not a whole, appearances notwithstanding. It opened out at points I could not see—not only on the Muslim peoples we had left behind and who awaited our return, but also, above all, on the place where the interrogation concerned "who." A place without space that no longer acknowledged an exterior.

The rite, language through and through, occurred in this place, showing what was unfolding within it, as you show something in the hollow of your hand by uncurling your fingers and opening your palm. There, showing was not the same as pointing; or, if one insisted on "pointing" and "indicating," one had to understand these two words in the sense of "calling attention to something." A hand opens and calls attention to the thing in its palm. The rite, by unfolding, calls attention to what is said within it, to what is said in and through its words, the words we speak together and to each other. This being the case, we never cease bearing witness to what we say, to what comes with our words—always in excess, making for repetition and commentary to the far extremes of language.

Symbols are, first, constructions of this "who." I, someone

else, the other, others, the Other, are ways of calling that "who" and answering to "who." Shaping, formative answers. Forms emerge with each accomplished action. Interpretation follows, seeking itself in and through the actions, inaugurating its own recurrences, constantly making them anew. Order is also always in the process of coming about. This mimesis starts at daybreak, when the nocturnal curtain enveloping our universe rises. The sun rises on us, on each of us.

Who was this "we," this "I?" Intention counts above all, Islam proclaims. Differences don't fade away; Islam tells us only that each of us is solely responsible for his or her differences. I knew a few of mine. Brought up a Muslim, in the freedom of tribal life and worship and, later, in urbanized forms, I was educated in Arabic and French. The colonial order shaped our idioms, our landscape, and our bodily and moral lives. When Morocco became independent, I discovered my true nationality, which made clear that the European nationalisms were myths. When I began the pilgrimage, I was an anthropologist as well, with philosophical pursuits and dreams. Islam was my home—I said and ritually repeated—but I inhabited it as a homeless man. It forever went beyond me and I beyond it. Every day we sent each other back to our mutual strangeness, which linked us through the memory of a kinship evoked in images. The images often blended into new scenes and were recomposed in representations that took time to get used to. I had distanced myself long ago from the practices and faith of my childhood and youth, but I was convinced, by my own experiences, that my existence was constantly being transformed into something it was not, something that came before it. Was this something that also touched my Muslim brothers and sisters, inhabiting Islam, their home(s), in their own ways?

Ibrahim and Ismail walked in the direction that the vision

foretold; they were going toward the image that had been revealed, the scene of a violence that deferred all commentary.
It eclipsed all relationships and led all reproduction to a dead
end. It put love between brackets and yet kept it intact. Paradoxically, it excluded hatred, as it did despair. Going against
all hope, it locked itself into order, and in this reality everything was a given. Faith remained: for when reality closes in
on itself there are still possibilities, even when nothing possible can be detected. It closes in all the more for having re-
jected the worldly truth, which would be to turn back, safe
and sound, and to disobey—legitimately, according to all
prevailing criteria (human and divine). But father and son
had to disqualify this legitimate truth, scorn it, and destroy
its common forms and representations. Three times Satan
spread all life's seductions before Ismail's eyes. According to
some versions, he also showed him his own corpse, a head-
less cadaver covered in blood. We went over the stages of
that reality, which Ibrahim and Ismail brought into the
world, by following the plan of the vision and the exposed
image. Meanwhile, we had learned the outcome as they
walked toward the unknown. But nothing conflicted with
what for them, as for me, appeared in silhouette against the
dark background of confinement: a world that could have
happened. And indeed it did happen. Substitution, compensation, promise. And it came to pass, indeed, manifesting the
future as inscribed in the ordeal of past action.

At once, this end of the story, which ushered in historiog-
raphy and history, as well as philosophies of history, made
clear the trace of debt, or the trace *as* debt. The memory of
the self as active sufferer, toying with the violence of which it
was also the victim. The two scenes came one after the other,
although they were the same. They divided in two. Time was
precisely in this dividing, and with it came the rite, spelling
out its signs. Ibrahim and Ismail were walking to the end:

that of the son, which was that of the father, that of the father and son. They wrought violence upon themselves—themselves as mark of a ripping out and "dismemberment" of an origin. Memory of a self re-creating itself, rediscovering its imagined traces, rebelling against maps, seeking meaning in direct, empirical transcriptions, positively confirmed. Perhaps I could have guessed some of the reasons why that memory resonated with my own, the memory that haunted me and prompted me to seek in myself the being who was not there, at least not yet.

The stages of the sacrifice bore witness to the non-occurring origin, which nonetheless could not escape its image of dismemberment. In the recital of these stages, the development of the themes was recapitulated in finales that evoked and revoked the openings. Reciting, recitation, was appropriate for the finitude of being that emerged as what it had always had within it, not just as a repeated future but as the very mark of emergence. It was normal for memory to seek its mark at the place where beginning and end returned and overlapped.

We walked on, treading in the steps of Ibrahim and Ismail, father and son, father-and-son, observing "halts" where they had halted. Like the pilgrimage as a whole, the sacrifice was a halt and prepared a new departure. I saw few women there; the sacrifice was men's business, as Ibrahim's had been. Hajar, who had sacrificed everything so her son could live, was mute and absent. (According to a well-known tradition, the patriarch had made the mother leave under a false pretense.) Once again, I saw in my mind's eye all the sacrifices I had participated in—presenting themselves in a sort of procession, each with a man and his knife, or another man carrying out the sacrifice in his name, as the law required. This was decidedly a site for the father, and certainly the best-guarded site of the father's memory.

My God, so many sanctuaries! Mina and its sacrifice were therefore the sanctuary of other sanctuaries, the sanctuary of otherness, which I had just encountered in violence and adversity. Everything followed from that: the anxieties, the symbols and their construction of the world—of image, of creation of the self, of the creation of others and of lifeforms. Yet I found it hard to understand the piety of the women, excluded as they were from this rite at Mina and distanced from conducting many others, including that of prayer. I registered certain facts, although reluctantly: that Muslim women didn't put themselves forward yet had plenty of authority, which some called power, in their behind-the-scenes division of labor—in sexuality, in reproduction, in the very formation of the father, in masculine fantasies and obsessions. These points spared me the dilemmas of ideology, mystification, and "false consciousness." They also relieved me of the obligation to investigate the brute force I saw applied to women every day, which appeared to be taken for granted. Certainly, women always defended themselves against the harms inflicted on them and had their own ways of returning or dodging blows. But these exchanges still happened too often, and only with difficulty—and recently—had we been learning the ways to recognize and transcend them. This new work was long, and the way was not straight.

Still, I found the explanations unsatisfactory, and the issue sharpened for me during the pilgrimage—especially since, in the Holy Places and times, on clearly defined thresholds, the gender norms were applied so very strictly. And yet these were precisely the places where women's initiative and *initium* could be seen vigorously at work. Social difference, warranted by the ritual, somehow distanced all *Gesellschaft*, all community. Ismail's sacrifice took place long after Hajar's effort and ordeal with her baby, long after God had given her the gift of restored life when he guided her steps in her desperate race between Safa and Marwa, toward the well of Zamzam, which saved Ismail.

Even though other rituals framed this episode, history distanced the historical, insinuating itself into it, cracking it open. That fissure, locus of invention, was able to make a passage for history—not a ready-made history, which one could recognize for what it was, but history (collective or personal) as something still being created, on which more light could always be shed. Psychoanalytic and Marxist approaches had certain difficulties here, especially when in contact with ritual. Although they came quite late to our societies, they arrived steeped in ready-made historicity, recurrence, and predicted structures: the "return of the repressed," tradition transformed by new "modes of production." Moreover, they adapted to an environment of ideas in which "Islamic society" was conceived, at the outset, as being polarized between men and women. Hence these approaches quite naturally recognized subjects that divided in two: precapitalist/capitalist, masculine/feminine (the first all-powerful vis-à-vis the second), or a self in two parts thrown off balance by the dialectic of narcissism and of the assumption of the father's symbols and values.

But the phenomenology of the world's pre-reflexive configurations, of the perspectives of a consciousness immanent in action and in movements of one's own body, put me on the path to something that goes beyond these histories conceived as the simple development of initial structures or seeds. By appropriating the idea that consciousness is always already in action, in the lived world, I could not but conclude that it carried with it the unbridled mark of its own emergence. Something of its passivity, borne by its movement, was constantly active in cultural constructs.

At the fateful halt, Ismail and Ibrahim reached that mark: the end of a world which brought them to its outer edge.

They did not take a single step farther; following their example, nor did we. They went through this world backward; starting with an interpretation and following it, they stopped at its limit, which gave onto the exterior of all interpretation, onto the view of an image and the sound of a silence that anticipated only language. Wasn't it this halt at the edge of our life-forms, this view, and this sound that caused us men and women to receive images and anticipated languages? Wasn't it here that we were going to receive our borrowed symbols anew, be enjoined to bring them to safety and to change them?

These thoughts freed me from a certain unease. They didn't resolve the uncertainties, but they dispelled my feeling of resignation. I had now exchanged the pain of this resignation for the perspective of working painfully along the path of truth. I made my sacrifice on that path, whereas before I had simply been trapped in suffering.

In these backlit silhouettes, and by the repetitions and condensations of the features of the sacrifice and my picture of them, the colors and contours grew clearer as the composition advanced, as our life-forms showed themselves: neither fabricated nor arbitrary, as the social sciences too often claim. Nor were these traces of a writing that appeared only to be dispersed forthwith. For they never stopped proliferating for us, as no doubt they were created by our predecessors and, at the same time, simply received and accepted by them: specific configurations of the human—happening, persevering in this future *to come*, passive-active in the realization of their own movements still to come. I wanted the life-forms I claimed for their future, just as the women who were kept away from the sacrifice were free to want it for all time. The past and the present of these coalescing customs were insufficient criteria to judge their success or failure. Instead of giving in to a prejudice, I was learning to wait for what they were becoming, with a kind of patience that drew its energy from the patience shown by Hajar, Ismail, and Ibrahim. I could glimpse the sacrifice as power and as limit, and I sought to take up my position in its future.

Metaphor, that's what the sacrifice was, in the first place of violence turned against the self, at the limit of knowledge and interpretation, at the gap between borrowing and conscience, in the movement toward clarity when the lines converge at the point where perspective ends. That the sacrifice was ordained did nothing to diminish the freedom of the prophets whose action confirmed its character as an absolute commandment. It was definitely this other-than-self whose authority was adduced, putting three instances onstage: the source of the command, myself, and my other-than-self. Every thrust of life is a blooming that creates a debt, destroying other possible blooms, thus making of every being a lack of being, an inability to be—oneself and others. To my companions and also to the other pilgrims, to all humanity, I was a figure of this lack, since I was always waiting for humanity to define me. The risks were always enormous, for one could always pin the blame for the lack on someone other than oneself.

Our institutions and symbols—unstable, shifting incarnations of what was virtual in the initial defect—can at any time project otherness outside themselves and metamorphose it into an absolute figure of evil, thus transferring the debt in its entirety and the obligation to pay it back. In an extreme case of twentieth-century barbarity, a system that claimed legitimacy in languages extrapolated from extreme sacrifice conceived and executed a program along these lines. An insane machinery of restitution by extermination was set against certain peoples designated as quintessentially other, then expelled from humanity, anticipating their complete removal; they were, according to the engineers, the ultimate other: Jews. It is easy to recognize a perversion of religion in this sinister plan. But it is just as easy to see that many other religions based on sacrifice can be similarly transformed if they move from the recognition of virulence in the self to the projection of it onto others, transforming their difference into stigmata.

Islam's jurists did not hide the fact that violence lay at the heart of sacrifice, that murder was its identity. Still, they sought to contain the violence with restrictions and precautions. They worked to mark the line between what is allowed and what is forbidden, making an orderly classification of what things, being sanctioned by the sacrifice itself, might be broken or killed in order to eat, use, or defend oneself. Violence was thereby in a sense turned against itself, in a systematic complementarity that gave preeminence to masculinity and presumed humanity's domination over other orders of creation. According to the legal experts, our sacrifice at Mina was an offering and a gift. Being an inauguration, it was what followed the curtain being raised on the action. That was why we had to be there at first light of day. Moreover, our offering coincided with the great Feast of the Sacrifice that all Muslim communities were celebrating at the same time—an observance that in Arabic is still called the "dawn feast."

Everything took place with a double orientation—toward community fervor and toward a practical relativism of association with individuals, groups, societies, and religious communities (first among them Jews and Christians). This dual orientation, which widened the circles of belonging and alliance, was fatally accompanied by a family war with the two other monotheisms of the Near East, inasmuch as Islam challenged them openly, modifying the rules for customary behavior in the world, rejecting any form of communication with God but revelation, and rejecting the archaic pact between the divinity and a particular group. Moreover, worship and submission left little room for even the idea of a covenant.

One might have expected that Christianity's self-sacrificing God would not accept, other than in simple words, the substitution of the lamb, that, in short, He would not accept that the sacred carcass, the whole carcass, along with the bread and wine, would become a standard-bearing totem with consequences on a mass social scale: theological empires, universal churches, colonial nation-states with imperial powers, grand totalitarian constructs, a universal network of radical Islamic reform, lust for and acts of ethnic cleansing, a new imperialism of redemption. Advocates of absolute purity, advocates of closed communities, with a mission to save all humanity, time and again discovering their taste for ostracism and for victory foretold.

Sacrifice moved along three poles: the vision, the father-son pair, and the lamb substituted for the sacrificial father-son. It directed life's violence toward creatures other than human. It authorized violence but did so while seeking refuge, as one would from evil, in God. It invited us to do the same, to act as it did, going one step at a time, and to show patience in the hope that in time our vision would become clearer. Otherness was in us, and there was no guarantee that interpretation would always be able to distinguish between God and Satan—especially as the confusions became more threatening with our communities growing, our territories adjoining, and the sources of our satisfaction coming closer to or being planned for sites we must share.

If sacrifice showed us anything, it was that the morale of a human being who knew how to wait patiently would persist despite the systematic, generalized rationalities of the new nation-states. These must coexist with something that is the archaic value par excellence, whose integrity violence cannot harm: love kept intact, and the eventuality that father and son, self and other, will be saved by time—the one thing offering respite. It was therefore within its power to disclose the debts of ambition and desire and to recall us to redemption. Sacrifice did not reveal things lying "hidden since the world was created," as a literary prophet had declaimed. Nor did it deliver us from violence, which was presumed permanent and endemic in so-called primitive societies. This prejudice persisted, although actually the societies for a while classified as such managed to practice violence and contain it through mutual distancing and ritual, until modern men, all too often boasting of God's self-sacrifice, came and unleashed it systematically against them.

The sacrifice in which I took part at Mina went in these two directions. Alas, the allegedly technical modern rationalization of it replaced the old ethic of going one step at a time, and a massive, blind, industrial death machine was substituted for an initial sensitivity to human and animal suffering. Even the charity that flowed from it did not lessen the difficult mystery of the kill, while the gift of meat marked with the donor's name put a finishing touch on the assimilation of one life by another. Despite everything, while the sites, eruptions, and uses of violence might be recognized and circumscribed, their mystery remained complete.

I had no recipe for moderating specific anxieties and fears, for keeping the salvation thus attained from degenerating into a witch hunt, for holding the internal enemy at bay and preventing him from emerging to take on the features of a threatening enemy at the borders—of self, religion, culture, civilization, or nation. But perhaps I could seek some help by exploring the metaphor of sacrifice more deeply, then returning to this figure of speech. Two sacrifices took place in one: that of Ismail and that of the lamb given to the patriarch, one replacing the other. Above all, something of each was expressed in the other. The first preserved the possible in confinement itself. The second made regulated, undisguised violence a condition of the human life force. One gave a religious meaning to humanity, the other a human meaning to religion, making it unable to save itself or to endure without destroying and consuming lives quite close to its own. Ritual thus turned on itself and for itself: that was indeed its characteristic movement. It challenged us with the sense of its meanings, which were hardly hidden secrets or stars in the sky that one need only contemplate. I use the word "sense" with the meaning of direction: I had to go toward precarious meanings, which depended on dialogue, disagreement, and intertwined testimonies.

One direction gave people a down payment on life, transferring immolation and destruction to an animal: preferably a lamb, a male ovine, without defects, *complete*, a domestic animal, with cloven hooves, a ruminant. Sheep, goats, camels, all the herbivorous species that had these characteristics were acceptable for the sacrifice. No carnivores, no nonruminants, no shod animals, no cloven-hoofed that weren't ruminant, like pigs. No sea beasts, no wild animals obtained through hunting—not even ruminants. It was also forbidden to sacrifice certain domestic animals, and their consumption was greatly discouraged because it was "repugnant": horses and donkeys, for instance; shod animals that were not ruminants. But above all, pigs were the most strongly prohibited. No sacrifice of pig, no consumption of pork. Pigs were horrible. Yes, they are domesticated, have cloven hooves like the purest animals, but they have other characteristics: they feed on everything, even things contaminated by blood and excrement. Perhaps pork, rather than being an incarnation of confusion in the world's systematic, was the intermediate in the three monotheisms, a life-form close to and yet different from the other two. A domestic animal with cloven hooves that feeds indiscriminately—and not a ruminant. Furthermore, like certain wild animals, it fed on carrion, displaying, as it were, a form of animal cannibalism. Slitting the throat and processing the blood of a pig would be as fermentation is to certain plants and to the processing of alcoholic beverages. So it was not surprising that pork and wine became metonyms for Christians, powerful near neighbors with whom we Muslims have exchanged centuries of hospitality but also, all too often, invective and rejection. Pork became the point against which a very marked hostility was projected. But that was not because the enemy was consigned to the side of nature. This enemy was, rather, an intimate savage, unendurable and yet indispensable to our self-image: out of nature, out of culture, and thereby part of both, keeping the definition of each in suspense.

As a metaphor for consumption and giving, the sacrifice rite ordered me to eat part of the carcass and give the rest to charity. Many of my companions took pieces home with them. The carnage carried out annually thus remained circumscribed. The use of animals—beyond that, of all creation—was limited. Between nature and us circulated this third factor which did not let us use it as a thing, void of being, waiting to appear, a simple ingredient in a chain of consumption and production. Domestic animals I always felt very close to, transmitters as they were of the life of all living things. The sacrifice allowed me to take the life of one, but it came back to remake mine and to remind me of my life as of a debt, returning me to myself as an inability to be, persisting through destruction.

The other direction led me to sacrifice as a figure of speech. Violence and language were no longer at polar opposites for me. The first came from the Word, which deployed it and yet surpassed it in narration and recitation. The heroes' progress, and then our own, which ended with the killing of an animal, did not occur as it would if we had been following a formal or experimental method of verification. Other extremely effective realities were invoked. They encouraged me not to restrict my relation to what are usually called positive realities. Sacrifice was a relationship among us, the pilgrims, and it was transmitted through Qur'anic recitation. Before undertaking this trip, I had thought it could be summed up as a process of persuasion. But I still meant by that a kind of acquisition of beliefs and a deepening of one's convictions. I quickly realized, once I was here, that I was alone in thinking about this deepening.

Our sacrifice referred to Ibrahim's, and the lamb to Ismail. Other people emphasized and I mentioned that metaphor was a creative transfer via "as if." All ritual was about behaving as if by accomplishing a thing one was accomplishing another thing. This doing "as if" could not be summarized by comparing isolated aspects that were already there. Metaphor created new structures of experience. It transcended similarity. My own description of the hajj—once it identified and isolated various fragments and noted each detail—simultaneously tried for a redescription that made a picture, to which successive strokes added depth and direction. The result could be recognized progressively (and only in part): a "thick description" not only, or even especially, in the wealth of detail, but in terms of enriching the realities that symbols and signs invoked. I demanded not only that metaphor give shape to the shapeless, but that it evoke and invoke the possible forms of reality of which the real world might be capable.

This was a request, not a decision. My will took this as its goal but had to receive the involuntary, just as societies had to receive it in accepting their own creations. I thus had no other choice but to abandon a certain language: "arbitrary choices," "construction," "fabrication," "invention" of the self, of tradition, of institutions, of humanity. Put simply: the emergent being, human being, being human, does not choose, build, create. If one wants to keep those words, one must use them to mean "working at" something received, as a painter works at colors, an inexhaustible memory. Like a painter, but with no doubt fewer options, I had to take myth and ritual as inspiration, and stop repeatedly, try and try again, start and start over, hoping to provoke forms whose arrival I awaited.

While memory was not always comforting, metaphor gave me assurances that could scarcely be denied. All I had to do was remember them. Even when metaphor passed into common usage, it always bore me along, as faithfully as my own legs. More important, it preserved a refuge ready to receive me. Each time that political-theological machines or groups forced the violence of sacrifice onto perverted paths, painting the victims as the guilty ones, thus preparing for aggression, those who did not accept these sinister drives —making sure always to question their own feeling of innocence—could invoke the sacrifice so as to bar the way to lynchings. A rampart against the making of enemies, their voices will not be extinguished. They will demand an end to hostilities, crying to the world that the metaphor of sacrifice always overflows its interpretations.

12

EPILOGUES

OUR RETURN TO MECCA FROM ARAFAT VIA MUZDALIFAH HAD followed an elliptical pattern, you will recall. We thus went back to the beginning, but by discovering new places and prayers that prepared us for the stoning. I was starting to understand that from now on, all my returns—to the sources of myself, to this pilgrimage experience, to my travel notes, to Morocco, then to the United States—would be elliptical. Nothing from now on would escape that form—which, as in an elliptical sentence, subtracted certain elements so as to lead to new, wider territories and to concentrations whereby one could leap into the unknown. It would conjugate actions, all our actions, in every tense. In sum, its economy would become abundance, excess.

And so I was on the road to Mecca once again, after the stoning. Along with Abbas and his wife, I decided to go on foot so as to avoid the traffic jams. We walked in the midst of the white-clad crowd, the power of its torrential mass spreading everywhere. There was no pushing or shoving.

We stopped several times to drink and rest. Many people paused at the numerous charity stations where food and drink were handed out. They ate what they could and left behind yogurt containers, bottles, cardboard boxes, and wrappers. We moved slowly, avoiding as best we could the refuse strewn on our path.

Near the big tunnel that led directly to the holy city, we exchanged a few remarks about an accident that had happened at this very spot, so I had been told, the previous year. According to the most widespread version of the story, a sudden electricity blackout had plunged the crowd into darkness and blocked the ventilation system. Dozens of pilgrims were said to have been crushed in the ensuing panic or to have suffocated for lack of air. On the way out of the tunnel, we took a wide avenue, then another that led us to the mosque for the circumambulation and the running between Safa and Marwa. After that I left the state of *ihram* for good. I had partially abandoned it, according to what is allowed, after the first stoning, when I had my hair cut.

The following day, when I attended the farewell circumambulation, I plunged once again into the crowd, where emotion was peaking. I went to meditate afterward, in peace, beneath the arcades. Leaving the mosque, I couldn't help gazing at the black cube one last time. Visiting it repeatedly had been to no avail: the "House of God" appeared to me in a guise that resisted familiarity. It was a house that was not a house, it was not a mosque, and it occupied the center of the quintessential mosque. We prayed turned toward it, but not within its walls, and we revolved around it. On one side of it had been inset a stone that came from paradise according to Muslim tradition: it came from a "time" preceding time. This "house" was also, as I said, clothed—a unique quality and privilege. And we bade it farewell before leaving it, without tarrying long. It welcomed you so as to send you right

away with the memory of its presence and the duty to pray in
its direction. A few moments later, going back to our lodgings, I felt clearly that something was missing. I missed the
black cube I had left behind me. The memory I would preserve of it would be one of loss. It would thrust me into further wanderings, lead me onto unexpected paths. The black
cube, and the image of the black cube, would remind me that
I had lost something for all time and that it is written that I
shall always seek it.

This feeling added to the horror of my trip back home.
The imperious command to leave Mecca as quickly as possible, the relaxation after intense effort, the exhaustion, and
the feeling that I had completed a cycle—all this prompted
me to get back to Morocco quickly and rest there, especially
since a misunderstanding with one of my companions had
poisoned the end of my stay in Mecca and was growing more
complicated with each passing day. The pilgrimage had
strained our relations, then clarified our differences so
sharply that it had led to a break. This was a common situation, and, luckily, the rituals made separation easier, with a
minimum of violence. Under the circumstances, I decided to
take care of things alone, and since I wanted to avoid long
waits and aborted arrangements, I hired a taxi to drive me to
Jeddah airport. This took me almost an entire day, since the
driver had to go with me to the hajj administration office to
get his identity checked. Only on this condition would I receive the letter for the airport police that would get me back
my passport and other travel documents. When someone
agreed to take me to the office, in the middle of the afternoon, we had to wait for a long time; he stood in the street
and I in the waiting room. After some deliberation, the officials told me that the Indian driver I had found would not be
allowed to take me to the airport, that I should find a Saudi
national to do so! I had to pay off the driver, who was no less

distressed than I, and let him go, postponing until the next
day the job of looking for another taxi. Worn out, I went to
see the people in charge and tell them how impatient I was.
They offered me a car with a driver, and this new, Saudi
driver duly arrived to pick me up. I noticed as we drove off
that he had with him a young man from his family; both were
close relatives of the functionary who had dealt with my case.

On the way to the airport the two men in front talked to
each other for a long while, paying no attention to my presence. Conversation was limited to a few laconic answers to
my questions about the airport, customs, and retrieving my
papers. Then, at one point, the driver asked me where I lived
in Morocco.

"I have a house in Morocco, but I live in the United
States," I answered.

"Oh, the United States! I've always wanted to go there.
You can make a good living there, right?"

"Yes, you can make a good living . . ."

"Oh! I've always wanted . . . Here I teach in a secondary
school; it's not bad. But I have to moonlight. For instance,
drive a taxi from time to time, like today."

"Why? Don't you make enough?"

"No . . . Are you going to Morocco this time?"

"Yes."

"Do you know Jeddah airport?"

"No. Do you?"

"No, neither do I. But we'll find out . . . We'll manage . . ."

The two men resumed their conversation. I looked out at
the arid landscape and fought off anxiety. After a long silence, the driver's young companion turned around to talk
to me.

"Where do you live in Morocco?"

"In Rabat," I said.

"Rabat, not Casablanca?"

"No, not Casablanca."

"What about Tangiers? Is Tangiers nice? Do you know it?"

"Yes, I like it a lot . . ."

"There's the sea and everything. Can you have a good time in Tangiers?"

"Yes. It depends what you mean. I go there because it's a beautiful and interesting city. And I like the people . . ."

"Which is the most impure city in Morocco? Casablanca or Tangiers?"

"I don't know what you mean . . ."

"I mean, the place where there's the most vice, the most turpitude and lust."

"I wouldn't know . . . What's the most impure city in Saudi Arabia?"

"They're all pure!" He flung this answer back at me and turned again to the front.

We drove for a long time in silence. Near the airport, the two men began to consult each other nonstop, taking one road only to abandon it for another, asking for directions from time to time from other drivers. Night fell and we were still looking for the right terminal. We stopped at several buildings. Toward midnight, we still hadn't found the hajj terminal, and the driver had dropped any pretense of knowing the place. It was very late when we happened on the right location.

My two guardian angels handed me over to the police. We had planned to have a cup of coffee together after the formalities were completed, but the police sent the two men away at once. "You don't have anything to do here, go home!" We barely had time to mumble goodbye.

After lengthy verification procedures, I received my tickets and travel papers. Tired and disoriented by my long adventure, I went to lie down on a bench not far from a prayer room. The noise and the comings and goings of the crowd kept me from sleeping. I had to be content with drowsing as I waited to board the Rabat flight, scheduled for eleven the following morning. When the offices opened for business, though, the crowd was already enormous, and confusion reigned everywhere. Flights had been canceled, and groups of travelers had been waiting for ten, twenty, or forty-eight hours without explanation. I took my place in line at around ten o'clock. We spent practically the whole day waiting, since the counter at the gate only opened at about six in the evening. Excess baggage, jostling, fighting, and constant movement ended up making everyone irritated.

As we boarded, suitcases, bags, and containers of miraculous water took up all the space. And then the plane was overloaded. Everything was filled: seats, aisles, and the overhead compartments. Pilgrims had stuffed big bottles of Zamzam water into some of these, from which the beneficial liquid was now leaking.

Once wedged into my seat between an elderly man and a woman draped in white veils, I could not move at all. The aisles filled up with still more suitcases, cardboard boxes, bags, container bottles. After hours of negotiations, maneuvers, and squabbles, the crew gave up trying to control this. I refused to imagine what might happen if we had to make an emergency landing: we would trample each other. The pilgrims were stuck, like me, but impassive in the face of danger. Some of them even dared to scramble and slalom through the luggage to reach the lavatories. We took off around midnight.

I was half-asleep when my neighbor woke me. She asked me to check the expiration date on her passport. I was surprised, but complied without asking questions.

"Do you travel much?" she inquired abruptly.

"Yes, why?"

"No, no, nothing, you can tell when . . . Come see us in

Casablanca, you'll enjoy your stay . . . I'm sure you're married, but come anyway . . ."

"But weren't you just on pilgrimage?"

"Oh, come on, aren't we all human?"

I shifted in my seat and noticed that her veil was now gaping open over her chest, adorned with a gold necklace and no longer very young.

As if in response to my astonishment, the woman continued: "I go there for business, and I've brought up lots of children. Many women go for other things. Money, money, money . . . There's lots of money to be made. And we've got lots of women at home . . . In the East, men don't mind running after us. God forgive us!"

This exchange reminded me of several scenes. Young women from Beni Mellal, Casablanca, Marrakech, and elsewhere, whom I had seen in elevators, corridors, or phone booths, dressed in the latest fashions under their veils, making appointments to meet downtown or in nearby residences. I had met a good many women trading happily on the marriage market.

The piety and extreme abnegation I had encountered among men and women in Mecca and Medina carried the pilgrims far away from common desire, whether sexual or acquisitive, but my seat neighbor on the plane must have represented a particular group. In an earlier conversation, I had learned that she also traveled in Europe where, she claimed, two of her daughters were married to Frenchmen. She was originally from Safi, and asked if I had a family. I told her yes, and that we lived in the United States. Perhaps this information had emboldened her. Still, I would not exclude the possibility of a link between greater intensity in the ritual practice of sacrifice, on the one hand, and greater intensity in the life force, on the other. During the exercises and instructions we had received in preparation for the pilgrimage, I remember having been surprised by a sentence the legal experts often repeated: "Your women are licit for you the instant you leave *ihram*"—for us, clearly the period between *umra* and the hajj proper. I was amazed that the scholars had thought they must repeat this clarification several times, for I imagined that the pilgrims were preparing for a long period of abstinence. Perhaps I had poorly estimated the daily privations that a pious Muslim life implies. Perhaps I had been unable to appreciate that ritual intensified the life thrust toward death, imminent or deferred. Nothing surprising if this life thrust should continue in erotic or commercial expenditures! Its currents surfacing during the pilgrimage seemed powerful enough to sweep people into doing things that defied the extreme severity of Wahhabi surveillance and laws. But I had also often seen a sort of coexistence between obsession with purity and obsession with impurity (such as expressed by the relative of my driver), the twin obsessions making a way for each other, handily allowing for censure and also negating itself by making an ideal subject for the law.

My neighbor eventually curled up in her veils and went quickly to sleep. She awoke only for dinner, which was served in chaos. An infinitely long time followed the meal. I don't know when our imminent landing was announced. It was a moment impatiently longed for: deliverance, I thought. That was an illusion.

Still, as the night ended, after much shoving in a decrepit sort of hangar, I thought I saw the world bathed once more in enchanted hues. We walked through the crowds massed on either side to welcome the pilgrims. The beautiful, clean faces of the people clad in white seemed, despite the harsh lighting and the strong police presence, to float in a kind of transcendence, and voices blended naturally in sweet, re-

peated hymns, saluting the metamorphosis of the men and
women leaving the squalid building. This sort of epiphany,
which I had sometimes felt in Medina and Mecca, brought
me close to a feeling of the invisible manifested to the pilgrims after all the acts of their pilgrimage drama were over,
starting with the preparation and farewell.

This was—no doubt will be—one of the moments when I
would have worn my title of *haj* with a sort of joy I knew
well. It was like no other feeling. It never lasted very long.
All too often evanescent, it gave my other joys an end-of-
season flavor, with the pleasure from them rather like what I
used to feel as a child when toys were broken. This joy always came filled to the brim. It knew no half measures. It
made the self overflow in waves of dithyrambs. It needed
neither music nor dance, for it was both. It was entire because it came with its origin and was that origin's end. When
it was no longer there, I knew from experience that it would
return with the future, to which it always emigrated.

This time, its coming and passing gave meaning, equally
ephemeral, to my return and then quickly dissipated. For after the brief moment of generous welcome the crowd gave
each arriving pilgrim had passed, my return was not the
usual one. There was no party, no reception for me with a
group of friends and relatives come to congratulate me and
receive the gifts I had bought in Mecca and Medina, no
scene where the telling about my voyage unfolded in its own
time, where in the presence of witnesses it would have joined
a common theodicy. A few caps for my children, who were
waiting across the Atlantic, and a watch for my wife, who was
looking after them, far from the house where I was going to
rest in Morocco. A few prayer rugs for the neighbors and
two or three works of Qur'anic calligraphy under glass for
close friends. Unlike other pilgrimages I had celebrated with

other pilgrims over the years, this one received no social confirmation. For this reason, the title of *haj* was not added to my name.

I was comfortable with this, since the title, which for many people crowns and ends a life course, couldn't be the denouement of the adventure for me. More than ever, I was flung on the road and the horizon was moving pitilessly away, like the mirages on the hot steppes of my childhood. Besides, the custom may have begun late in the life of Muslim communities and had become a general one only as they moved away from Islam's Holy Places. The Prophet and his companions did not bear the title *haj*, nor did kings and presidents (with a few exceptions). I was willing to forgo this sign of salvation, though many other people saw it as a major stock in establishing capital and an insurance policy for the future; or it encouraged them to rethink their lives and put them in order according to their reconquest of self and/or world. My friend Lahcen liked to tell his companion, the *faqih* and notary public, that his pilgrimage was a license to "become even greedier," and everyone enjoyed the joke.

So each of us went off to discover his or her life, on the road that separated us from death. Surely the ongoing histories I had had the chance to accompany for a few episodes— the biographies still being written—would have happier endings than my own story. Without presuming uniformity, which it would surely be wrong to assert, I could see that happy endings were common, even though what was acquired in the pilgrimage still had to be consolidated in subsequent action. Despite everything, what the pilgrims seemed to have acquired in their versions of the story was, rather, hope. But even there, suspense remained; suffering had not been defeated. Faith, which is also the faith of others—of selves migrated to others and identified with them—thus confronted itself in forever new and renewed interpretations.

We were building arks of Noah. The travelers who boarded agreed on a destination. Everyone knew that this was an image of hope. But in the meantime, forms of life were being created. And the intertwined destinies of individual and collective existences became the concrete incarnation, proof, and portent of success.

Beyond the obvious difference between the other pilgrims' experience and mine, suspense, intrigue, passion, and suffering animated every life; my experience and the experiences I encountered were therefore signaling to each other: a relationship understood as dialogue, call, misunderstanding, and collision, of which the dynamics and meanings were not always within reach—far from it. The collisions brought into play doctrinal disagreements and shared symbolic structures, of course, but stakes, too: objects for debate and conflict, which also returned as mutually foreign fragments of memory in the *bricolages* of tradition. The references we tried to give them metamorphosed even as we pinned them down. Our powers of interpretation found their fulfillment here but also their limits: in symptoms that awaited individual stories to construct and reconstruct as identities. Powers of being that were also powers of making, or, if you like, powers to signify, to give a meaning, powers that until now did not have the means to work themselves out, powers without which no meaning could come into existence.

After I had performed the pilgrimage, I naturally tried to analyze it as a religious manifestation specific to Muslims living in the contemporary world—a world in which they and their religion are, on an unprecedented scale, permanently engaged with non-Muslims, their religions or systems of ideas, in a context of accommodation and conflict between ways of life, modes of production and consumption, and so forth. Understood, these practical forms are not separate from their images, nor are the latter separate from practices or from images of the self and individual, no more than from their articulations in all sorts of signs, including those of language.

It was difficult to articulate and classify this in the language of anthropology. Synoptic tables, where hitherto implicit links (in the description I had put in my notebooks) became clearly visible, proved fruitless. They soon became juxtapositions and collections of data ruled by dichotomies—ritual/practice, spiritual/material, sacred/profane—with the usual consequences: one had to find a means to reconcile or transcend them in a synthesis of the human postulated, according to one's theoretical inclinations, as pragmatic, rational, symbolic, and communicative. Or one could abandon such reconciliation and search instead in religious discourse for the principle of "disciplines" that would construct subjectivities and domesticate the desire for utilitarian or power goals—power of government and of the preemption of the thought and the unthought. Or else, in desperation, I might have to take the human to a breaking point, where one might just see traces of a quest for origin, pursuit of which would yield only more traces. In sum, religion and ritual would take their place in the ever-expanding merry-go-round of literature.

Either religion dissolved in the categories of reason, literature, or knowledge, or it became a system of interpretation and contemplation, a response to existential dilemmas and the feelings to which they might give rise. Or, again, I might have to break down the myths and rituals to rediscover a paradigmatic, formal logic, and then construe them as signs whose differences would serve to articulate general propositions. All that to attenuate, if not resolve, the antinomies of life/thought, past/present.

I had long ceased to consider signs and symbols in the equivalences of their opposition, whose signification would order itself along a paradigmatic axis. I preferred an approach that favored successive ritual acts conceived as words, phrases, and texts which always summoned their meaning in a sort of anticipation of words, phrases, and texts to come. With the central symbols were others subordinate to them, and others still that took care of transitions, pauses, and endings. In short, syntax and message: a style. In this view of things, ritual transforms the subject by giving him or her a world to inhabit that is shifted away from the empirical, social, and pragmatic world—hence also shifted vis-à-vis the world of conscious or unconscious rationality. Not that it eliminates the latter; rather, it relates to them in concealments or displacements, thus coloring life and action.

It goes without saying that these styles are also positions taken, precisely because they imply a search for totalization. Because it is always in the process of being achieved, and each accomplishment reaches the limits of the hitherto unachieved—is its virtual extension—style challenges itself and is thereby challenged. Styles are positions taken also because they seek themselves in the circumstances created by opposition and by social and political hegemonies. This is why they become deliberate gestures of will and power, and not only in the sense of the "I can" that is not possibly amenable to being subordinate to "I think." The immanence of the world in "I can" is a lesson that phenomenology teaches us. Nothing stops this new beginning for reflexivity, despite the silence that surrounds it today, from being extended into power dynamics—especially since such a return "to things themselves" can only shift the blind angle of consciousness, not take it over. Since we cannot recover this angle, perhaps we can at least examine its traces again, create a certain truth about the worlds they point to, that is, admit these worlds as our history. In that way, we would accept what takes place in us and through us—without us—and find a possible ending in it, which, in turn, retraces the course backward, just as one goes back over traces to find the line to a past action.

Proceeding in this way, I recognized that symbols not only served in the construction of different orders but also issued orders, that we were born and made ourselves under their rule and authority. Their orders authorized and hierarchized ritual roles, which were also, obviously, social roles. Did one, then, exclude symbolism and its interpretation in favor of strategic practices, in favor of "techniques" and disciplines of body and self deriving from and reinforcing a "discourse" of virtue? To have done so would have been to leave out of reflection on the hajj precisely what made it an utterly unique mode of action, life, and exchange: a re-displacement of biographies according to the symbols and to the orders they issue about human lives. Symbols and their interpretations arose in fields and followed styles, the logics of which were historically differentiated, linked by convergence and tension—in, for example, Muslim, Christian, Jewish, Hindu, Confucian, secular/Christian fields (which, for the past few centuries, might more accurately be called Christian/secular in Europe, America, and elsewhere), and so on. To omit these in favor of a mysterious creation and "production" of self would amount to projecting onto Muslims a discourse of academic power.

And indeed the self—or "subjectivity," to use the term common today—is the product of constructions whose principle can be found in education and the stakes put in training, as in dressage, and in types of knowledge linked to the powers that set the contours of what is thinkable and doable. Yet while these analytical remodelings may widen the scope of the lives we might wish for ourselves—just like their reconstruction, for that matter—they could miss out on what is both most common and most bewildering in our lives: that after the fact, and once they have gone in directions neither predicted nor even predictable, they can still seem like a possible outcome of what preceded it.

It is not in the least surprising that ritual—with its repetitions, admonitions, spatiotemporal rhythms and practices, structuring the body in permissions and prohibitions (of ingested substances, of other bodily practices, of colors and clothing)—makes for a general classification of things, of all the beings in this universe, including other human beings, and that all this leads to the elaboration of recognizable lifestyles and persons. Nothing distinguishes Muslims from other people in this respect. After all, it's a question of showing differences in an identity that wants to distinguish itself so as to succeed in this world and the next, an identity that religions postulate. These styles are thought out and stand out one in the other and in relation to each other, just as we are formed in and in relation to one another. Looked at from this point of view, the hajj repeats and reaffirms that Muslims are different from non-Muslims. With the hajj, Muslims empower themselves to display force and presence in the contemporary world even while being "absent" from the domination of powers that control, through military force, traffic in raw materials, labor, technology, goods, ideas, and images.

At the time I went on the pilgrimage, our states were becoming hypertrophied (a condition worsened by conflicts and impotence); the fragmentation of national structures and norms in the postcolonial period was accelerating; and we were dealing with the unprecedented, growing strength of extremist trends in some nations—notably the United States and Israel—that saw this strength as a sign of their divine election to represent a human ideal and to lead the world, especially the Middle East. Seen from where we were standing—that is, from Mecca—these new theodicies resembled the conquering and domineering powers of which colonial history and experience had already given us examples. Besides, a conquest from another age and a colonization-cum-ethnic cleansing were well under way against the Palestinian people, at the very moment when Arabs elsewhere had finally been liberated. These theodicies, which gave themselves out as the very history of humanity and democracy, collided at full force with Muslim will and with the Muslims' power to make their own ways of life. Like all theodicies, these claimed omniscient power, to predetermine the future and meaning of all styles of life. Among the pilgrims, responses to this claim varied, but most were hostile or distant, ranging from focusing on the self so as to maintain one's balance in this new environment, through dialogue, to opposition or to violent struggle—using stereotypes while waiting for weapons. But nothing comparable to the power of the states that sought to dominate them and take their resources, or to their even deadlier capacity to annihilate Muslim soldiers and civilians.

For a majority of the pilgrims with whom I shared daily life or had conversations, this was not simply a political history of Muslims and the world that was continuing, or happening now, before our eyes and in our lifetimes. It was a calamity, and not just a historical calamity, because for them it portended an imminent loss of salvation. In other words, to save the future of our ways of life was for them and for me not just a matter of saving the future of a civilization; it was a matter of saving oneself and of preventing the fall from being an eternal one.

It was at that point that I felt affected, and doubly so. First, I was moved because I recognized the dangers my companions felt were threatening their path, and I could also see that their lives were possible, desirable lives. Second, besides my difficulty in attaining salvation, I was realizing far more acutely than before how difficult it was to guarantee a continuation of this civilization beyond the ritual forms that had for generations given Muslim communities faith in their future. I suddenly understood that their death was going to be testimony to their efforts and that these efforts would survive in Muslim lives; this might in the end give birth to new, vigorous creations, which in turn might deliver future generations from the tyranny of absolutist thought—the kind that trumpeted the end of history with a particular form of democratic life and customs for the self and the world, as well as the kind that tried to limit Muslim life to a single type of community, imposed by powers that arrogated to themselves the exclusive right to interpretation.

But if these lives—interrupted yet paradoxically for a time prolonged in this huge rite of passage, which put ordinary life in brackets—if these lives had the combined strength and benefit of this testimony, to what was my own life preparing to testify? That was the principal question that amplified and replaced the questions I had asked myself when I left for the birthplace of Islam. And it became increasingly obvious to me that this problem of death and what it witnessed was the theme on which religion and the anthropology of religion were obliged to intersect, so long as the latter agreed to deal with the former without confounding it with its own languages, and if, above all, one acknowledged that because of this intersection the pilgrimage made political languages and the systematization of human life virulent, and not the other way around.

The pilgrimage gives the intersection between religion and anthropology an urgency that Islam's other canonical rituals rarely attain; besides, it unites them all, or their equivalents: prayers, invocations, sacrifices, profession of faith, alms, abstinences connected to fasting, and of course the prescribed purifications. The emphasis on intention, the rhythms, the halts, and the general sense of a break are juxtaposed with, and set against, the habits of daily life. All these rites develop in contrast to other religious traditions, but they also echo them. Moreover, Muslim and non-Muslim daily habits and observances not only affect each other but create outright collusions and contrasts: hence the polemics, rejoinders, reconsiderations, interpretations, pressures, dynamics of persuasion and war.

In these back-and-forths, the anthropologist was affected by the life of others; he lived it in a mode of recognition and simultaneously recognized it in what had been foreign to him. And, despite everything and insofar as it extended a tradition, he lived it as his former life. In the forms it took, it had no less a chance for a future than the life he had striven to make in his own choices, or than the lives informed by past and present traditions he had studied, or by traditions yet to come. Since the future successes of these forms of life depended on an imponderable, to what could the anthropologist's death hope to testify, if it was incapable of the same testimony as those of the other pilgrims? How did one justify accepting the life of others in a mode of recognition while nonetheless betting on a future for forms of existence detached from the ritual energy that presided over their birth?

The hajj, a singular rite the size of the planet, led me to another crossroads, as I have said. While I had believed I could go through it as an anthropologist, I had to accept that it was an event charged with unpredictability that had erupted into my life. A new excavation site thus opened up, leading me to search for a way to re-create myself as an anthropologist working on the horizon of Muslim tradition, like colleagues of mine all over the world who went on (whatever they may say) turning over the questions raised by their ancestors. The dangers of the enterprise were evident, given the extreme violence aroused by identities that play at denying their secret schisms; given also the lassitude and opportunism which have allowed such violence to multiply within the comfort of performative "little narratives." In the face of these perils, only creative freedom and faith in it enable us to persevere in the traces this freedom has left behind. We can always read some of those traces in the specific creation that is Islam as culture, civilization, and history, just as we may read them in other traditions. And so it becomes an urgent matter to apprehend this story, to return to the springs of its formation, to the will that overcame hazards.

I thus felt somewhat justified in my choices, my wagers. I had based them on reasons drawn from the past, on—must one repeat?—a certain awareness of history. Circular awareness, both cause and effect, created a certain truth about the past. This creation was a return that found something new in the old, although the novelty appeared only in the enterprise itself, one recovering the other without being confused with it. In fact, this was a break and not a reunion, with a historical meaning that might always have been present.

At this point in the narrative, where I have played the roles of both narrator and protagonist, I dare hope that this detour has clarified, for the reader and for myself, some of the motifs that inevitably made my position difficult. The fact is, when my pilgrimage was done, I no longer had either the courage or the desire to write as I had before. A certain savoir faire was still there, but the will and the belief were lacking. For a long time I resisted a story that kept coming back, asking insistently to be written. Certainly I had always thought it was illusory to try to get rid of narrativity in our descriptions and analyses—and, even more, in the daily effort that we make to hold our lives together (past and future), to embrace them in a glance, in a global gesture of inspection (retrospective as well as prospective). Narrative, a particular manner of speaking—which clearly imposed its own constraints, as has rightly been pointed out—offered symbolic constructs that were so many configurations of self and others, and of self through others, with a three-way dynamic that distilled human lives, already begun, toward their progress and their end. At each stage, its fabrications accounted for themselves to themselves by giving meaning to the previous stage and anticipating the next one. Succession and anticipation, knotted together in the plot, kept taut the unfolding line of a life that always knew it was over.

These successions, these anticipations, these plots on the horizon of finitude—did they have a religious or other virtue that could bring the testimony of a pure faith in Islam's ways of life together with testimonies animated by the motivation of salvation after death?

Certainly, the two hopes driving the two positions were not identical. But it was not out of the question that civilization's possibilities would allow them to meet, which thereby would keep the promise of renewal. From this perspective, narrative—with its passion for detail, conversation, questioning, and even challenge—revealed itself more and more as an appropriate means of approaching pilgrimage and pilgrims. The scene, filling up from one step to the next, becomes a *tableau vivant*, adjusting itself to theoretical prospects and to sketches picking up where others left off—so that women, men, and their actions are not reduced to generic categories.

The reader will understand that the story told here starts with a transformation, and precisely because of this transformation the protagonist/narrator possesses neither the beginning nor the end. On the other hand, the author is trying to write a conclusion. His only consolation—no Hollywood happy ending, this—is that the narrative unfurls the story and presents it as the history of a possible existence. Writing on this threshold has the function of a prayer calling this possible existence into being and, when that takes too long, of a magic incantation that casts signs toward the unknown, summoning it to give a sign.

It would surely have been inappropriate to try to hide the kinship this narrative had with the theological one, to which it returned nonetheless in order to face it, taking a position that only detachment made possible. Related to and distant from tradition: a moment of mourning and therefore also of remembrance. The hajj, the story of Ibrahim, of intrigue about the sacrifice, of suspense and conclusion, exercised its paternal rights over my narrative. And that is why it sought to mourn these rights, in hopes of preserving a memory of them. Memory of the religious act overhanging them, which always overhangs the laws in the black and white of the circumambulation of the Kaaba: with its striking contrast between fertility and life, on the one hand (certain accounts explicitly link the black of the famous Black Stone to women and menstruation), and, on the other, the pure white joy in finitude, in a life pouring out beyond the body-self. Memory therefore of a relationship that time always carries away, that knows to settle only temporarily in the spaces where law is settled and applied. Memory of mourning life, at Arafat, and of the denouement of resurrection, with the temporary flight and the search for a foretaste of life at the approach of the burial scene. Joy of deliverance, after the double success of this flight and of the triumphant stoning of Satan. Memory of the woman, the mother, Hajar, and her running to save and create the son, therefore also creating the father, since (as we often forget) fatherhood cannot be defined without progeny. Memory of two terms in collusion and conflict, whose ambivalences express far more than simply a son's camouflaged guilt in desiring to murder the father. Memory of a scene in which all the terms are unstable and anticipatory. Memory of the father himself, on the ambiguous paths leading to clarification of his law. For, one must recall, this father had known to mourn in agreeing to the sacrifice of his son and his exile in apparently unmarked, hostile territory. No doubt future narratives will be written there, where the stories are mutually articulated, where the plots come together in one plot. Notwithstanding structures, groups, and laws, narrative will perhaps assume again its "creative evolution." New narrative configurations will arise to retrace and modify the limits of what was created. The course of history will reveal, as any conclusions do, after the fact, the logics of action and the unexpected consequences of familiar premises.

Suspense and surprise join and cross the actions of Ibrahim's narrative in an extraordinary intrigue. Their meaning, revealed at the end, responds to an error in interpretation that will always be made but is nonetheless established only at the conclusion, since until the very end of the story the meaning is intractable for the hero. A voice from on high reveals to him at the end of the road that he has believed in a dream, that he has mistaken a dream order for a real order. This lapse, common to all interpretation, insinuates uncertainty into knowledge and refers every subject back to its will, to its possible worlds as "will and representation."

The hajj took us back to our will to exist beyond the worlds we ascribed to ourselves, in our differences—race, class, nation, or gender—called us to bring forth our pasts and the pasts we had to summon in the form of something to come. Its story—or rather, its stories, since there were several—took hold of our lives. They made us retell the Qur'anic narratives that retraced our past and anticipated its conclusions. In these repeated progressions, which ramified in many directions, each person tried to search for who he (or she) really was to confirm some wager he had made about himself, bringing himself into existence. The endless repetition and rewriting of the narrative—like those of the rituals, and there isn't much difference, in this respect, between ritual and myth—look back to that past where we once were without ever having been present to it. Dead time, time of death in our lives. Time when we had been, although we were still waiting for it at the closed horizon of our life stories. All these narratives, including mine, returned to the sites of ancient and future worlds, in the world that inspired and transcended them, borne out in it, with no hope of reaching its limits.

The hajj received the story of our life in a typical three-part evolution, braiding together its episodes according to a plot with a weighty ending. The final part luxuriated in contingencies yet resisted decipherment, though Ibrahim's narrative did furnish an interpretation that seemed to have a happy ending. And no doubt most of the men and women I met at the holy sites sought to make of their lives stories analogous to those of Hajar, Ibrahim, and Ismail. World events and historical contingencies—the hajj administrations, the transformation of the hajj into a product and a commodity, its metamorphoses into rites and power struggles between a social and a political body radically differentiated in and through the body—these were taken by each pilgrim for what they were: trials and tribulations, which a happy ending would transform into obligatory hurdles, and which for that reason partook of the holiness of the moment. They had a dual valence, though, and in the world itself one awaited the scintillating lights of their other side, despite the delays and apprehensions shadowing it. Uncertainty enclosed and radicalized the hope that analogy with the Qur'anic narrative would be verified, that life and death for each person would be analogous to what they had been for

Ismail: miracle and resurrection. In sum, that an origin and a relationship would be revealed at the end of the story and prove it was there; that we were like a mark in time which had always been our own being: beings in displaced existences.

As for the lives resembling mine, another narrative, analogous to the one I have just told, and yet different, intruded. It didn't have to be written—or at least not in this way. But it was essential that, as a possible narrative path, it existed. For those lives, too, a return and a reversal to the mark they were learning by following the rite induced them to decode something without any guarantee; but it also condemned them to repeat, until death, the narrative of what was happening to them. This was now the only way of getting it, gathering the events into historical plots converging toward a memory. Burial rites, testimonies to a will to live that escaped the illusion of historical inevitability, spreading through what had been and corroding its determinisms.

The parallels between this journey and the journey of the hajj couldn't be more striking. But the two types of narrative that animated, indeed consecrated, a transformation did not simply work to make a link from nature to culture or to interpret culture. The hajj left ordinary time behind and offered its own scansion, which confused times and tied their urgencies to the succession of day and night—to what, in human perception, was the journey of the sun. The hajj took its own time, but there was this anxiety always at work in its rhythms, and it overtook us. Through it, the concern with time linked our being with a time before awareness of time. And if one wanted to preserve the words of interpretation or of duality and difference, one had to keep them together, therefore off balance in relation to themselves. Something would then appear that intervened before interpretation, turning up in the aftermath of a decoding that cannot be complete, since it requires positions and positioning; something which, from this perspective, would be confused with religion, inasmuch as religion always seems to be hanging over the life that created it. We may well see this as transcendence—or, on the contrary, as an antidote to the misfortunes of history. Whether as ideology, mystification, conservation, or on the contrary as subversion and the anti-hegemonic power of making oneself in relation and/or opposition to dominant systems, ritual and religion seem constantly to be taking a step back so as to reappear above.

Through this connection, the hajj, a ritual narrative, is a family story—like the narrative I am now leading into its last phase, although it is being a rebel to closure. Both follow affiliations and both have signposts. One recalls Ibrahim begging God to give him a son who would make a father of him and make a mother of his woman—his women (wife and concubine)—and of them together a family. A foundation, an origin in a story with no origin. An institution that was going to allow them to live in the place where humanity had landed, long ago, after the Fall. A family story with its tensions and jealousies, which sent Hajar and Ismail, the longed-for eldest son, into exile in the desert. The rest is well known: a story of patience and the will to live; of Hajar, the woman scorned, saving her offspring and ensuring continuity for the lineage . . . Life force that burst into the cube clad in black and gold, sheltering the stone blackened by contact with the indivisible powers of transformation-pollution and fertilization. Now, as the story clearly says, building the cube was the refoundation of a house of God, making the earth a habitation after the family of Hajar, Ismail, and Ibrahim had been reunited (in any case the family in the Muslim version). Return of the father after the mother had saved the son—who became Hajar's desire, after having been a demand and a gift. A return of the father thanks to

the mother's work, which would make a man of Ismail, helping him to fulfill the law of which his father had also been
the name and the transmitter.

Ritual and religion interpret this limit well, this access to
law as its own fulfillment, posed resoundingly in and through
sacrifice. However, this whole family story as it unfolds
brings about something (in a sort of response) on which the
lineage can get only an imaginary purchase—neither more
nor less than a hypothesis about a form of life. It transforms
fertility and procreation into regulated reproduction, and in-
serts the gift as the foundation of a lineage that was intended
to be purely patrilineal, disregarding the fact that God had
given Ismail to Hajar, too, and that she rose, far more than
the other protagonists, to the responsibility which came with
the son. All this in a drama of new beginnings that gave back
what had come before, having transformed it. Transfers of
energy between a man and a woman who came from each
other? Or even before, in the first scene of copulation, and
no doubt before. A time the memory of which would have
been preserved before anyone was born, before one had
moved far enough away to turn back to it. If this were the
case, every family story, including the one Freud invented
without seeming to consider the story of Sarah, Hajar, Ismail, Ishaq, and Ibrahim—and whatever the interpretations,
the danger of pathology and of complete closure on itself—
would lose its status as a precedent and its illusory claims to
be the first and last interpretation.

The family saga of Hajar and Ibrahim, like the others,
therefore continues. Like all family stories, it is liable to nur-
ture surprising offspring and episodes which may take it
away from its familiar terrain. And it is possible that one day
a new Hajar story may arise, which would continue her migration and the migration of her name (itself a derivation

from an Arabic root for *migration*); one in which the divisions established between the will to live and the masculine guardianship that watches over the law recast themselves in unprecedented plots and come to unexpected endings. Hajar . . . the story continues.

ACKNOWLEDGMENTS

This book constitutes one stage in a wider research project on pilgrimage. My initial investigations were facilitated by a grant from the J. S. Guggenheim Foundation, which I would like to thank for its invaluable assistance.

Subsequently, and in accordance with the Islamic precept, I financed my trip to the Holy Cities with my own means. Throughout this difficult experience, the vital support was and still is the affection and understanding shown by my family, especially my wife, Miriam Lowi-Hammoudi, and our two children, Jazia and Ismail.

Friends and colleagues encouraged me by agreeing to offer comments and suggestions that improved the results of this work. Mohammed Zernine generously helped me and made several enlightening remarks in our friendly dialogues. Adonis, through his friendship and careful reading, helped me polish the text. I owe the final choice of title to his suggestion. I am happy to thank both of them warmly.

Clifford Geertz graciously took the time to read this book

at an advanced stage and to share his remarks and encouragement with me; I am most grateful. I would also like to thank Miriam Lowi-Hammoudi and Stefania Pandolfo, who enriched my work by suggesting corrections and making comments, as well as my colleague Jim Boon, who agreed to go over an earlier version. Laurence Rosen read the manuscript very closely and made judicious observations; I am grateful to him and to Elaine Pagels, with whom I had conversations that were intellectually very stimulating, as well as to Isabelle and Jim Clark Deces, who generously shared their enthusiasm with me. Good thanks also to Professor Hossein Modarressi, who was kind enough to refer me to works on Islamic law regarding the pilgrimage and sacrifice; and to Samer Traboulsi and Ahmed Assad for their help in reading sources in Arabic. After two presentations of my work at Harvard University, I benefited from the remarks and reactions of Roger Owen, Bill Graham, Byron and Mary Jo Good, and João Biehl. I would like to take this opportunity to thank them.

Friends accompanied this research, in their own way, through enlightening discussions on Islam, the Muslim world, and the Near East today, in the new regional and global context. Richard Falk and Hilal Elver, Mohammed Allaoui, Faouzi Senhaji, Mohammed Naciri, and Jamila Buret all discussed these subjects with me and listened, with a degree of selflessness, as I frequently digressed. I wish to acknowledge my debt to them for the moral and intellectual comfort they offered me.

This book would not have seen the light of day without help from Princeton University's department of anthropology and Institute for the Transregional Study of the Contemporary Middle East, North Africa, and Central Asia. Carol Zanca and Gabriella Drinovan helped unstintingly. Gregory Bell was an extraordinary collaborator, and G.

Drinovan had the patience of typing the first draft of the manuscript. I hope all of them will accept my thanks for the cooperation they so graciously offered.

Finally, I would like to emphasize that I bear sole responsibility for the ideas and opinions expressed herein.

A. H.